普通高等教育『十一五』国家级规划教材
教育部教师工作司组织专家审定
高等院校小学教育专业教材

小学英语教学法教程

（第3版）

主　编　王　蔷
编写者　王　蔷　敖娜仁图雅
陈则航　马　欣　赵春生

高等教育出版社·北京

内容提要

本书是《小学英语教学法教程》的第3版，第1版入选普通高等教育“十一五”国家级规划教材。第3版教材基于近年来小学英语课程与教学发生的变化，依据《义务教育英语课程标准（2022年版）》的理念和要求进行编写，主要内容包括：通过对第一语言和第二语言的不同学习特点的讨论，引导学习者充分认识小学生英语学习的特点；对小学英语课程的价值、学生核心素养的培育和课程目标要求进行解析；对小学英语教学设计，课堂教学管理的技能和技巧，词汇、语法、语音教学，听、说、读、写技能教学，适合低龄儿童的语言教学技巧，小学英语的评价与测试，以及教材的评价与使用等进行详细阐述。

本书主要用英文编写，行文明快流畅，内容翔实生动，教学设计实用、有效，编者力求从学习者已有知识和经验出发，帮助学习者逐步建构小学英语教学的专业知识与能力。希望学习者通过使用这本书，在小学英语教师专业化道路上取得进步的同时，提高自身的英语语言运用能力，为可持续发展奠定良好的基础。

本书可作为小学教育专业英语方向课程的教材，也可作为小学英语教师新课标培训用书。

图书在版编目（CIP）数据

小学英语教学法教程 / 王蔷主编 . -- 3版 . -- 北京：高等教育出版社，2023.7（2024.2重印）

ISBN 978-7-04-055762-6

Ⅰ . ①小… Ⅱ . ①王… Ⅲ . ①英语课－教学法－小学 Ⅳ . ① G623.312

中国版本图书馆 CIP 数据核字（2021）第 036447 号

小学英语教学法教程（第3版）
Xiaoxue Yingyu Jiaoxuefa Jiaocheng

策划编辑 王雅君　责任编辑 王雅君　封面设计 姜 磊　版式设计 杜微言
责任绘图 于 博　责任校对 高 歌　责任印制 沈心怡

出版发行 高等教育出版社
社　　址 北京市西城区德外大街4号
邮政编码 100120
印　　刷 涿州市星河印刷有限公司
开　　本 787mm×1092mm 1/16
印　　张 22.25
字　　数 540千字
购书热线 010-58581118
咨询电话 400-810-0598
网　　址 http://www.hep.edu.cn
　　　　 http://www.hep.com.cn
网上订购 http://www.hepmall.com.cn
　　　　 http://www.hepmall.com
　　　　 http://www.hepmall.cn
版　　次 2003年6月第1版
　　　　 2023年7月第3版
印　　次 2024年2月第2次印刷
定　　价 45.00元

物 料 号 55762-00

高等院校小学教育专业教材总序

我国已进入全面建设社会主义现代化国家的新的历史阶段。在这样一个历史阶段，教育越来越成为促进社会全面发展、推动科技迅猛进步，进而不断增强综合国力的重要力量，成为我国从人口大国逐步走向人力资源强国的关键因素。我国的教师教育正面临着前所未有的机遇和挑战。教师教育的改革与发展直接关系到千百万教师的成长，关系到素质教育的全面推进，关系到一代新人思想道德、创新精神和实践能力的培养和提高，最终关系到推动科学发展、促进社会和谐、全面建成社会主义现代化强国目标的实现。

培养具有较高学历的小学教师是适应基础教育课程改革与发展的迫切需要，也是我国教师教育课程改革与发展的必然趋势。为了适应基础教育课程改革与发展的需要，我国对培养较高学历小学教师工作进行了长时间的积极探索，取得了较大成绩，并积累了许多宝贵经验。党的二十大报告强调，要全面贯彻党的教育方针，落实立德树人根本任务；加强师德师风建设，培养高素质教师队伍。中共中央、国务院《关于全面深化新时代教师队伍建设改革的意见》提出:“全面提高中小学教师质量，建设一支高素质专业化的教师队伍。”“根据基础教育改革发展需要，以实践为导向优化教师教育课程体系。”为此，要结合教师专业标准等的要求，依据《教师教育课程标准（试行）》，优化教师教育课程结构，改革课程教学内容，开发优质课程资源等。

开展小学教师培养工作，课程与教材建设是关键。当务之急是组织教育科研机构、高等师范院校的专家学者和教师联合编写出一套高水平的、规范化的、专门用于培养较高学历小学教师的教材。

编写高等院校小学教育专业教材，应该遵循以下原则：

一、时代性与前瞻性。教材要面向现代化、面向世界、面向未来，反映当代社会经济、文化和科技发展的趋势，贴近国际教育改革和我国基础教育课程改革的前沿，体现新的教育理念。

二、基础性与专业性。教材要体现高等教育的基础性，同时要紧密结合当今小学教育课程改革的趋势和实施素质教育的要求，针对小学教育专业的特征和小学教师的职业特点，力求构建科学的教材体系，提高小学教师的专业化水平。

三、综合性与学有专长。教材要根据现代科技发展和基础教育课程改革综合化的趋势，强化综合素质教育，加强文理渗透，注重科学素养，体现人文精神，加强学科间的相互融合以及信息技术与各学科的整合；同时，根据小学教育的需要，综合性教育与单科性教育相结合，使学生文理兼通，学有专长，一专多能。

四、理论与实践相结合。教材要根据小学教师职前教育的要求，既要科学地安排文化知识课和教育理论课，又要加强实践环节，注重教育实践和科学实验，重视对师范生教师职业能力的培养。

五、充分体现教材的权威性、专业性、通用性和创新性。教材应以教育部制定的《教师教育课程标准（试行）》为编写依据，以教师培养、培训沟通为目的，在体系框架、内容、呈现方式等方面开拓创新，加大改革力度，充分体现以学生为本的教育理念，使教材从能用、好用提升到教师、学生喜欢用。

高等教育出版社根据以上原则组织编写了有关教材，这些教材经过专家审定，请有关单位和学校酌情选用。

第 3 版前言

《小学英语教学法教程》第 1 版于 2003 年出版，第 2 版于 2009 年出版。至今第 2 版也走过十余个春夏秋冬。在这十余年中，我国小学英语课程的开设规模和课程质量取得了长足的进步，《小学英语教学法教程》也陪伴了一批又一批小学英语新教师的成长。

《义务教育英语课程标准（2011 年版）》（以下简称“义教课标 2011”）颁布之后，对提升小学英语的教育质量起到了重要的指导和促进作用。经过广大小学英语教师的共同努力，小学英语课程质量得到快速提升，小学英语教师队伍的整体水平也在不断提高，小学英语课程资源更加丰富，学生的英语理解和表达能力也都有长足的进步，“聋哑英语”在小学阶段已经得到全面改观。近年来，随着英语阅读素养概念的提出和英语分级阅读的实践，小学生的英语阅读兴趣、阅读习惯、阅读体验受到前所未有的重视，学生的英语阅读和表达能力也明显提高，小学英语展现出更好的发展前景。孩子们更喜欢英语了，更乐于通过阅读汲取语言营养、发展认知能力和思辨能力，他们不但获得了更丰富的人文知识和科学知识，而且更乐于用英语去表达自己的感受和想法了。

2022 年 4 月，教育部颁布了新修订的《义务教育英语课程标准（2022 年版）》（以下简称“义教课标 2022”）。“义教课标 2022”的颁布为“综合语言运用能力”目标画上了一个句号，揭开了以落实立德树人为根本任务、以学科育人为宗旨的核心素养时代的新篇章。

2022 年 10 月，党的二十大胜利召开，在实现中华民族伟大复兴中国梦的征程中，国家对教育事业寄予了厚望。党的二十大报告强调，“教育、科技、人才是全面建设社会主义现代化国家的基础性、战略性支撑”，首次将教育、科技、人才一体安排部署，赋予教育新的战略地位、历史使命和发展格局。在深入践行我国教育发展新方向的过程中，培养高质量的小学英语师资，服务国家发展战略，落实立德树人根本任务，是建设高质量基础教育人才培养体系的重要任务，所有教育工作者都要凝聚智慧，提供思路，贡献力量。

本教材的修订全面融入了“义教课标 2022”的新要求，重点探讨了课程目标的变化、课程内容的重组、学业质量的要求和教学方式等内容，也增加了一些新的专题，还补充或替换了相关的阅读材料。教材在整体结构上突出了“义教课标 2022”对教学理念、教学设计、教学方法的指导作用，并将教学设计独立出来作为第三单元的内容，探讨了教学内容分析、学情分析、教学目标设计、教学活动设计、单元整体教学设计等问题，附有新的教学设计案例。此外，本次修订还加入了有关绘本阅读的内容讨论和方法介绍，以及绘本阅读教学设计的案例。希望本次修订能充分地反映“义教课标 2022”的新要求，以及近年来小学英语课程的发展需求和小学英语教师职前培养及职后专业发展的需求。

修订后，本教材共9个单元。前两个单元聚焦理念学习。第1单元探讨了小学开设英语的价值和意义、儿童学习英语特点和小学英语教师的基本素养。第2单元聚焦课程标准，一方面，帮助小学英语新教师了解过去四十余年我国基础教育课程改革的发展脉络；另一方面，重点讨论了“义教课标2022”的要求，明确了课程的出发点和落脚点，从而为基于核心素养培养目标的教学设计、教材研读等奠定理论基础。为了更好地帮助新教师学习和把握“义教课标2022”的课程理念、内容和要求，本次修订补充了一系列课标解读文章和微课作为拓展资料。第3单元聚焦教学设计，力求从教师专业素养的角度，帮助未来小学英语教师明确教学设计的有关要求。第4单元聚焦课堂教学管理。第5~7单元聚焦小学阶段的语言知识和语言技能教学。第8单元和第9单元分别聚焦教学评价、教材评价与使用。

与第2版教材相同的是，第3版教材保留了大量的学生活动，通过讨论活动和阅读材料帮助学生深化对小学英语课程和教学中一些关键问题的认识，在此基础上，教师应把重点放在对学生教学实践能力的培养方面。因此，建议教师在教学过程中，坚持以学生活动和教师引导下的讨论交流为主，在涉及具体课堂教学的内容时，要突出正确理念引领下的教学设计实践与反思性学习。教师可以遵循以下步骤开展教学：第一步，组织学生围绕特定内容进行教学设计实践；第二步，组织学生在课堂上分享自己的教学设计，在此基础上，引导学生基于本教材的讨论要点和阅读资源，对学生教学设计中的问题进行分析和讨论，并提出解决问题的方案，明确改进方向；第三步，引导学生改进教学设计后，在实践中进一步与同伴交流与反思，提炼并总结做好教学设计的原则和方法。这样开展教学，学习才能真正发生，学生才能深度参与和深度反思，学生的实践能力才能得到提升。

第3版教材的修订工作主要由王蔷和敖娜仁图雅共同完成。希望第3版教材能充分地反映“义教课标2022”的要求，也能更好地适应小学英语课程和教学的快速发展，从而更好地满足小学英语教师发展的需要。由于修订时间比较仓促，恳请读者和教材使用者为我们提出宝贵的意见和建议，如有获取教学课件的需要可发送邮件至责任编辑王雅君的邮箱 wangyj@hep.com.cn。

最后，感谢广大教师教育工作者和学生长期以来给予本教材的大力支持！感谢上海市教委教研室朱浦先生及其团队为本教材提供的课例示范；感谢广东省东莞市教育局教研室张凝女士为本教材推荐了优秀的绘本资源和课例示范。感谢高等教育出版社的编辑团队为这次修订工作所付出的心血。

王蔷

2023年2月

第1、2版前言

CONTENTS

Unit 1 Children as Language Learners **1**

1.1 How do we learn our first language? 2

1.2 What differences and similarities are there between learning an L1 and an L2? 5

1.3 What are the characteristics of Children as language learners? 10

1.4 How do Children's individual differences affect their learning? 15

1.5 Why should teachers treat children as equal human beings? 20

1.6 What makes a good primary English teacher? 22

Reading 27

Unit 2 Understanding the National English Curriculum **33**

2.1 Why is English offered in primary schools? 35

2.2 What are the main goals for primary English? 38

2.3 How is the content of the 2022 Curriculum organized? 46

2.4 What academic achievement standards are specified for Levels 1 & 2 in the 2022 Curriculum? 53

2.5 What are suggested for teaching the Preparatory Level and Levels 1 & 2? 57

2.6 What general teaching suggestions are specified in the 2022 Curriculum? 61

2.7 Summary: implications for the future 65

Reading 68

Unit 3 Instructional Design **83**

3.1 What is instructional design? 83

3.2 How to do text analysis 86

3.3 How to do student analysis 93

3.4 How to design lesson objectives 98

3.5 How to design lesson activities 102

3.6 How to do overall unit design 106

Reading 108

Unit 4 Classroom Management **119**

4.1 How to motivate children to learn English 120

4.2 How to give effective classroom instructions 125

4.3 How to ask effective questions 132

4.4 How to set up classroom discipline 141
4.5 What should teachers do when teaching large classes? 147
4.6 How to manage classroom interaction 150
4.7 How to organize activities in a lesson 156
4.8 How to treat children's errors in the classroom 165
Reading 170

Unit 5 Teaching Vocabulary,Grammar and Pronunciation 175
5.1 How to teach vocabulary to young Learners 175
5.2 How to teach grammar to young learners 183
5.3 How to teach pronunciation to young learners 191
Reading 201

Unit 6 Teaching Language Skills 205
6.1 How to teach listening to children 206
6.2 How to teach speaking to children 212
6.3 How to teach reading to children 219
6.4 How to use stories for teaching English to children 228
6.5 How to teach writing to children 241
6.6 How to integrate the four skills 247
Reading 250

Unit 7 Practical Techniques for Teaching Young Learners 257
7.1 How to use songs and rhymes 258
7.2 How to use games in the classroom 263
7.3 How to use mind maps 267
7.4 How to use projects in teaching 271
7.5 How to use board writing in teaching 279
7.6 How to use resources in teaching 286
Reading 292

Unit 8 Assessing Learning with Children 295
8.1 What are assessment, tests and evaluation? 296
8.2 How can we set up targets and design assessment tasks? 301
8.3 What can we use to assess learning? 307
8.4 How can we give feedback to learners about their learning? 311
8.5 How can we use tests to assess learning? 316

Unit 9 Adapting and Evaluating Textbooks **329**
9.1 How to evaluate textbooks 330
9.2 How to select textbooks 332
9.3 How to use textbooks effectively 337

References **343**

Unit 1

Children as Language Learners

Aims of the unit

In this unit, we are going to focus on the following:

1.1 How do we learn our first language?

1.1.1 How do children acquire their first language in general?

1.1.2 How did you learn to speak Chinese as your first language?

1.2 What differences and similarities are there between learning an L1 and an L2?

1.2.1 In what ways are they different or similar?

1.2.2 How can we better help children learn a foreign language?

1.2.3 What are the principles for designing activities used in the primary classroom?

1.3 What are the characteristics of children as language learners?

1.3.1 What characteristics do we know about children's learning?

1.3.2 What are the major differences between children and adults in learning a foreign language?

1.3.3 When should children start learning a foreign language?

1.4 How do children's individual differences affect their learning?

1.4.1 What are you good at and what are your classmates good at?

1.4.2 What activities can we design to meet different needs?

1.4.3 What type of person are you?

1.4.4 What is your aptitude for learning a foreign language?

1.5 Why should teachers treat children as equal human beings?

1.5.1 How should teachers treat children?

1.5.2 How do you understand humanistic education?

1.6 What makes a good primary English teacher?

1.6.1 What role does a primary school teacher have to play?

1.6.2 What is a good primary English teacher like?

1.6.3 Do you have the potential to be a good primary English teacher?

We all know that learning a foreign language in a school context is not an easy task. As we all learned our first language without much difficulty, it is naturally helpful for us to look at the ways how we learned our first language so that implications can be drawn for teaching and learning a foreign language. Then we will move on to look at children as language learners in terms of how different they are compared with adults in learning languages. Children have their own ways of seeing, thinking and doing things and the way we teach children a foreign language should definitely be different from the way we teach adults. This is a big challenge for teachers of young learners. Therefore, it is necessary to discuss what qualities a good English teacher of young learners should have.

1.1 How do we learn our first language?

There are many differences between learning one's first language (L1) and a foreign language (L2), but there are also similarities. Let us first look at how people learn their L1 and see what we can learn from such experiences for teaching L2.

1.1.1 How do children acquire their first language in general?

Task 1.1.1

The following are some statements made by different people about the ways people learn L1. Check the box below if you agree with it. Add more, if you have observed others and try to give some examples for your statements. Then discuss them with a partner.

- ☐ By imitations.
- ☐ By repetitions.
- ☐ By listening to stories.
- ☐ By talking to others.
- ☐ By talking to oneself.
- ☐ By talking about pictures.
- ☐ By singing songs.
- ☐ By reciting poems.
- ☐ By acting and performing.
- ☐ By watching television cartoons.
- ☐ By playing games.
- ☐ By being corrected by parents.
- ☐ By learning language rules.
- ☐

☐

☐

Discussion Point

We can definitely learn something from the way children acquire their first language. Children learn L1 by listening to adults, imitating what adults say, listening to stories, and so on. Research into L1 shows that the most important factor for L1 development is when children are interacting with people around them and when they are involved in using the language for doing things—listening, speaking, playing, singing, viewing, acting, etc. That is to say, sitting in front of a television only provides them with the input; it is their engagement in conversation with others and getting things done with the language that drives their language development. Therefore, language learning process is a socializing process. Interaction and experimenting with the language in communication are important ways of language learning. In L1 learning, mothers play an important role. They are normally very patient and try to interpret their children's intention from the context. They talk to children using simple language, the context and body language to help children understand.

In teaching L2 to children, we should always remember how we can engage children in learning by using similar experience they have had with L1. Young children can develop a fascination for language if the methodology of the classroom is stimulating and involves the learners as fully as possible. To engage them as much as possible, teachers need to give the learners something to:

— look and say
— listen to
— sort or set
— solve
— match
— choose
— make
— repeat
— read silently
— write/copy
— hold and say
— do as you say
— pass to someone
— perform/act out
— compete in groups
— imagine
— respond to
— sequence/order
— compare
— guess
— draw and describe
— count
— read aloud
— memorize/recite
— spell orally
— touch and guess
— chant and sing
— mime
— research/find out

Adapted from Cheater & Farren, 2001.

1.1.2 How did you learn to speak Chinese as your first language?

TASK 1.1.2

How did you learn to speak Chinese? If you cannot remember, think of a young child that you know and recall the way he or she learns Chinese. Can you find any instances when children said something that was totally unexpected or interesting but grammatically unacceptable? Put together a few examples and discuss the following questions.

a) Where do the incorrect examples come from?

b) What in general are the parent's attitude toward them?

c) What do they tell us about the process of learning?

d) How would you relate this to learning a foreign language?

Discussion Point

The following are some utterances made by Chinese children as well as English children acquiring their mother tongue. Do you find them interesting? Can you add more examples?

A.

a) 他打你呀？意思是：他打我呀。（你、我不分）

b) 我也没要了。意思是：我也不要了。

c) 天白了。意思是：天亮了。

B.

a) Don't running. It means: don't run.

b) Switch off the dark. I don't like the dark shining. It means: switch off the light, I don't like the light shining in the dark.

c) Mama a girl. It means: mama is female.

We can see that children are able to produce utterances which cannot possibly be learned from an adult. Obviously, they themselves have created them! Children are active and creative language learners. They do not need to hear every sentence to be able to say it. They can make sense of the world from what they see and hear and create their own utterances when there is a need for them to communicate their own meaning. Parents seldom try to correct children. They often feel very amused at children's creativity. Foreign language learners, we believe, can be just as creative as first language learners. We simply need to create the opportunity for them to do so.

According to Peccei (2000), mothers interpret children's meanings from their incomplete utterances and expand their utterances to provide correct language input. They "rarely call attention to grammatical errors in an explicit way". Research by Shatz (1982, in Peccei, 2000) has shown that "only about 4 percent of all children's errors are explicitly corrected by parents and the overwhelming majority of these are vocabulary errors". The research results indicate that it is very important to make language learning experience a positive and encouraging one.

1.2 What differences and similarities are there between learning an L1 and an L2?

Having looked at the way how L1 is learned, we now move to look at the ways most people learn an L2. Compared to the fact that most children learn their L1 successfully, the reality that some children can't learn an L2 successfully is a bit worrying.

1.2.1 In what ways are they different or similar?

We have all had the experience of learning both Chinese and English with Chinese as our L1 and English as our L2. Do you agree that learning English as a foreign language is more difficult than learning Chinese? Why is it so?

TASK 1.2.1A

Think about the differences that exist between children learning their L1 and children learning an L2. Make a list of the differences in the space given below and discuss them with a partner. Then, think about the ways by which we can minimize the differences so as to make learning another language easier and with more success.

Items	L1 learning	L2 learning	What can we do?
Exposure to language	Natural and adequate		
Length of time	All day long		
Learning context	Supportive, friendly, and tolerant		
Types of input	Natural and in context		
Strategies for learning	Listening before speaking		

continued

Items	L1 learning	L2 learning	What can we do?
Motivation for learning	Remain high for communicative needs		
Value of error correction	Not of much value		
Support and guidance	Constant and patient		
Opportunities for experimenting with the language	Opportunities all the time round		
Feedback forms	Always encouraging		

TASK 1.2.1B

What are the similarities between the learning of L1 and L2? Discuss with your partner and make a list in the space below.

Similarities between the learning of L1 and L2:

Discussion Point

The acquisition of L1 and L2 is quite different in many aspects. For L2 learners, the language input is limited. The time spent on learning L2 is much shorter. The learning context is formal and errors are often corrected. Also, the development of the four skills begins almost at the same time. Moreover, L2 learners often do not have the need to communicate in the target language; therefore, there are few opportunities for pupils to interact except in the classroom and little real context for children to experiment with the language. With 30–40 pupils in one class for just a few hours a week to learn the language, teachers are not able to check on the progress with every pupil and be patient and supportive to every child.

However, there are some similarities between the learning of L1 and L2. Rich context and input, opportunities for using the language, interaction with others, etc. are important in learning any languages. Teachers should create a nice environment and interesting activities for pupils to use the language to do things.

1.2.2 How can we better help children learn a foreign language?

TASK 1.2.2

Which is a better way for children to learn a foreign language? Please check from the speech bubbles below. Then read **Reading 1.2.2**[1] and make a list of suggestions for teaching English to children based on that reading.

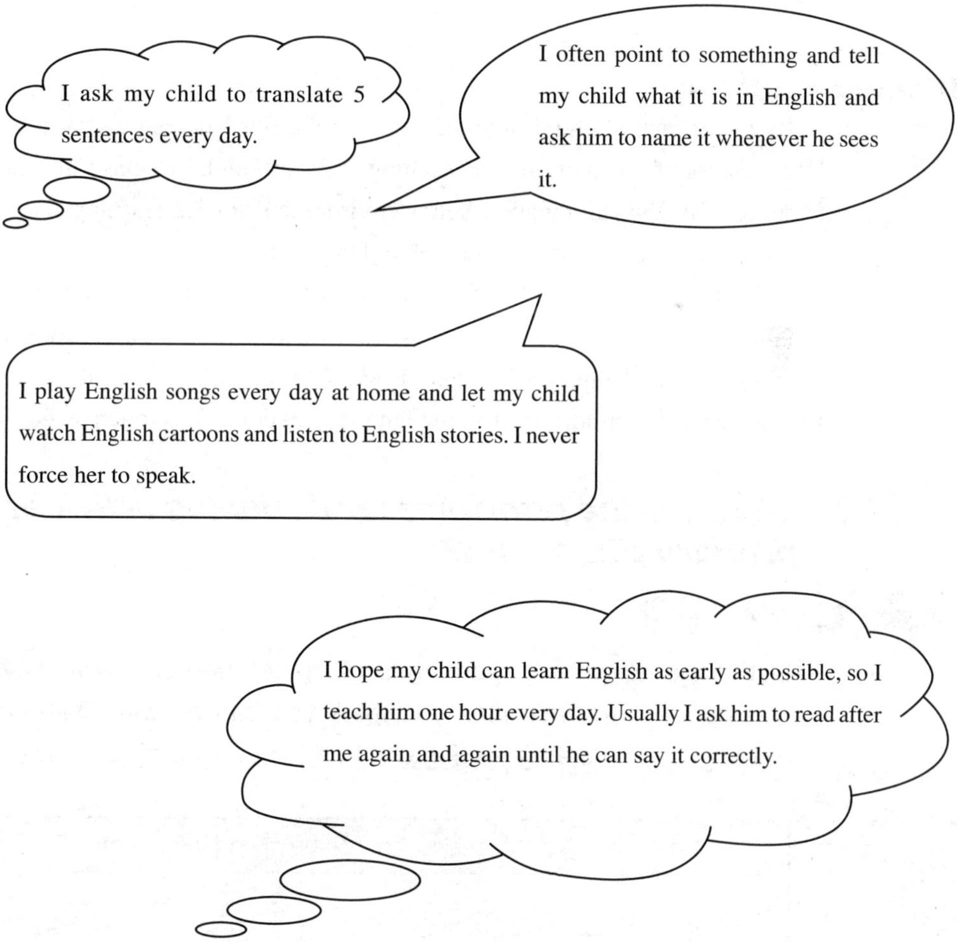

---

① All of the Readings can be found at the end of chapters or in the QR codes (the same below).

I think grammar and vocabulary are the most important in learning a foreign language. They are the focus of my teaching.

I often organize games for my pupils to do role-play in the class. They learn to use the language to do shopping, order food, ask for directions, etc.

Discussion Point

By understanding the differences and similarities between learning L1 and L2, we can draw a lot of implications for teaching and learning L2 to make the learning of L2 more successful. We can create a better environment for L2 learning. For example, we can try to create a supportive situation and be tolerant of our learners' errors when they are trying to communicate. We can also provide more opportunities for children to hear the language before asking them to say the words and give them more chances to experiment with the language. We can design activities which are interesting and motivating and encourage children to use the language in context as much as possible.

1.2.3 What are the principles for designing activities used in the primary classroom?

TASK 1.2.3

List all the activities in learning English that are commonly used in the primary classroom or the activities you think you can do with children. For example, reading aloud a dialog, asking children to act out a dialog, etc.

Activities that can be done with children	
1.	6.
2.	7.
3.	8.
4.	9.
5.	10.

Discussion Point

How many types of activities have you listed out? Do you think they are all appropriate for children? Traditionally, teachers teach children by starting to teach them the International Phonetic Alphabets (IPA) with the hope that IPA will help children get the correct pronunciation. As a result, there are a lot of activities done in the classroom with a focus on helping children recognize phonetic symbols and practice and repeat sounds of individual words. Also, teachers tend to put a lot of emphasis on teaching the English structures so that children can remember the rules and write down the correct forms of verbs, pronouns, or other grammatical forms in doing exercises or tests. The target of teaching the language is often put on the memorization of words and dialogs and on doing written English exams.

The point is that remembering all the phonetic symbols does not automatically guarantee good pronunciation, and getting to know the rules of grammar does not guarantee good communication. What's more, children often become tired and bored by learning and reciting the phonetic symbols or structure-based dialogs. They gradually lose interest and confidence in learning the language when they can not enjoy it and fail to do the tests well.

In order to teach children well, we need to understand what interests them and how they learn better. Children are naturally interested in language when they are very young with their native language. That includes listening to stories, reciting nursery rhymes, singing songs, recognizing and saying words and phrases for fun. We believe it is the same for children learning a foreign language. Those activities that involve children in singing songs and saying rhymes, telling stories and doing chants games would present no problems to children but rather add to the excitement and interest of learning.

Understanding how children learn another language is an important starting point for developing skills and strategies for teaching children. The following principles are summarized to provide an understanding of teaching language to young learners.

Principle 1: Children learn best when feeling happy and secure.

Principle 2: Children are naturally imaginative, active and creative.

Principle 3: Learning is often a mutual accomplishment. Learning is collaborative, not adult driven. Children participate at their own level of understanding with mothers' help.

Principle 4: Children often learn through guided participation and they profit from the support and encouragement of more competent people.

Principle 5: Children learn best when they are involved both physically and mentally.

Principle 6: Children need plenty of opportunities to use the language again and again.

Principle 7: It is not interaction itself but the quality of interaction that contributes to better learning.

Principle 8: Language is the means through which self-regulation of learning behavior develops.

Principle 9: Learning depends upon the negotiation of meaning.

Principle 10: Children learn in a similar way as they acquire their mother tongue. They learn the whole language rather than through analyzing language rules.

1.3 What are the characteristics of Children as language learners?

Do we understand children? What is special about them? When do they learn best and when not? What kind of help do they need most? As a teacher of children, we need to understand how they learn so that we have a better chance to support them in learning better.

1.3.1 What characteristics do we know about children's learning?

TASK 1.3.1

The following are some statements about children's characteristics and suggestions for teachers. Please match them and discuss with your group members whether you agree with them or not.

Children's characteristics

a) It's difficult for children to understand verbal instructions to begin with.

b) Children's attention span is very limited.

c) Children do not often have a clear purpose for learning. They learn simply because they are happy and enjoy the activity.

d) Children like to do things with their hands, bodies and minds.

e) Children like to do things with achievable targets because they want to feel sure that it is not something beyond their ability.

f) Children are imaginative, creative, and like new things and participating in activities.

g) Children are not good at analyzing language rules.

Suggestions for teachers

1. Make the learning enjoyable and pleasant.

2. Keep instructions very simple and support them with body language.
3. Organize some hands-on activities for children to do. Use Total Physical Response (TPR) if necessary.
4. Use many short and simple activities instead of long activities.
5. Do not explain complicated grammar to children. Guide children to discover rules by themselves.
6. Do not make tasks too difficult for children. Tasks should always have definite outcomes and repeated elements to ensure security and participation.
7. Give children opportunities to imagine and create, e.g. invite them to draw a monster or imagine seeing something through a telescope and tell others about it.

a — ____ b — ____ c — ____ d — ____

e — ____ f — ____ g — ____

Discussion Point

Children are naturally curious and active. They are full of enthusiasm and often show a lot of eagerness to participate. If children are happy, feel secure and stay in a threat-free environment, they are more likely to enjoy learning. It is often said that children' s attention span is short but we sometimes find that small children can concentrate on one thing for a fairly long time but not on other things. So it really depends on what they do. Children will not concentrate if you lecture them! This means we need to consider how to create a real desire for children to learn English; we need to provide opportunities and sufficient time for children to experience and experiment with the new language; we also need to provide a variety of opportunities for children to use language in different contexts, and finally provide timely feedback for children to know how they have been performing and what aspects of language need to be improved (Moon, 2000).

Phillips (1993) also mentions that as a general rule, it can be assumed that the younger the children are, the more holistic learners they will be. Younger learners respond to the meaning underlying the sentences but not to make the analytical studies that older learners do. Younger learners have the advantage of being great mimics. They are usually prepared to enjoy the activities the teacher has prepared for them. These factors mean that it is important for teachers to think of different ways to nurture children' s motivation. Phillips (1993) makes the following suggestions:

- Provide a clear meaningful purpose for using the language in the activity.
- The activities should be simple enough for the children to understand what is expected of them.
- The task should be within their abilities: it needs to be achievable but at the same time sufficiently stimulating for them to feel satisfied with their work.

- The activities should be largely orally based—indeed, with very young children, listening activities will take up a large proportion of class time.
- Written activities should be used much less with younger children. Children of six or seven years old are often not yet proficient in the mechanics of writing in their own language.

It is common sense that if an activity is enjoyable, it will be memorable; the language involved will "stick", and children will have a sense of achievement which will enhance their motivation for further learning. The kinds of activities that work well with children are games and songs with actions, TPR activities, tasks that involve colouring, cutting, and sticking, simple repetitive stories, and simple speaking activities that have obvious communicative value. Enjoying learning is likely to lead to success while success will make learning more enjoyable. This cyclical process generates a positive attitude towards learning English, which is perhaps one of the most valuable things that primary teachers can build up with children, as the tasks and activities may stimulate a life-long learning desire in children.

1.3.2 What are the major differences between children and adults in learning a foreign language?

TASK 1.3.2

Make a list of the differences and discuss them in groups.

Children	Adults
1.	1.
2.	2.
3.	3.
4.	4.
5.	5.

Discussion Point

Children and adults are quite different in their approaches to learning another language. Some major differences are summarized as the following:

- Adults pay more attention to form while children pay more attention to meaning.
- Children are not as self-conscious as adults in speaking the language or in making errors in front of others.
- Adults can concentrate more on what they learn while children can not concentrate

on learning for very long periods.

- Adults often learn with a clear purpose or motivation in mind, while children do not usually have a clear purpose for learning another language as they may regard it just as another school subject.
- Adults can learn by listening attentively and by taking detailed notes about vocabulary and grammar, while children often can not sit still for a very long time and they need to move and do things.
- Adults are good at regulating themselves in learning; they plan for revision and they use other sources to help them. Children, on the other hand, are less able to regulate themselves; they are not good at planning and monitoring their learning and need to develop such abilities.
- Adults are good at conceptualizing, generalizing and theorizing things, while children are good at understanding concrete things instead of abstract concepts.

With all the above differences in mind, we realize that working with children and working with adults are very different. Teaching children requires more energy and care in the understanding of how children think and learn, because "children are still developing; their bodies are still growing; their minds are still developing; some aspects of their first language are still developing" (Moon, 2000). When we are teaching the language, we are not only teaching the language, we are taking care of the whole child in his/her process of overall development.

As teachers we play an important role in that development and we can only achieve it through our way of interacting with children, by planning our activities which will facilitate their development, by creating a classroom environment in which children can explore their understanding, discover meaning in life, become aware of the differences in cultural values and life styles, and can experiment with the new language without being afraid of making mistakes. We also need to help children learn how to learn. With all these tasks, we conclude that children are more difficult to teach than adults.

1.3.3 When should children start learning a foreign language?

TASK 1.3.3

Read the following three stories and **Reading 1.3.3** individually first. Then share your opinions and comments in a group.

Story 1

I work in a foreign company and I know the importance of English. Although my wife and I do not have very high income, we decide to put our only son into a bilingual kindergarten, which costs us 100,000 RMB each year. We just want to provide him with the best education and hopefully he can pick up English quickly.

— Li Ping

Story 2

I'm an English teacher. I started teaching my daughter English when she was 3. I tried to talk to her in English as much as I can. I made her watch English cartoons and listen to tapes everyday and I often read English stories to her. She's now 7 and seems to be enjoying it and she is very good at it. I'm glad I started early.

— Zhen Feng

Story 3

Neither my husband nor I am good at English so we hope our son can achieve a lot in this field, but we don't know how we can help. Many of our friends put their children into English classes on weekends to learn Cambridge Young Learner's English. A lot of my son's classmates go to all kinds of English classes in their spare time, too. We don't want our son to be left behind so we sign in a class on Saturday too. Soon we find out that there are so many different tests, CYLE（Cambridge Younger Learners English）, PETS（Public English Test System）, etc., we have no idea which one we should go for. Meanwhile, our son is working very hard to memorize all those difficult words and grammar rules. I feel that he is very tired and wants to give up. I don't know whether we are doing the right thing.

Reading 1.3.3 孩子多大学外语合适?

— Xiao Qing

Discussion Point

Since there are many differences between adult learners and young learners, many parents want their children to start learning English as early as possible. They don't want their children to suffer from learning in the formal classroom when they grow up. They think it is much easier for children to acquire a language when they are young and they are able to acquire it in an unconscious way. However, this kind of preschool learning usually happens at home and children are usually surrounded by anxious parents. Their learning experiences are more often than not boring and the level of their language proficiency is related to their parents' level of proficiency. As we all understand, if parents cannot pronounce English properly, children will develop unnatural pronunciation and intonation which can be hard to get rid of later and good pronunciation is an important foundation for children's future learning. Apart from pronunciation, motivation is another factor that needs great care. If we bombard our children with new words, they might easily lose their interest in learning that language. And they will suffer even more when they need to learn it in formal classroom learning.

Therefore, young children should not be forced to learn another language at their early years if they are not in good circumstances.

1.4 How do Children's individual differences affect their learning?

Every individual is unique. Howard Gardner (1983, 1993) in his theory of multiple intelligences points out that people have different intelligences, therefore, it is unfair to treat them as the same. Some people may not be good at one thing but can be talented in another. Children will need special care and encouragement for they are too young to realize their potential. Also, they can be easily hurt or demotivating if they do not get the right support and understanding. It is, therefore, very important for teachers to try different teaching approaches to meet the needs of different children.

1.4.1 What are you good at and what are your classmates good at?

TASK 1.4.1

Please interview your classmates and find out who is good at the things listed below. If one's answer to a certain question is "yes", ask him/her to sign his/her name for that particular question in the signature section. If the answer is "no", go to another person until you find someone who says "yes". For each question, you need to collect at least one name.

Activities: find someone who...	Signature
1. likes to keep a diary.	
2. can tell if someone is singing off-key.	
3. can calculate numbers easily in his/her head.	
4. likes to read books with many pictures.	
5. likes to dance.	
6. likes to do puzzles and mazes.	
7. can list three things that help him/her learn.	
8. can draw a picture of his/her favorite food.	
9. has an interesting joke to tell.	
10. can sing part of a favorite song.	
11. sings in the shower.	
12. can easily identify at least 10 different kinds of flowers.	
13. finds it hard to sit for long periods of time.	

continued

Activities: find someone who...	Signature
14. frequently creates new activities and materials for his/her classes.	
15. is often involved in social activities at night.	
16. loves to teach someone how to do something.	

Adapted from Christison, 1998.

Discussion Point

— Are you able to find someone in your class for each item listed above?

— Are all the 16 items true in your case?

— What do you learn from this activity?

People are born to be different. One cannot be good at everything. American psychologist Gardner has proposed the theory of multiple intelligences which has provided a new perception to the understanding of human intelligence and the development of children. The theory has led to a new understanding and re-justification of the goals in education and consequently it has had an important impact on the processes and evaluation in education. In China, our goal of education in schools has long been laid on the development of language and logical thinking, ignoring the development of other intelligences as they are not within the core subjects to be tested for entering higher levels of schooling. Using only one standard in judging all the pupils in terms of their success in school learning has many disadvantages, as many children become demotivated when they are not doing very well with logical thinking and are easily discarded as unable to learn properly. However, there may be other intelligences within them which would show them as very intelligent, but unfortunately these skills and abilities have not been discovered or recognized by the school system.

1.4.2 What activities can we design to meet different needs?

TASK 1.4.2A

Look at the eight intelligences and discuss with your group members possible activities that are suitable for involving children's different intelligences when teaching them English. Then read **Reading 1.4.2A** and add more if there are any.

Reading 1.4.2A What do you need to know about Multiple Intelligences?

Intelligence	Forms of learning	Learning activities
Linguistic intelligence	listening, speaking, viewing, and reading	vocabulary use, story telling, poetry reciting, debate, speech, etc.
Logical-mathematical intelligence	concept induction, numerical calculations	designing abstract symbols, discovering rules, designing graphic structures, designing outlines, analyzing statistics, etc.
Musical intelligence	singing, chanting	composing, listening to music, playing musical instruments, rhythm exercises, etc.
Spatial intelligence	painting, description, visual presentation	imagination, color design, painting, etc.
Bodily-kinesthetic intelligence	dance, hands-on activities	dancing, gymnastics, sports activities, etc.
Interpersonal intelligence	learning with peers or others	cooperative skills training, emotional participation, talking to people, etc.
Intrapersonal intelligence	activities that reflect the emotions and experiences of the inner world	independent thinking, self-understanding, self-regulation, thinking skills, writing diaries, etc.
Naturalist intelligence	observing things, classifying, appreciating	discovering and revealing problems, observing and watching natural phenomena, forecasting weather, etc.

TASK 1.4.2B

Reading 1.4.2B A Test on Multiple Intelligences

We have just looked at the eight intelligences. Now choose a topic from below and work in groups. Design some learning tasks involving different intelligences. Do not design one single task for one intelligence but try to put together a number of activities involving different intelligences for learning a particular topic. (If you would like to find out what a multiple intelligences test is like, you may refer to **Reading 1.4.2 B**).

- Numbers
- Colors
- Family
- Hobbies
- School
- Weather
- Seasons
- Countries and cities

➢ Shopping

Discussion Point

— Have you ever noticed that your pupils are different in terms of intelligences?

— Do you think multiple intelligences should be considered when you plan your lessons? If so, how do you achieve this in your teaching?

The above two tasks (Task 1.4.2A and B) intend to remind teachers that children are different, so different approaches and tasks should be adopted during the process of teaching. It would be useful if teachers put the topic in the center and think of possible activities suitable for different intelligences when planning their lessons. By doing so, children with different intelligences can all enjoy the learning process and make progress with the best support they can get.

1.4.3 What type of person are you?

TASK 1.4.3 A

Please do the following personality quiz to discover what type of person you are.

What type of person are you?	Y	N	S
1. Are you usually smiling and happy?			
2. Do you enjoy the company of other people?			
3. Do you find it difficult to get along with new people?			
4. Is it important for you to succeed in what you do?			
5. Does your mood change often and suddenly for no reason?			
6. Do you notice other people's feelings?			
7. Do you think the future will be good?			
8. Can your friends depend on you?			
9. Is your room often in a mess?			
10. Do you get annoyed if you have to wait for anyone or anything?			
11. Do you put off until tomorrow what you could do today?			
12. Do you work hard?			
13. Do you keep your feelings and ideas to yourself?			
14. Do you often give presents?			
15. Do you talk a lot?			
16. Are you usually calm and not worried about things?			

Note: Y for Yes, N for No, and S for Sometimes.

TASK 1.4.3B

Please tick the following adjectives that describe your personality according to the results from Task 1.4.3A, and write a short summary about your personality in the space provided below.

1. cheerful	___	9. untidy	___
2. sociable	___	10. impatient	___
3. shy	___	11. lazy	___
4. ambitious	___	12. hard-working	___
5. moody	___	13. reserved	___
6. sensitive	___	14. generous	___
7. optimistic	___	15. talkative	___
8. reliable	___	16. easy-going	___

My personality:

____

____

1.4.4 What is your aptitude for learning a foreign language?

TASK 1.4.4

Reading 1.4.4. is an aptitude test for finding out how talented you are for learning a foreign language. Finish the test and then, discuss with your group members the following questions.

a) Did you get the same score in this test? What makes the difference?

b) Can you think of any qualities (personalities, learning styles, etc.) that might help or hinder your language learning? Please add more to the following list.

☐ extrovert ☐ introvert ☐ risk-taking ☐ sociable ☐ ☐

c) Do you agree that children of the same age are basically the same in the way they learn new things? If your answer is NO, can you give some examples? Why is it important for a teacher to understand individual differences in language learning?

d) How can a teacher cope with children of different personalities? What is the possible influence on language learning? What can the teacher do?

Discussion Point

Howard Gardner's theory on multiple intelligences helps teachers realize the different intelligences pupils have, so that they would try different types of activities or teaching methods that cater for the different needs. As we all know that education should not try to make different people the same. In fact, we want everyone to maintain his/her own special character. Besides, we have to agree that we are born to be different. Therefore, we need to be treated differently. If a teacher can think of multiple intelligences when planning a lesson, his/her pupils will definitely benefit a lot from the lesson.

Learner difference is another important topic for language learning and teaching. Only when teachers realize the differences between their pupils are they able to teach according to the needs and the learning styles of the pupils.

1.5 Why should teachers treat children as equal human beings?

Compared with adults, children are small and weak. This makes parents and teachers almost automatically feel that they are at a superior status and they know what's best for children. It is difficult for adults to treat children's ideas and needs as equally important as theirs. Most of the time, adults choose either to ignore or to criticize children. In this section, we are going to look at some cases where children are treated equally.

1.5.1 How should teachers treat children?

Task 1.5.1A

Look at the following 9 statements and discuss with a partner whether you agree with them or not.

Statements	Agree/Disagree
1. Children know what they want.	
2. Children should do their own things by themselves.	
3. Children shouldn't be given too many restrictions.	
4. It is possible that parents can chat with their children like friends.	
5. Parents should respect children's own choices.	
6. Teachers should provide opportunities for children to try something they want to do.	
7. Teachers do not necessarily know more than children do. They can learn together.	
8. Teachers should be the best friends of children.	
9. Teachers have every reason to trust children.	

Task 1.5.1B

Reading 1.5.1
Two stories

Please read **Reading 1.5.1** and write down your opinions about the 2 teachers' stories below. Then share your opinions with your partner.

Discussion Point

In Task 1.5.1A and B, we introduced the idea that children should be treated respectfully as individuals. Parents should respect their children and try to help them become independent with good ability in solving problems and communicating with others. Similarly, teachers should also treat children equally and try to be their friends. Adults have to believe in children so that they can let them have more control over their own life. Some might say children do not know what's good for them and what's right to do. This could be true and they need guidance from adults. However, this does not mean that adults can ignore children's feelings and force things into their heads. We need to understand them, respect them, love them and look after them. If we treat our children in the appropriate way, they will give us a big surprise by showing how well they can take responsibility.

1.5.2 How do you understand humanistic education?

Task 1.5.2

Please try to answer the following questions and compare your understanding with **Reading 1.5.2**.

a) What do you think " humanistic education" is?
b) Does "humanistic education" guarantee good teaching?
c) Does "humanistic education" mean the teacher should not consider discipline?
d) "Humanistic education doesn't teach basic language skills." Do you agree?
e) What does "humanistic education" mean to children? Why do we need it?

Discussion Point

Treating children as human beings is easy to say but difficult to achieve. Parents tend to have strong desires to protect their children, to control them and to spoil them. As a parent, when you see a child doing something dangerous or doing something with difficulty, you would want to help him/her immediately. This intention is part of our human nature and should be respected. However, too much attention and care can destroy children's ability to create, to try new things and even to do basic things in life. When these children grow up, when they have to be independent in doing things and making decisions, and when their parents can't be with them, they would suffer a lot because they depend too much on their parents. That is, of course, not something we have desired. Therefore, we should learn to offer them opportunities to try and to create. This is the same with language learning. Children need to learn to try a new language and to become independent learners.

Meanwhile, teachers and parents tend to think that children are just like a blank piece of paper. They should be fed with knowledge which might be useful for their future life. As a result, children are given very little respect and freedom in choosing or developing their own way of thinking and learning. We believe that children should be respected in terms of what to learn and how to learn. Humanistic education requires teachers to treat children as human beings who have their own thoughts and needs. Teachers should never try to force their ideas into children's minds and should always try to think at the same level as children.

1.6 What makes a good primary English teacher?

In the previous sections, we have discussed the special features of children as language learners and realized the importance of meeting their different needs and treating them as equal human beings. This has put the primary English teachers in a situation where they have to face the challenge. Therefore, in this section we are going to explore the qualities that a good primary English teacher should have.

1.6.1 What role does a primary school teacher have to play?

TASK 1.6.1

A primary school teacher may have to play many different roles. Look at the following list and tick the ones that you agree with and then compare and discuss the meaning of each with your partner.

- ☐ A parent
- ☐ A guide
- ☐ A friend
- ☐ A motivator
- ☐ An organizer
- ☐ An observer
- ☐ A helper
- ☐ A singer
- ☐ A dancer
- ☐ An actor
- ☐ A story teller
- ☐ A participant
- ☐ A discipline controller
- ☐ An evaluator

Discussion Point

It is quite possible that you have ticked all of the above. Yes, being a good primary teacher is not an easy thing. It seems that there are many roles we need to play in teaching so as to motivate our learners and offer them the best educational opportunity. However, it is not always possible that we can play all these roles equally well. Our personal styles are different. Besides, you do not need to be a dancer or an actor to be able to teach in the primary school. Of course those capabilities will certainly add to your strength as a primary school teacher. The point we would like to make is: not everybody can be the same. Be yourself. You do not need to feel bad if you cannot sing or dance, you can always find a way to develop your strength. Dean (2001) invites all the teachers to develop their own styles in teaching. She says that the best way of working depends not only on what is important in the curriculum but also upon your strength, your personality, your experience, your beliefs and the situation in which you work.

1.6.2 What is a good primary English teacher like?

TASK 1.6.2

The following may be some of the qualities required/expected of a good primary English teacher. Tick the ones that you agree with and add more if you can. Compare what you have with a partner and give your reasons.

- ☐ She/He needs to be good-looking.
- ☐ She/He needs to have a very loud voice.
- ☐ She/He needs to be good at singing and dancing.
- ☐ She/He needs to be good at playing games.
- ☐ She/He needs to be good at drawing.
- ☐ She/He needs to be very young.
- ☐ She/He needs to be fond of children.
- ☐ She/He needs to be very encouraging.
- ☐ She/He needs to be good at controlling children.
- ☐ She/He needs to have a good command of English grammar.
- ☐ She/He needs to be good at acting.
- ☐ She/He needs to have good pronunciation.

Discussion Point

It is really not easy to be a good primary school teacher. A report of research into the effectiveness of primary school teachers by Hay McBer (2000 cited from Dean, 2001) reported in the *Times Educational Supplement* listed the following descriptions by children of a good teacher, which may be helpful for you to summarize your points.

A Good Teacher...

is kind
is generous
listens to you
encourages you
has faith in you
keeps confidence
likes teaching children
likes teaching their subject
takes time to explain things
helps you when you are stuck
tells you how you are doing
allows you to have your say
doesn't give up on you
cares for your opinion
makes you feel clever
treats everybody equally
tells the truth
is forgiving

As far as teaching English is concerned, besides many other qualities, a very important quality is obviously proficiency of the English language, that is to say, you should be competent in English, which means you must have reasonably good pronunciation and intonation, can communicate with the language in oral and written forms and can understand some basic English grammar. Besides, you also need to be good at using different teaching techniques which work with children. You can not use the same method for teaching adults to teach children. That will definitely lead your teaching to failure. You need to be versatile, have the ability to sing and act, good at telling stories and acting out in drama, even at drawing and dancing. Also, you need to be able to organize games and activities. To teach adults, you do not need to worry about all these. As long as you are competent in the language, knowledgeable, and can explain the language well, in general, you will survive in an adult class.

1.6.3 Do you have the potential to be a good primary English teacher?

TASK 1.6.3

Make a list of the qualities that you think you possess in the left column and the qualities you would like to further develop in the right column. Then discuss what you have written with a partner.

Qualities that you think you possess to be a good primary English teacher	Qualities you wish to develop further
1.	1.
2.	2.
3.	3.
4.	4.
5.	5.

Discussion Point

Primary school English teachers need to possess special qualities in addition to language competence and teaching capabilities. Primary school teachers need to understand how children think and learn. You need to care for the whole child instead of just caring for the language that you are teaching. You need to help children develop in an all round way—linguistically, intellectually, culturally, and morally. You need to guide them in mastering learning strategies and learning how to learn, and help them develop the ability of using imagination and learn to solve problems. You also need to teach them to care for others and respect others. Language is both a target for teaching and a tool that should carry rich educational content for children.

Phillips (1993) points out that teachers of young learners "need special skills, many of which have little to do with the language, which becomes a by-product of learning activities rather than a centrepiece. Helping children learn and develop becomes more important than simply teaching the language. The approach and techniques are therefore drawn from good general educational theory and practice rather than from a narrow TEFL (Teaching English as a Foreign Language) repertoire".

From the above discussions, we can see that a good primary school English teacher needs to develop competence in at least three areas: the English language, the understanding of children and the techniques and methods for teaching English to children. Knowing the language and knowing how to communicate with the language are essential to an English teacher. Understanding how children think and learn is the key to undertake primary education. Techniques and methods for teaching English to children are necessary skills for a primary school English teacher and they can be trained and developed.

Reading

Reading 1.2.2

第一语言与第二语言的学习过程及其启示

教学法的探讨需回归到最根本的问题：儿童是如何学会说话的？人类是如何学习第二语言的？

一、儿童是如何学会说话的？

早期的语言学家认为，人类语言的形成来自不断的示范及模仿。孩子在牙牙学语时，若发出某些声音与成人的语言相类似，如 Ma-Ma, Ba-Ba 等音，便得到回应，在许多次回应及鼓励之后，他们便知道：下次看到这个人就叫 Ma-Ma(妈妈)，看到那个人就叫 Ba-Ba(爸爸)。儿童语言的发展是儿童自己对声音的实验、成人不断地给予示范及正强化的结果。

也有语言学家相信人类的语言架构与生俱来，随着年龄的增长及生理的成熟，内在的语言能力便逐渐被开发出来。所以不论外在的语言环境如何，只要渐趋成熟，人便能展现语言的能力。

心理学家皮亚杰和维果茨基提出的儿童认知发展理论使语言学家对语言发展有了新的看法：语言是人类借由各项活动与环境互动的产物，是具有社会性的，是一种主动且持续进行的过程。当然，示范、正强化及年龄对语言发展都有影响，但是儿童并非一味模仿成人的语言，成人在适当时机给予协助，往往能成为关键性的助力。儿童主动使用语言进行有意义的表达，其语言能力也是随着他们生活需要及对周围人和事的兴趣的增加而逐渐提高的。

二、人类是如何学习第二语言的？

事实上，学习第二语言的过程与第一语言相当类似。要学好英语，首先就要置身在英语的环境中，让儿童熟悉这种语言的声音与音调，英语对话为儿童提供了丰富的词汇及句型来源。所谓的“英语的环境”，可以是在家中听、看英语绘本，浏览英语网站或是到以英语为主要语言的国家旅游等。当然身处英语的环境中的时间越长，效果越显著。

其次，我们还要检视英语的学习方式。因为儿童学习语言是一种主动的过程，需要与环境进行有意义的互动，所以全语言教学法（whole language approach）是一种值得参考的语言教学观念。学校英语课程融入听、说、读、写技巧，以生活化的主题呈现内容。换言之，语言的学习融入对生活知识的探索中，活动内容对儿童而言有趣且有意义。随着生活阅历、知识的增加，儿童掌握的词汇及句型也越来越多。活动内容要根据儿童的年龄及英语能力而调整，重点是将听、说、读、写技巧自然地融入这些活动。儿童在进行各项讨论、扮演各种角色或查询资料时，因为要表达、要沟通，加上有教师在语言上的引导及辅助，便自然地将词汇及句型加以运用，这样的效果远超过传统式的教学。家长在为孩子选择英语课程时，不妨多了解教师的教学方式，看看是不是能提供这样生活化、有意义，并能让孩子主动参与的课程。

Reading 1.4.4

A Quiz: Test Your Language Aptitude

Interpret your score

Below is a quiz for testing your language aptitude. It is adapted from the *Sunday Times Magazine*. Write your answers on a piece of paper and then add up your scores to find out how good a language learner you are.

1. Learn the following Samoan words (The Independent State of Samoa is in the South Pacific):

   toalua husband
   tamaloa man
   tamaitiiti child
   taulealea youth
   loomatua old woman

   Did you find this task
   a) easy and fascinating?
   b) very difficult?
   c) not easy; the words look the same?
   d) so boring you didn't even try?

2. Exhausted after swimming in the river, Fred decided to get some sleep, but the ***boolles*** made it impossible, and even the smoke from his camp fire didn't keep them away.

   What is a ***boolle***?
   a) a wild animal b) a giant mosquito
   c) a kind of noise d) don't know

3. Someone asks you the way in very bad English. When he/she doesn't understand your reply, do you
   a) say it again but louder?
   b) get irritated and give up?
   c) draw him/her a map?
   d) find out if he/she speaks another language you know?

4. Here is a new language:
   ek kum chuchu — the train is coming
   ek namas chuchu — the train is very big

nek kum niva chuchu — the train isn't coming

ek chuchu — it's a train

How would you say " it's not a train" ?

a) *nek chuchu niva*

b) *ek niva chuchu*

c) *nek niva chuchu*

d) don't know

5. How many foreign languages can you greet someone in?

6. Your boss tells you that you have been chosen to go on a six-month course to learn a completely new language. Do you

   a) plan to look for another job?

   b) say he/she has chosen the wrong person?

   c) worry a bit but reckon you'll cope?

   d) long to get started?

7. You go to an evening class to learn a language. The class lasts two hours a week. List the sorts of practice you might do on your own at home.

8. How good are you at expressing yourself in your own language, both in speaking and in writing?

   a) I can always put into words exactly what I want to say.

   b) I don't know.

   c) It depends on the situation.

   d) People sometimes say I am not clear.

9. When did you last read a book for pleasure (in any language)?

   a) Yesterday.

   b) I can't remember.

   c) Last week.

   d) Last month.

10. Have you got

    a) a bilingual dictionary (English into your language)?

    b) a monolingual dictionary (English-English)?

    c) both a bilingual and a monolingual dictionary?

    d) no dictionary at all?

11. Read through this list of words, then write down as many of them as you can without looking.

    Pin church identify luxury accelerate carefully miscalculate occasional anxious know daffodil impertinent

12. In one minute write a list of things you could do with a cabbage (apart from cooking or eating it).

13. In one minute write down as many reasons as you can why it might be useful to learn Eskimo.

14. Fill in the blank with one of the words below.
    Shakucomespiteare isos wonone ovofef tehe wororolid's grematerest's wririterners. Hehe wasis ____ onin Staratarafoorrd-inon-Aravont.
    a) borotone b) born c) shororit d) don't know

15. What is your attitude to learning about British culture (arts, institutions, ways of life)?
    a) I'm not interested in the slightest. I just need to learn the language.
    b) I'm interested a little bit, but only out of curiosity.
    c) I'm very interested in finding out about the people behind the language.

16. What do the following words in Samoan mean?
    toalua tamaloa tamaitiiti taulealea Loomatua

17. Are you male or female?

Reading 1.5.2

What Humanistic Education Is...And Is Not

In the field of education and especially in today's society, "humanistic education" is the subject of considerable interest and controversy. Many people of goodwill immediately react "for it" or "against it," depending on previous experience with the term. Actually, the term means many different things to different people. What follows is a very brief attempt by a number of educators to clarify the term "humanistic education" by describing what it is and what it is not.

Humanistic education is an educational approach. Most educators who advocate humanistic education typically intend this approach to mean one or more of three things:

(1) Humanistic education teaches a wide variety of skills which are needed to function in today's world—basic skills such as reading, writing and computation, as well as skills in communicating, thinking, decision-making, problem-solving and knowing oneself.

(2) Humanistic education is a humane approach to education—one that helps students believe in themselves and their potential, that encourages compassion and understanding, that fosters self-respect and respect for others.

(3) Humanistic education deals with basic human concerns—with the issues throughout history and today that are of concern to human beings trying to improve the quality of life—to pursue knowledge, to grow, to love, to find meaning for one's existence.

Humanistic education methods are used in public and private schools, the family, religious education, business and other settings.

Humanistic education enhances the teaching of the basics. Rather than ignoring the basics, humanistic educators seek to expand our concept of what basic education is, saying that basic skills for surviving in today's world go beyond reading, writing, computation, and vocational skills and include skills for communicating, problem-solving and decision-making.

Humanistic education is supported by years of research and experience. One of the strongest reasons for supporting humanistic education is that, when done effectively, students do learn! Considerable evidence shows that cooperative learning structures higher self-concepts, and the student's motivation and interest in learning are related to greater academic achievement. These results do show that humanistic education is a valid educational approach that deserves serious attention and respect.

Humanistic education supports many goals of parents. Does a parent sometimes wish his or her children would listen more respectfully, choose less impulsively, calm down when overexcited, learn to be assertive without being aggressive, and make better use of their time? Many methods of humanistic education teach students how to do these things. Several approaches of humanistic education teach students to relax and control their nervous energy and to plan and take more responsibility for their time.

Humanistic education encourages parent involvement in the schools. Humanistic educators believe that parents should be knowledgeable about their children's curriculum, active in parent-teaching activities, able to visit the school and observe, should have a way to make suggestions or register complaints about their child's program, and within reasonable limits, should be allowed to request alternative learning options for their children when they disagree strongly with school practices.

Humanistic educators believe that schools have a role to play in the "values education" of students. Few parents have ever questioned the school's role in encouraging the values of punctuality, fairness, health, courtesy, respect for property, neatness and the like. Humanistic educators believe schools also should encourage the democratic and humanitarian values of tolerance, self-respect, freedom of thought, respect for others, social responsibility and the like. Schools cannot and should not be "value-free."

Humanistic education is not psychotherapy. Teachers do not need to be trained psychologists to conduct humanistic education activities. They do require sensitivity to students needs, classroom management skills, and the ability to conduct a class discussion. These skills are within the grasp of all good teachers.

Humanistic education is not a panacea. No one claims that implementing methods and approaches of humanistic education will instantly, or even eventually solve all of a society's problems. There are many problems in our communities, country and society which require complex and long-term solutions. At best, humanistic education can better equip young people with the skills and attitudes to play a more effective role in seeking these solutions.

Humanistic education is not necessarily synonymous with good teaching. Just as there are many "traditional" teachers who do a poor job of teaching reading and writing, there are also ineffective "humanistic" educators. We should encourage all teachers to get the training they need to do the best possible job. And the government should provide the support and funds to help the schools continue attracting qualified and competent professionals.

Humanistic education is essential for preparing young people to be citizens. Citizens must know how to gather information, distinguish fact from opinion, understand many different viewpoints, understand justice, think for themselves, communicate their opinions clearly, and work with others for the common good. These are among the most important skills that humanistic education seeks to teach our youth.

Unit 2

Understanding the National English Curriculum

Aims of the unit

In this unit, we are going to focus on the following:

2.1 Why is English offered in primary schools?

2.1.1 What are the values of offering English in primary schools?

2.1.2 What supports are needed to ensure a successful provision of a foreign language in primary schools?

2.2 What are the main goals for primary English?

2.2.1 What do you think should be the main goals and objectives for primary English?

2.2.2 What are the main goals of English education for schools in China over the past 40 years or so?

2.2.3 What does each aspect of the core competencies mean and how do they relate to each other?

2.2.4 How is the overall curriculum structure presented in the 2022 Curriculum?

2.2.5 How are the levels designed in the 2011 and 2022 Curricula ?

2.3 How is the content of the 2022 Curriculum organized?

2.3.1 How do we understand the content structure of the 2022 Curriculum?

2.3.2 What does each content element in the 2022 Curriculum refer to ?

2.3.3 What highlights can be found in the content requirements of the 2022 Curriculum for Levels 1 & 2?

2.4 What academic achievement standards are specified for Levels 1 & 2 in the 2022 Curriculum?

2.4.1 What are the functions of academic achievements?

2.4.2 How is the EAAS presented and why?

2.5 What are suggested for teaching the Preparatory Level and Levels 1 & 2?

2.5.1 Suggestions for teaching the Preparatory Level

2.5.2 Specific learning activities and requirements for the Preparatory Level

2.5.3 Suggestions for teaching Levels 1 & 2 learners

2.6 What general teaching suggestions are specified in the 2022 Curriculum?

2.7 Summary: implications for the future

[微课]
课程发展背景

China's national curriculum reform in basic education has witnessed rapid development. Specifically, it has gone through three stages. The first stage began in the 1990s with the goals focusing on developing students' basic language knowledge and skills, known as the "Double Basics Goals" stage. This stage, which lasted for about 10 years, focused on memorizing vocabulary and grammar rules, in addition to developing students' four language skills—listening, speaking, reading and writing with inadequate attention paid to educating the person.

In 2001, a nation-wide curriculum reform was initiated which signaled the beginning of the second stage known as the "Three Dimensional Goals" stage. This stage advocated a more student-oriented education which stressed not only the teaching of basic knowledge and skills, but also attending to processes and strategies, as well as cultivating students' positive emotions, right attitudes and value building. Under the guidance of the "Three Dimensional Goals" , the English curriculum shifted its goals from the "Double Basics" to the "Overall Language Ability" , a more student-centered orientation, reflecting a care for whole person development and quality-oriented education. The goal of "Overall Language Ability" has five components, i.e. language skills, language knowledge, emotional attitudes, learning strategies, and cultural awareness. The revised English curriculum entitled *English Curriculum Standards for Compulsory Education (2011 Edition),* (hereafter 2011 Curriculum) continued with the same goal until a newly revised edition of the English curriculum was released in April, 2022.

This newly issued *English Curriculum Standards for Compulsory Education (2022 Edition),* (hereafter 2022 Curriculum) has designated a new shift of goals from developing students' "Overall Language Ability" to cultivating students' "Core Competencies" through the subject of English. This signaled the beginning of the third stage — the "Core Competencies Goals" stage. The "Core Competencies Goals" in the English curriculum consist of four components, namely, language ability, cultural awareness, thinking capacity, and learning ability (Figure 2.0.1).

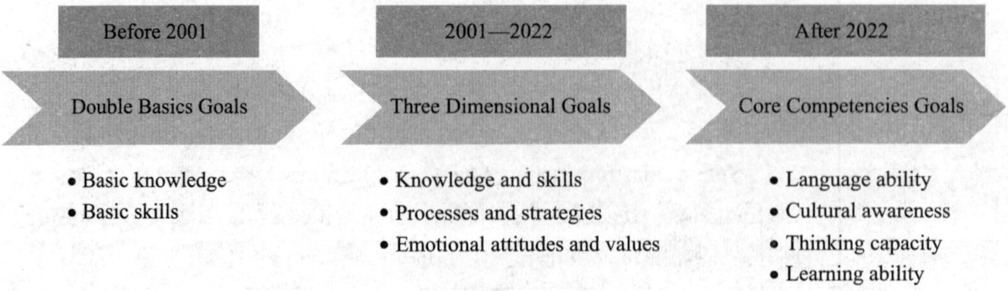

Figure 2.0.1 An overview of the English curriculum development

Such a shift serves as a new guiding compass for advancing China's English education at the school level in the new era. Along with the new goals, both the curricular content and instructional approaches have been restructured. To successfully implement the curriculum, English teachers need to understand what has been changed, why these changes are made and how we can transform the English curriculum blueprint into classroom practice.

2.1 Why is English offered in primary schools?

It is commonly believed that for learning a foreign language, the younger the better. In fact, researches have so far shown controversial results. Despite many different views about when the best age is for learning a foreign language, the introduction of a foreign language to young learners is developing rapidly all over the world. At the turn of the century, a lot of governments in the world began to offer a foreign language in primary schools. China is among them. From 2001, English has become a required course in primary schools from grade 3. Why are so many countries eager to have a foreign language included in the school curriculum? There must be some reasons for doing so.

2.1.1 What are the values of offering English in primary schools?

TASK 2.1.1A

Discuss the values and benefits of introducing English at the primary level in China. Write them down in the space provided and then compare your list with **Reading 2.1.1**.

The values and benefits of introducing English at the primary level
1.
2.
3.
4.

Discussion Point

One of the major needs for introducing a foreign language to primary school pupils is that the world is becoming a global village. People from different countries and cultures need to communicate far more frequently in order to live together. World peace and advances in business and technology also depend more and more on the understanding among different people and cultures. Every world citizen is faced with the challenge to gain the abilities to live and communicate in this multilingual and multicultural international society. Furthermore, people need to be educated from childhood to understand this multicultural world, and become prepared linguistically and attitudinally to communicate with others in the world open-mindedly.

The 2022 Curriculum states explicitly at the very beginning of the values and benefits for introducing English to students at the compulsory stage. It is reclaimed to follow the 2011 Curriculum that the English curriculum has both an instrumental and a humanistic nature as shown below.

The English curriculum for compulsory education is an integration of instrumentality and humanity, and is characterized by being foundational, practical, and comprehensive. Learning and using English provides an opportunity for students to learn about different cultures, conduct cross-cultural comparison, and capture the best of world cultures. It enables them to develop an awareness and ability to engage in cross-cultural communication and exchange, learn to perceive the world objectively and sensibly, and shape their international perspectives. It helps them develop a sense of family and national identity, enhance cultural confidence, form correct world views, life views, and values, thus laying a foundation for students' lifelong learning and future success.

TASK 2.1.1B

[微课]
课程性质的比较

Read the following two descriptions regarding the nature of the English curriculum (Table 2.1.1). What difference can you find between the 2011 and 2022 editions?

Table 2.1.1 The nature of the English curriculum

2011 Curriculum	2022 Curriculum
义务教育阶段的英语课程具有**工具性和人文性双重性质**。**就工具性而言**，英语课程承担着培养学生基本英语素养和发展学生思维能力的任务，即学生通过英语课程掌握基本的	义务教育英语课程体现**工具性和人文性的统一**，具有**基础性**、**实践性和综合性**特征。学习和运用英语有助于学生了解不同文化，比较文化异同，汲取文化精华，逐步形成

continued

2011 Curriculum	2022 Curriculum
英语语言知识，发展基本的英语听、说、读、写技能，初步形成用英语与他人交流的能力，进一步促进思维能力的发展，为今后继续学习英语和用英语学习其他相关科学文化知识奠定基础。**就人文性而言**，英语课程承担着提高学生综合人文素养的任务，即学生通过英语课程能够开阔视野，丰富生活经历，形成跨文化意识，增强爱国主义精神，发展创新能力，形成良好的品格和正确的人生观与价值观。工具性和人文性统一的英语课程有利于为学生的终身发展奠定基础	跨文化沟通与交流的意识和能力，学会客观、理性看待世界，树立国际视野，涵养家国情怀，坚定文化自信，形成正确的世界观、人生观和价值观，为学生终身学习、适应未来社会发展奠定基础

Discussion Point

Although both curricula state that the English curriculum enjoys a dual nature of instrumentality and humanity, the way how such a nature was described is different. For the 2011 Curriculum, its instrumental and humanistic nature was stated separately one by one, while the 2022 Curriculum describes its dual nature in an integrated way. This is quite a significant difference as the implementation of the 2011 Curriculum has witnessed some pressing issues in classroom teaching. That is, the instrumental nature of the curriculum has been prominently influential while the humanistic nature reflects a much weaker presence with little impact on students' development. The reason for this is that the two natures have been attended separately in classroom teaching, as an overall majority of classroom teaching time has been devoted to teaching language knowledge and skills with little attention paid to meaning of life behind the language. More often than not, activities related to value judgment or forming good attitudes are only added as a flavor at the end of a lesson with typically a slogan, a song, or a famous quote, leaving little time for students to engage in thinking and discussions of the deep meaning presented in the texts. The result is that teaching is conducted in a superficial, fragmented and modular manner with little learning taking place.

2.1.2 What supports are needed to ensure a successful provision of a foreign language in primary schools?

In the above section, we discussed the values and benefits for young children to learn a foreign language. Then, we will talk about: can a young age automatically guarantee the success of learning a foreign language?

TASK 2.1.2

Discuss the questions below in groups:

1. Do you agree that for learning a foreign language, the younger the better? Why?
2. What supports are needed to ensure the success of learning English in primary schools?

Discussion Point

Children have unique advantages over adults in learning another language, especially in acquiring good pronunciation and intonation. Other advantages include: they are good at imitation and not shy in speaking up. They are curious about learning and trying new things. However, age alone cannot guarantee the success of learning a foreign language. To ensure success, the introduction of primary English in schools needs much more support. First, qualified English teachers are needed, who should speak good English with adequate language knowledge and integrated skills. Second, teachers should understand how children think and learn so that appropriate methods can be selected, as children are different in many ways from adolescents and adults in learning a foreign language. In addition, a positive environment and relaxed and warm contexts are needed. Teachers need to develop special skills in managing, guiding, and facilitating children in learning. Finally, clear goals and objectives for teaching English to children should be established. For a better understanding of the international studies regarding offering foreign language for younger learners, please go to **Reading 2.1.2** for more information.

Reading 2.1.2 《国际小学外语教学研究及其启示》

2.2 What are the main goals for primary English?

2.2.1 What do you think should be the main goals and objectives for primary English?

TASK 2.2.1

The following are some statements concerning the goals of primary school English language teaching. Read them carefully and decide whether you agree with them. Add your opinions if you have more.

- ☐ To provide valuable experience for future language learning.
- ☐ To teach more vocabulary and structures to children.
- ☐ To help them obtain good pronunciation and intonation.

- ☐ To raise children's awareness of a different language and different cultures.
- ☐ To help children form good habits in learning a foreign language.
- ☐ To add interest and increase motivation for children learning another language.
- ☐ To lay a good basis for spoken English.
- ☐
- ☐
- ☐
- ☐
- ☐
- ☐

Discussion Point

Some people say that the fundamental goal for introducing English to primary school children is to help them develop English language skills and knowledge so that they are able to use English to communicate with others. We will say that this is only partly true. What should not be neglected at the same time is children's overall development as human beings. By offering a foreign language at the primary level, we are aiming to educate the whole child rather than only teach them the language. Therefore, the first priority for teaching English at the primary level is to cultivate children's interest in learning, motivate them to work hard, help them get into good learning habit and develop useful learning strategies so that they are ready to continue with further learning when they move into secondary schools. Introducing a foreign language to children is like opening up another window for them to see the other side of the world. This will arouse their interest and curiosity in different cultures and different ways of communication. It is hard to imagine that a child who gets tired of the subject will work hard and make efforts in learning it. In other words, if a child, after learning English in the primary school, hates it, you would not expect him/her to work hard on it and be motivated to continue learning it when he/she moves on to the secondary school. Therefore, motivation and interest in learning are fundamental to ensure success in learning a foreign language for children.

Children in primary schools are developing physically, emotionally, intellectually as well as linguistically. As language teachers, we need to care for children in an all round way, not only teaching the language for the sake of the language. Children, through learning the language, should be able to develop cross-cultural awareness, linguistic competence, self-esteem, confidence in learning, cognitive abilities as well as cooperative spirit. All these are important qualities to be developed for life-long learning.

2.2.2 *What are the main goals of English education for schools in China over the past 40 years or so?*

TASK 2.2.2A

Study the overall goals of English Language Teaching for schools in China presented in **Reading 2.2.2A** from 1978 to 2001. Discuss the major changes and their significance.

Discussion Point

As far as the overall goals are concerned, the previous syllabi before 2001 all put the mastery of language knowledge and language skills as the priority, reflecting a clear instrumental orientation, whereas the 2001 Curriculum focuses on developing students' comprehensive ability of language use, taking into consideration the development of students' interest, motivation, confidence and learning strategies in learning. In particular, the 2001 Curriculum indicates that the English curriculum for primary and secondary school students has both instrumental and humanistic nature, giving clear emphasis on developing students' whole being through the English subject rather than just teaching language knowledge and skills.

TASK 2.2.2B

The following presents the overall goals of the 2011 and 2022 Curricula for compulsory education in China. Study Figure 2.2.1 and Table 2.2.1 carefully along with the descriptions of the two sets of goals below. Discuss the differences and significance of the two sets of goals.

[微课]课程目标的比较

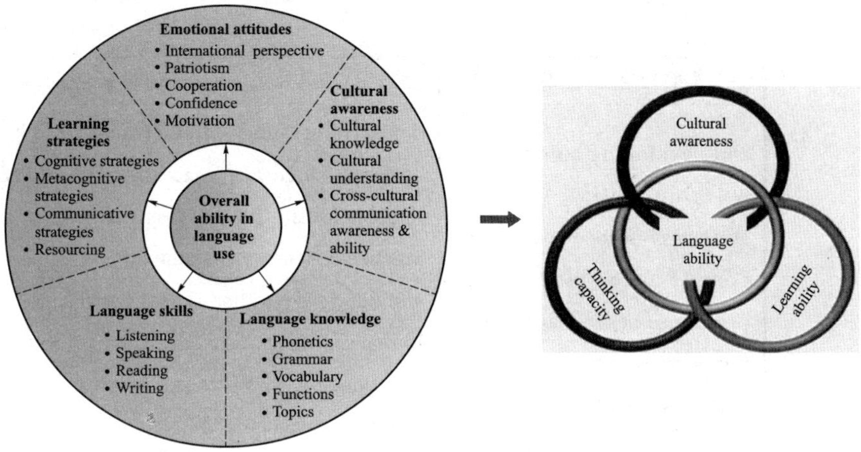

(a) 2011 Curriculum (b) 2022 Curriculum

Figure 2.2.1 The overall goals for the 2011 and 2022 Curricula

Table 2.2.1 The descriptions of overall goals for the 2011 and 2022 Curricula

2011 Curriculum	2022 Curriculum
The overall goal is to enable students to form a preliminary comprehensive language ability through English learning, promote mental development and improve comprehensive humanistic quality. The formation of comprehensive language ability is based on the overall development of language skills, language knowledge, emotional attitudes, learning strategies and cultural awareness. Language skills and knowledge are the basis of comprehensive language ability; Positive emotional attitude is conducive to promoting active learning and sustainable development; Effective learning strategies are conducive to improving learning efficiency	**1. Language ability development** To develop awareness of similarities and differences between the Chinese and English languages through language practice activities aimed at perceiving, experiencing, accumulating, and applying what they have learned, begin to establish a sense of the English language gradually, and increase experience of using the language for meaningful communication and exchange. **2. Cultural awareness cultivation** To learn about outstanding cultural achievements in different countries, compare cultural similarities and differences, develop cross-cultural communication ability, and form healthy and positive aesthetic tastes and correct values. To develop a deeper understanding of, and sense of identity with, Chinese culture, establish international perspectives, and build confidence in sharing culture. **3. Thinking capacity building** To develop the ability to think through learning English and to improve English learning while building thinking capacity; to observe and understand the world and look at things from multiple dimensions, and express views supported by evidence and facts in a coherent way; to develop logical thinking, dialectical thinking, and innovative thinking, and demonstrate a degree of being quick-witted, flexible, creative, critical, and profound when they think.

continued

2011 Curriculum	2022 Curriculum
and developing autonomous learning ability; Cultural awareness is conducive to the correct understanding and proper use of language. These five aspects complement each other and jointly promote the formation and development of students' comprehensive language ability	**4. Learning ability enhancement** To establish correct goals for English learning, keep sustained interest in English learning, and actively engage in language practice activities; listen attentively, be active in communication, and boldly try to use English in the process of learning; learn to explore things through their own initiative while be keen to collaborate with others and help each other; learn to reflect and evaluate on students' progress and adjust learning approaches as required; and learn about self-management for improving learning efficiency so that students are both passionate about learning and good at learning.

Discussion Point

The first difference lies in the fact that the two curriculua take two different positions. The 2011 Curriculum positioned itself from a disciplinary perspective with a focus on developing students' overall use of language ability based on language skills and language knowledge while the 2022 Curriculum positioned itself from the perspective of a students' development focusing on core competencies. Specifically, the goals for 2011 Curriculum are designed to develop students' overall language ability composed language skills, language knowledge, emotional attitudes, learning strategies and cultural awareness. However, it is not clear how these five parts may work together to contribute to students' overall language ability. The 2022 Curriculum aims at developing students' core competencies composed of language ability, cultural awareness, thinking capacity and learning ability. The overall goals are presented around each of the four aspects of core competencies with clear target descriptions and achievable objectives.

2.2.3 What does each aspect of the core competencies mean and how do they relate to each other?

TASK 2.2.3

How can we understand the meaning of each aspect of the core competencies which is to be developed through the English subject? What is the role of each aspect of the core competencies? Discuss in groups.

[微课]
核心素养的内涵与价值

Discussion Point

Reading 2.2.3A 谈核心素养（王守仁）

As we can see, the core competencies the English subject seeks to cultivate include four aspects, i.e. language ability, cultural awareness, thinking capacity, and learning ability. Among these aspects, language ability is the foundation; cultural awareness concerns value orientation; thinking capacity embodies the characteristics of mental and intellectual development; and learning ability is the key driving force behind them all. The core competencies are intertwined with one another and work with each other to develop learners in a coordinated manner.

The following presents the definitions of each aspect of the core competencies in the curriculum goals. Each definition consists of two parts. The first part defines a specific aspect. The second part defines the roles of each aspect in promoting the core competencies.

Language ability is the ability to understand and express meaning in specific contexts by using linguistic and non-linguistic knowledge as well as a range of strategies. Improving language ability helps students enhance cultural awareness, thinking capacity, and learning ability, and develop their ability to participate in cross-cultural communication.

Cultural awareness consists of an understanding of Chinese and foreign cultures, recognition and appreciation of fine cultures, and cross-cultural cognition, attitudes, and behaviors which students demonstrate in the new era. Developing cultural awareness helps students enhance their national identity and develop a sense of a global community and shared future. It also helps students learn to enhance their self-development, therefore becoming educated and responsible citizens.

Thinking capacity refers to students' skills employed in thinking and the quality of their thinking in terms of understanding, analyzing, inferring, judging, critiquing, and creating. Cultivating thinking capacity helps students learn to identify, analyze, and solve problems, and make correct value judgments.

Reading 2.2.3B 《义务教育英语课程中的思维品质培养》（陈则航）

Learning ability refers to students' awareness and ability to use and adjust English learning strategies actively, and expand English learning channels so as to increase the efficiency of English learning. Developing learning ability helps students master effective methods of English learning and develop good habits to enable life-long learning.

2.2.4 How is the overall curriculum structure presented in the 2022 Curriculum?

TASK 2.2.4

Look at the contents pages of the 2011 and 2022 Curricular below (Table 2.2.2). What differences can you find?

[微课]
新旧课标结构的比较

Table 2.2.2 The contents pages of the 2011 and 2022 Curricular

2011 年版目录	2022 年版目录
第一部分　前言	一、课程性质
一、课程性质	二、课程理念
二、课程基本理念	三、课程目标
三、课程设计思路	（一）核心素养内涵
第二部分　课程目标	（二）总目标
一、总目标	（三）学段目标
二、分级目标	四、课程内容
第三部分　分级标准	（一）内容要求
一、语言技能	（二）教学提示
二、语言知识	五、学业质量
三、情感态度	（一）学业质量内涵
四、学习策略	（二）学业质量描述
五、文化意识	六、课程实施
第四部分　实施建议	（一）教学建议
一、教学建议	（二）评价建议
二、评价建议	（三）教材编写建议
三、教材编写建议	（四）课程资源开发与利用
四、课程资源开发与利用建议	（五）教学研究与教师培训
附录	附录
1. 语音项目表；2. 语法项目表；3. 词汇表；4. 功能意念项目表；5. 话题项目表；6. 课堂教学实例；7. 评价方法与案例；8. 技能教学参考表；9. 课堂用语	1. 核心素养学段特征；2. 语音项目表；3. 词汇表；4. 语法项目表；5. 教学案例

Discussion Point

Four differences can be found from the contents pages of the two curricular. First of all, they have different organizational structures. The 2011 Curriculum has four sections, which are: Section I, Forward; Section II, Curriculum Goals; Section III, Standards Requirements by Levels; Section IV, Suggestions for Implementation, as well as

Appendices. The 2022 Curriculum has six sections, which are: Section I, Curriculum Nature; Section II, Curriculum Rationale; Section III, Curriculum Goals;Section IV, Curriculum Contents; Section V, Academic Acheviement Standards; Section VI, Suggestions for Implementation, followed by a few Appendices. It is obvious that the 2022 Curriculum begins with a statement of the curriculum and some guiding principles for the design of curriculum goals, curriculum contents, as well as teaching and assessment methods, etc.

Secondly, the 2011 Curriculum does not have a clear content section while the 2022 Curriculum has an independent content section.

Thirdly, a new academic achievement section is added to the 2022 Curriculum providing assessment guidance to ensure the quality of teaching and learning.

Finally, in the Suggestions for Implementation Section, a new subsection is added to the 2022 Curriculum giving suggestions on teaching research and teacher training. This is also the first time that teaching research and teacher training are included in the national curriculum and we can see a much greater emphasis from the Ministry of Education on the effectiveness and efficiency of teacher training to help teachers transform the curriculum blueprint into reality.

2.2.5 How are the levels designed in the 2011 and 2022 Curricula?

TASK 2.2.5

Look at the two figures below (Figure 2.2.2). How do you understand the leveled structures of the two curricula? What changes have been made?

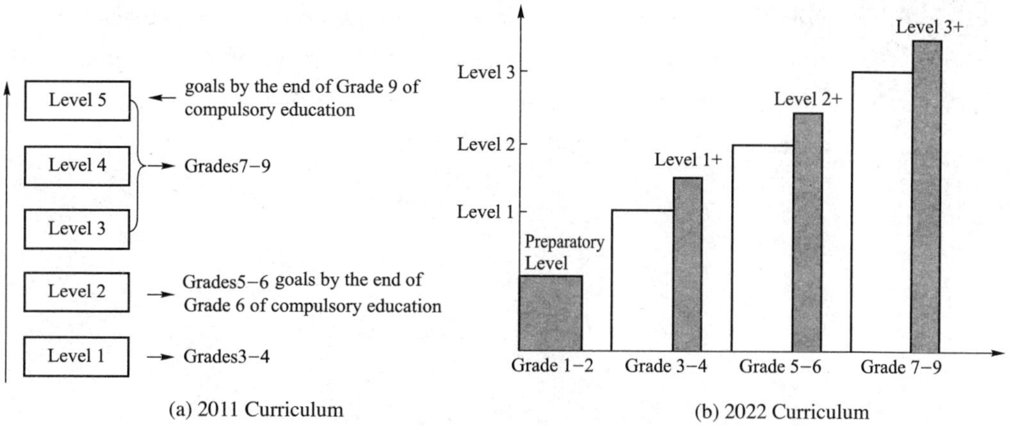

Figure 2.2.2 A Comparison of the leveled structures

Discussion Point

[微课]
分级课程设计的比较

As we all know, since 2001, a leveled system of curriculum structure has been introduced. For the 2011 Curriculum, they both used a 5 leveled structure for the 9-year compulsory education. Level One is aimed for primary grades 3–4 and Level Two is aimed for primary grades 5–6. Level Three, Four and Five are aimed at Grade 7–9 for the junior high school. As we can see, the leveled structure covers (two stages at the primary sector covering four grades), while the junior phase is divided into 3 basic levels covering three grades.

The newly issued the 2022 Curriculum optimized the leveled structures by dividing the 9-year compulsory education for English into three basic levels based on the key learning stages. Level 1 and Level 2 cover two learning stages at the primary phase with Level 1 targeting grades 3–4 and Level 2 at grades 5–6. Level 3 targets learning at stage three of grades 7–9 at the junior high school phase. With the newly designed level system, the English curriculum content requirements are presented around three levels, with Level 1 for Grade 3 and 4 students, Level 2 for Grade 5 and 6, and Level 3 for Grades 7–8 and 9. Taking into account of regional differences in the starting year of the English subject in primary schools, the 2022 Curriculum adds a preparatory level and three advanced levels in place (Figure 2.2.2 b). The Preparatory Level is designed to meet the teaching needs of Grade 1 and 2, mainly through activities such as viewing, listening, and speaking, while the advanced levels provide options for students capable of pursuing further studies. Content requirements for each advanced level are marked with a "+".

2.3 How is the content of the 2022 Curriculum organized?

全面和准确把握课程内容

With the 2022 Curriculum, developing students core competencies on language ability, cultural awareness, thinking capacity and learning ability through the subject of English have become the optimal goals. In order to achieve the goals, the curriculum content are carefully selected and restructured.

2.3.1 How do we understand the content structure of the 2022 Curriculum?

TASK 2.3.1

[微课]
课程内容结构与课程内容六要素的内涵

Curriculum content is an indispensable part in the curriculum. Look at Figure 2.3.1 below which shows the content structure of the 2022 Curriculum. How many content elements are there? What is the function of each element? What can you see in the outer circle? Why are they included as of the content structure?

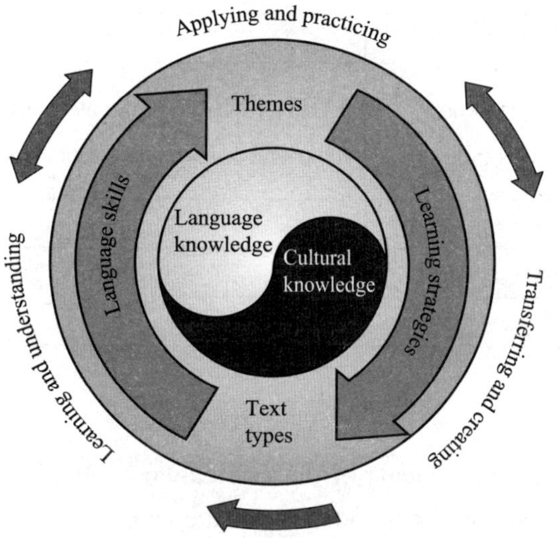

Figure 2.3.1 Content structure of the 2022 Curriculum

Discussion Point

The content of the English curriculum consists of six elements: **themes, text types, language knowledge, cultural knowledge, language skills, and learning strategies**. Built around these elements are the activities through which the contents are organized and processed by the students. The design of the curriculum content aims to advance the development of students' core competencies throughout the years of compulsory education. The activities that promote content learning include three major types. They are **learning and understanding, applying and practicing, and transferring and creating**.

2.3.2 What does each content element in the 2022 Curriculum refer to?

TASK 2.3.2

Read section IV in the 2022 Curriculum. Complete the information in the following table regarding the functions of each element. Then, discuss their relations with a partner.

Elements	Functions	What do they refer to?
Themes	Themes play the role of linking and unifying the other elements, providing the thematic contexts for language learning and student development.	man and self man and society man and nature
Text types		
Language knowledge	It provides the linguistic elements for the composition and expression of meaning.	
Cultural knowledge		
Language skills		
Learning strategies		

Discussion Point

The six components of the curriculum content are interconnected, and together they form the content foundation for the core competencies to be developed. Themes play the role of linking and unifying the other elements, providing the thematic contexts for language learning and student development. Text types are vehicles of language and cultural knowledge to elaborate the themes. Language knowledge provides the linguistic elements for the composition and expression of meaning. Cultural knowledge forms a source of knowledge for students to cultivate humanistic and scientific spirit, and develop good character and correct values. Language skills provide the means for students to collect information, construct knowledge, express ideas, and communicate feelings and emotions. Learning strategies provide specific measures for students to improve their learning with efficiency and effectiveness.

The following introduces the six elements in the content of the 2022 Curriculum, focusing on what each element refers to and what they include.

Themes. There are three broad categories of thematic contexts—**man and self, man and society, man and nature**. The theme of "man and self" takes the perspective of "I" and includes thematic clusters of "life and learning" and "learning to be and learning to do" . The theme of "man and society" takes the perspective of "society" and includes thematic clusters of "social services and interpersonal communication" , "literature, art, and sports" , "history, society, and culture" , and "science and technology" . The theme of "man and nature" takes the perspective of "nature" and includes the thematic clusters of "natural ecology" , "environmental protection" , "disaster prevention" , and "space exploration" . Each thematic cluster has several further sub-themes.

Text types. There are different types of text, including both **continuous texts**, such as dialogs, interviews, narration, exposition, argumentation, practical writing, songs, ballads, and children's rhymes, and **discontinuous texts**, such as charts, diagrams, web pages, and advertisements. Text types can also refer to spoken or written multimodal texts, such as words, recordings, videos, and digital forms.

Language knowledge refers to knowledge in pronunciation, vocabulary, grammar, discourse, and pragmatics, and serves as the foundation of language skills development. Specifically, **phonetic knowledge** is about the relationship between sounds and meaning which are inseparable, and language relies on sounds to realize its social communication function. English phonetic features include vowels, consonants, stress, units of meaning, intonation, rhythm, and so on (see Appendix II in the 2022 Curriculum). Through phonetic changes, the speaker expresses meaning and opinions as well as conveys attitudes, intentions, emotions, and so on. **Vocabulary knowledge** is the sum of all words and phrases in a language. Any word in the vocabulary is related to other words through a certain syntactic and semantic relationship, and it conveys information in the context. Learning vocabulary does not simply mean memorizing the sound, spelling, and meaning of the words. More importantly, it means using words in contextualized activities such as listening, speaking, reading, viewing, and writing to understand and express information or opinions related to various topics. **Grammar knowledge** includes morphology and syntax knowledge (see Appendix IV in the 2022 Curriculum). Morphology concerns the morphological changes of words, such as the number and case of nouns, the tense and aspect of verbs, while syntax concerns the structure of sentences, such as type of sentence, constituents of sentences, and word order. The relationship between morphology and syntax is very close. In language use, grammar is a unity of form, meaning, and use, which is also closely related to sounds, lexicon, discourse, and pragmatics, and directly affects the accuracy and appropriateness of understanding and expression. **Discourse knowledge** is a language unit that expresses meaning, and is the most common way people use language. In the process of using language, language users need to organize language into coherent texts with the use of discourse knowledge. Discourse knowledge is knowledge of how a text is constructed, how a text expresses meaning, and how people use texts in the process of communication. Discourse knowledge plays an important role in comprehension and expression, and helps language users understand the discourses they hear or read effectively. It also helps language users choose the appropriate text type, design a reasonable textual structure, plan the discourse components, and obtain textual cohesion and coherence so as to meet the needs of communication. **Pragmatic knowledge** refers to knowledge that helps language users understand others accurately and express themselves appropriately in specific contexts. Mastering pragmatic knowledge helps students choose formal or informal, direct or indirect, spoken or written language according to the purpose of communication, the degree of formalness of the communication occasion, and the identity and role of the participants, so as to communicate with others appropriately in order to achieve the purpose of communication.

Cultural knowledge covers knowledge about both material and spiritual cultures. The **material cultures** mainly include food, clothing, architecture, transportation, and inventions and creations in these areas. The **spiritual cultures** mainly include philosophy, science, history, language, literature, art, education, as well as values, moral cultivation, aesthetic taste, awareness of physical work, social conventions, and customs and traditions. Learning cultural knowledge is not limited to understanding and memorizing specific facts. Rather, it is more important to identify and judge the embedded attitudes and values.

Language skills consist of receptive and productive skills, including skills of listening, speaking, reading, viewing, writing, and integrated skills. Listening, reading, and viewing are **receptive skills**, while speaking and writing are **productive skills**. In the context of language skills, viewing skills are those of understanding meaning by making use of graphics, tables, animations, symbols, and videos in multimodal texts. In order to understand multimodal texts, students not only need to use traditional skills of text reading, but also need to study information from charts and tables to understand the meaning of symbols and animations. Receptive and productive skills mutually support and reinforce each other in the process of language learning.

Learning strategies refer mainly to meta-cognitive strategies, cognitive strategies, communication strategies, and affective strategies. Among these, **metacognitive strategies** are the strategies that students use to plan, monitor, evaluate, reflect on, and adjust the learning process or learning outcomes in order to develop learner autonomy. **Cognitive strategies** are the appropriate learning approaches, methods, and techniques students take to process linguistic information in order to improve the efficiency of

English learning. **Communication strategies** are the strategies adopted by students to gain more communication opportunities, maintain communication, and improve communication effectiveness. **Affective strategies** are the strategies used by students to regulate emotions in learning and maintain a positive learning attitude.

2.3.3 What highlights can be found in the content requirements of the 2022 Curriculum for Levels 1 & 2?

TASK 2.3.3

Work in groups. Read the content requirements of the 2022 Curriculum along with **Readings 2.3.3A** and **Reading 2.3.3B**. Make a list of the main highlights you can identify and discuss their implications. Then, share in class.

Reading 2.3.3B
《课程育人视角下英语课程内容的选择与组织》(张宏丽)

Main highlights:
1.
2.
3.
…

Discussion Point

The main highlights for the content requirements are summarized below:

Firstly, there is a strong emphasis on contextualized teaching of phonetic, vocabulary, and grammar knowledge. It stresses on guiding students to learn to use these types of knowledge for understanding and expressing meaning. The implications are that the teaching of phonetics, vocabulary and grammar knowledge to primary students should involve students in experiencing and using the language rather than telling them about the rules. More activities that can activate students' interests should be used such as listening and speaking activities, singing, chanting, acting, playing games, telling stories,and role-playing, as well as imitating, etc.

Secondly, new requirements are added for discourse knowledge and pragmatic knowledge as a foundation for developing effective receptive and productive skills. Discourse knowledge includes knowledge related to text types and their related features in organization and language use. Pragmatic knowledge includes knowledge related to the setting, participants, the purpose, etc. of communication events for determining whether the language or register used is formal or informal, direct or indirect so as to ensure the appropriateness in communication. The implications would be that when we teach the language, we should not teach phonetics, vocabulary or grammar separately from a text or a piece of discourse. Instead, we should focus our teaching on helping students understand the meaning conveyed by the text, either oral or written. Also, when we design speaking tasks, we need to make clear the setting, the participants, and the purpose of communication, so as to raise students' awareness about what language (e.g. formal or informal) should be used for that particular setting.

Thirdly, more specific requirements are provided regarding vocabulary and grammar knowledge at Level 1 and Level 2. For example, vocabulary requirements for Level 2 are 500 words and students are expected to learn to use them for oral and written communication. These 500 words are presented in the vocabulary list of Appendix 3 on page 87 in the 2022 Curriculum. Besides, 100–300 words may be learned through class learning and after class reading. In addition, a quantified requirement for out-of-class reading within Level 1 is 1 500–2 000 words and 4 000–5 000 words for Level 2. For Level 3 it reaches 150 000 words. The new curriculum continues to emphasize the importance of in-class guided reading and out-of-class free reading for helping students form good reading habits in order to prepare them for lifelong learning. A slight increase in vocabulary requirements at Level 1 and Level 2 indicates that the teaching of vocabulary should focus more on its use rather than on its usage. In other words, we should teach vocabulary in context for meaning so that students will not learn words through pure memorization and mechanical drilling, but through understanding and expressing meaning with vocabulary learned as a whole. In this way teachers can help learners build a vocabulary network around a particular topic. Also, additional reading after class becomes a very important way to support students to use the language they learned for real world reading and reading for interests. This can also help students consolidate and expand their vocabulary.

Last but not the least, the 2022 Curriculum redesigned the learning strategies requirements—highlighting the importance of metacognitive strategies and also adding affective strategies. The implications would be for the teacher to provide more guidance in supporting students to learn how to learn. Particularly, we can help students learn to make learning plans, carry out their plans, reflect on how well they do and what can be improved. In this way, we can gradually educate more autonomous and independent learners.

2.4 What academic achievement standards are specified for Levels 1 & 2 in the 2022 Curriculum?

2.4.1 What are the functions of academic achievements?

TASK 2.4.1

What is academic achievement? Do you think it is important to have academic achievement standards in the curriculum? Why?

Discussion Point

What is academic achievement? It is students' academic performance after they have completed their study of a subject at a certain level. Academic achievement standards are an overall portrayal of students' academic achievement built around the core competencies and the curriculum content. The English academic achievement standards are based on the core competencies, namely, language ability, cultural awareness, thinking capacity, and learning ability, and the developmental goals of these core competencies at each level. The standards also take into account the English curriculum content and the progressive outcomes of students' English learning at the stage of compulsory education, highlighting students' typical academic achievement in terms of learning outcomes at each level.

The English Academic Achievement Standards (EAAS) is a new section added to the 2022 Curriculum. It is also one of the significant changes in the 2022 Curriculum compared to the previous ones. With the EAAS, teachers will have a clearer idea as to what to aim for or what outcomes are expected of the students at each level after they complete their study at a certain level. Moreover, with the guidance of the EAAS, teachers will understand better how to assess students' learning regarding the students' core competencies. This will in turn influence teachers' ways of teaching, because in order to help students to reach the leveled achievement standards, teachers will have to change their ways of teaching. Therefore, the EAAS functions not only as a guide for teaching and learning, but also for assessment.

2.4.2 How is the EAAS presented and why?

TASK 2.4.2

Read Section V of the 2022 Curriculum on the EAAS. Discuss in groups: How is the EAAS presented and why?

Discussion Point

The EAAS describes specific learning outcomes in three levels according to the characteristics of students' academic performance at each level. The EAAS for each level in the 2022 Curriculum is presented in two parts. The first part provides a holistic picture of students' performance regarding their core competencies' i.e. language ability, cultural awareness, thinking capacity and learning ability, at a specific level. The second part provides a list of detailed performance criteria for assessing students' core competencies based on their linguistic and non-linguistic performances through receptive and productive activities. See Table 2.4.1、Table 2.4.2 and Table 2.4.3 for a detailed description for Level 1 and Level 2.

Table 2.4.1 Overall descriptions of the EAAS for Level 1 and Level 2

Level 1	Level 2
Level 1 (Grades 3–4)	Within the framework of the themes required at this level, with regard to the relevant thematic clusters and sub-topics, and according to the content requirements of language and cultural knowledge, students should be able to: start using language skills of listening, reading, speaking, and writing and learning strategies; perceive different linguistic and cultural phenomena based on text types of Level 1; obtain basic information; carry out short and simple communication with others; develop an initial awareness of questioning; try to reflect on how they learn; possess curiosity about learning English; take an active part in classroom activities, and be keen to collaborate and communicate with peers.
Level 2 (Grades 5–6)	Within the framework of the themes required at this level, with regard to the relevant thematic clusters and sub-topics, and according to the content requirements of language and cultural knowledge, students should be able to: use language skills of listening, reading, speaking, and writing and learning strategies effectively; learn about different linguistic and cultural phenomena based on text types of Level 2; compare similarities and differences of information; carry out communication with others orally or in writing; develop awareness of questioning; reflect on how they learn; take the initiative to discuss with others and ask for help when encountering difficulties in study.

Table 2.4.2 Specific descriptions of the EAAS for Level 1 (Grades 3–4)

No.	Academic achievement descriptions
1-1	Students can understand and respond to greetings in everyday life and use the language generally appropriately.
1-2	Students can interact with others and respond to praise, apologies, and acknowledgments using polite language.
1-3	Students can understand and respond to simple instructions with the help of pictures, gestures, and so on.
1-4	Students can learn about local customs of major countries in the world through simple animations, illustrated stories, and other types of text.
1-5	Students can possess curiosity about the English language, think actively when reading simple texts such as illustrated stories and dialogs, and try to ask questions about things they do not understand.
1-6	Students can imitate the pronunciation and intonation of speakers when following short audio and video materials.
1-7	Students can use simple language to introduce basic information about themselves and familiar things (e.g. personal preferences, school life, and so on).
1-8	Students can recognize or name typical Chinese and foreign cultural symbols when reading about and seeing them.
1-9	Students can write words and sentences they have learned correctly.
1-10	Students can model examples to write simple sentences.
1-11	Students are willing to observe linguistic and cultural phenomena in life, and try to look at things from different perspectives.
1-12	Students are willing to participate in classroom activities, and learn English with peers through imitation and performance.

Table 2.4.3 Specific descriptions of the EAAS for Level 2 (Grades 5–6)

No.	Academic achievement descriptions
2-1	Students can respond to others' invitations, wishes, requests, and so on using the language appropriately.
2-2	Students can infer the opinions and attitudes of a speaker with the help of key words.
2-3	Students can obtain basic information such as people, time, place, and event when listening to or watching simple audio and video materials.

continued

No.	Academic achievement descriptions
2-4	Students can learn about customs, dietary habits, and cultural traditions of major countries in the world through simple texts, and carry out an initial comparison of cultural similarities and differences.
2-5	Students can infer meaning of unknown words in a text with the help of pictures and contextual clues.
2-6	Students can sort out information about people, situations, and plots when reading texts of relevant themes, think independently, and put forward their own opinions.
2-7	Students can read aloud fluently the learned texts with clear articulation and generally correct pronunciation and intonation.
2-8	Students can communicate with others on relevant themes, express their own emotions, attitudes, and opinions, and generally achieve their communicative purpose.
2-9	Students can use simple sentences to describe specific phenomena and things related to Chinese and foreign cultures using generally coherent language.
2-10	Students can use learned words and sentence structures to tell simple and short stories with generally clear meaning.
2-11	Students can use capital and small letters and punctuation correctly in written expression with generally correct spelling.
2-12	Students can model examples to write simple greeting cards, invitation cards, and so on using generally accurate language.
2-13	Students can describe content of pictures in simple phrases and sentences with coherent meaning and generally correct sentence structures.
2-14	Students are willing to learn about different linguistic and cultural phenomena through reading and other ways, and try to analyze problems from different perspectives.
2-15	Students can develop interest in learning English, actively participate in classroom activities, discuss relevant themes with peers, and collaborate to complete learning tasks.

2.5 What are suggested for teaching the Preparatory Level and Levels 1 & 2?

2.5.1 Suggestions for teaching the Preparatory Level

TASK 2.5.1

Discuss in groups: What suggestions would you like to give for teachers teaching at the Preparatory Level (Grades 1–2)? Make a list and give your reasons.

Discussion Point

The following summarizes some tips for teaching at the Preparatory Level (Grades 1–2).

Firstly, it is very important for teachers to create a good learning environment to guide students to listen actively, encourage them to imitate, and facilitate them to express themselves freely. The teaching activities should focus mainly on viewing, listening, and speaking.

Secondly, teachers should support students to build up their vocabulary through listening and speaking activities, with understanding meaning as the priority. And it is important to engage children in simple everyday communications, and help them develop good learning habits.

Thirdly, teachers are suggested to choose themes close to students' everyday life, such as family and school life, plants and animals, and engage students' multiple senses in learning through direct, visualized, vivid, and engaging teaching methods. Teachers can also read stories, sing songs, and say children's rhymes with them to actively engage children in language learning and practice.

Finally, teachers should focus on students' classroom performance and participation when assessing their learning. It is very important to encourage students to speak up in English and participate in learning activities. Teachers can encourage students by giving them some verbal praises and useing "English-learning point cards" etc. to boost students' motivation for English learning, help build their confidence, and give them a sense of achievement.

2.5.2 Specific learning activities and requirements for the Preparatory Level

Table 2.5.1 provides a reference to learning activities and requirements of the Preparatory Level. Do you find them practical? What can you learn from the list? What implications can you draw? Share with a partner.

Table 2.5.1 Learning activities and requirements for Preparatory Level

Learning activities	Learning requirements
Listening and doing	1. Understand short classroom instructions and respond appropriately; 2. Act on words or instructions heard, such as pointing out the right pictures or objects, coloring, drawing, and doing something; 3. Understand simple, short stories with prompts of pictures and actions and respond appropriately.
Speaking and singing	1. Imitate to speak English following recordings; 2. Greet each other in simple language; 3. Exchange simple personal information, such as names and ages; 4. Guess the meaning and say the word according to miming; 5. Sing learned songs and children's rhymes individually or with others; 6. Say words or phrases based on pictures; 7. Express simple feelings, such as likes and dislikes.
Playing and performing	1. Play games in English as guided by the teacher and engage in simple communication with each other in the games; 2. Perform simple role-plays as guided by the teacher.
Viewing and listening	1. Watch English-speaking cartoons or English teaching programs with simple language, understand the main ideas, and imitate simple lines in them; 2. Carry out in-class listening and video-watching activities of at least 20 minutes per week.

2.5.3 Suggestions for teaching Levels 1 & 2 learners

TASK 2.5.3

What teaching notes are given for Level 1 and Level 2? What major differences can you find between Level 1 and Level 2? Complete the notes in the table below and then discuss in groups.

Level 1	Level 2

Discussion Point

The focal point of teaching for all levels stresses that the learning activities should be designed according to the curriculum content and should be related to real-life issues, so as to guide students to use their knowledge of English and knowledge of other subjects to solve problems through practice and investigation while developing and deepening their understanding of self, society, and nature. Table 2.5.2 highlights some specific teaching suggestions for Level 1 and Level 2.

Table 2.5.2 Main teaching notes for Level 1 and Level 2

Main teaching notes for Level 1	Main teaching notes for Level 2
1. Create a relaxing, equal, harmonious, classroom environment, fostering a good teacher-student relationship and mutual respect. In this way, students will not be afraid of making mistakes, and be brave to express their own views.	1. Attention should be given to boost students' interest in learning English and to create opportunities for them to experience success. Teachers should devise lively and diverse activities, such as exchanging dialogs, performing short plays, singing songs, creating stories, and designing posters, to support students with dif-

continued

Main teaching notes for Level 1	Main teaching notes for Level 2
2. Develop good learning habits, e.g. helping students develop simple study plans in the early stage of English learning, is just as important as developing their language skills. It is important for teachers to support students' learning with the help of pictures, videos, sketches, gestures and using activities such as listening to rhymed texts and sentences, listening to and singing songs, and listening to recordings of textbook passages. 3. In terms of vocabulary teaching, teachers should adopt the approach of integrating sound, form, meaning, and use, guiding students to perceive the pronunciation of words in context. Besides, creat opportunities for students to recycle the vocabulary in different contexts, but try to avoid simple memorization or isolated word practice out of context. As for grammar teaching, teachers should follow the principle of form-meaning-use unity, enabling students to see and experience the connections between form and meaning, allowing students to use the grammar learned in communication and expression. 4. Language learning activities should be designed in context with clear themes supported by different text types. Teachers should make good use of classroom activities and board work to help students internalize the language and cultural knowledge learned	ferent abilities and learning styles. For students with learning difficulties, teachers should provide more support, and fully acknowledge the efforts and progress they have made and help them learn to set achievable short-term goals, and work toward these goals through personal efforts. 2. Meaningful learning materials and activities should be used to develop students' spelling ability and phonological awareness and guide them to perceive and experience the stress, units of meaning, intonation, and rhythm of English through various language practice activities. 3. Emphasis should be given to coach students in developing learning skills, e.g. guide students to do an effective preview before the class and review after the class; sort out, organize, and summarize the learned content timely using charts and diagrams; carry out out-of-class English reading, listening, and video-watching on their own initiatives; use spelling rules to memorize words; and use dictionaries and other reference books to facilitate learning. 4. Integrated practice activities should be deployed to promote the overall development of the students' core competencies. Teachers should follow the principle of "learning and using English go hand in hand, in-class and out-of-class learning go hand in hand, and learning of different disciplines go hand in hand" to introduce integrated English practice activities, and broaden the scope of learning from textbooks to the much wider real world

2.6 What general teaching suggestions are specified in the 2022 Curriculum?

TASK 2.6

Go through the teaching suggestions in the 2022 Curriculum and find the focus of each suggestion. Are these suggestions related to each other? How? Refer to **Reading 2.6** for more information.

Reading 2.6
课程实施

Discussion Point

As we can see, there are altogether seven pieces of advice provided for classroom teachers. They cover almost all aspects of teaching.

The first suggestion is "**To adhere to educating people as the foundation**" . This suggestion serves as the guiding principle for setting teaching objectives, organizing teaching content, designing teaching activities and selecting assessment methods. It emphasizes that teachers should take the establishment of morality and cultivation of people as a fundamental task of English language teaching, accurately understand the core competencies and grasp the value of educating people through English lessons.

The second suggestion is **"To strengthen the integrity of unit teaching"** . It calls for integrated teaching of the content under the unit thematic theme. To do so, teachers should conduct in-depth analysis of the texts in each unit and perform necessary integration or reorganization of the content based on students' cognitive and life experience so as to establish a connection between the content and educational functions of each text in the unit so as to form an integrated, relevant and developmental unit blueprint for educating people. By doing so, teachers can guide students to explore the meaning of the themes so that they can gradually construct and generate deeper understanding, form positive attitudes and value judgment around the theme of the unit, and achieve comprehensive development of the core competencies.

The third suggestion is "**To carry out indepth study of various text type in a unit**" . This suggestion calls on teachers to carry out a comprehensive study of various texts in a unit. Specifically, teachers are advised to answer three basic questions. Firstly, "What" the theme and content of the text are. Secondly, for the question of "Why" , we focus on what meaning the text conveys, as both spoken and written discourses have their communicative purposes, such as the intentions, emotional attitudes, or value orientations of the author or speaker. Thirdly, the "How" question. This question focuses on what stylistic features, content structures and language characteristics the text has. If the text comes with pictures or tables, what kind of meaning or function they have. When studying a spoken text, teachers should also pay attention to the degree of formality of the context and the ways and functions of language expression. For example, the formality of the dialog situation, the identities of the speakers, whether the language expression is casual, direct, polite or euphemistic, and what communicative strategies the speakers may have used. When analyzing the accompanying pictures, teachers should focus on the meanings conveyed by the actions, expressions, psychological states, and color matching of the characters or animals, as well as by the scene layout. Teachers should realize that when finding answers to questions of "Why" and "How" , there may not be definite answers. Teachers should actively discuss among themselves and learn from each other.

The fourth suggestion is **"To organize and implement teaching by respecting the principles for English learning activities"**. The design and implementation of teaching should be guided by themes and supported by various text types, encouraging students to learn language and cultural knowledge in an integrated manner through activities such as learning and understanding, applying and practicing, and transferring and creating.

The purpose is to enable students to use the knowledge, skills and strategies they have learned to express personal views and attitudes around the theme, solve real problems, and achieve the teaching purpose of cultivating their core competencies.

As far as these English learning activities are concerned. They contain three inter-related levels of activities, namely, learning and understanding, applying and practicing, and transferring and creating. Under each level, another three types of activities are further provided.

Regarding **learning and understanding activities,** they include: perception and attention, acquisition and sorting, and summarizing and integration. Through perception and attention activities, teachers activate students' existing knowledge and experiences based on the theme of the text content, introduce necessary language and cultural background knowledge, and clarify the problems to be solved, so that students can connect their existing knowledge and experience with the learning themes, discover cognition gaps, and form learning expectations. Then, teachers may guide students to learn and apply language knowledge and skills through activities such as acquisition and sorting, summarizing and integration, etc., in order to help them obtain cultural knowledge related to the theme of the text at hand, connect the dots, form new knowledge structures, and perceive and comprehend the meanings expressed by the language.

As for **applying and practicing activities,** they include activities such as description and interpretation, analysis and judgment, and internalization and application. On the basis of learning and comprehension activities, students are guided to use their structured knowledge to carry out a variety of meaningful language practice activities such as description, interpretation, analysis, and application, to internalize language and cultural knowledge, deepen their understanding of cultural meaning, consolidate existing structured knowledge, and facilitate the transformation of knowledge into competence. The advancement from learning and understanding activities to applying and practicing activities can be completed at one time or in multiple cycles.

Finally, regarding **transferring and creating activities,** they include reasoning and argumentation, criticism and assessment, and imagination and creation. Students should be guided to carry out reasoning and argumentation activities based on the value orientation behind the text and the attitudes and behaviors of the author or main characters, learn to appreciate the stylistic features of the discourse, grasp the structure of the discourse, discover the means and characteristics of language expression, evaluate the views and behaviors of the author or the main characters through thoughtful analysis, deepen the understanding of the meaning of the theme, and use the learned knowledge, skills, methods, strategies and ideas to understand the world from multiple perspectives; creatively solve problems in new situations, rationally express emotions, attitudes and views, and promote the transformation of ability into personal quality.

A final point to be remembered is that evaluation activities should run throughout the process of teaching and learning, focusing on the students' comprehensive application of language and cultural knowledge learned at the end of the study, understanding of the meaning of themes, well-founded expression of personal views and attitudes, and demonstration of correct values, thereby meeting the course objectives.

The fifth suggestion is **"To guide students to love learning and be good at learning"**. The point is that English teaching should not only focus on "what to learn", but also on whether students "like to learn" and know "how to learn". To do so, teachers should design multi-sensory language practice activities to allow students to experience the fun of learning English through viewing, imitating, observing, communicating etc. in rich and interesting situations. It is important for teachers to understand that assessment and evaluation of students' learning should take students' efforts, learning attitude and performance in competence development as the main indicators, and it is vital for teachers to discover students' learning advantages, affirming their progress in a timely fashion, and guide students to overcome difficulties, solve problems, and enhance their self-confidence in learning. In addition, teachers should help students learn to manage their own studies, clarifying learning goals, determining learning plans and ensuring time management; remind students to take the initiative to preview before class, and review and summarize in time after class; encourage students to use various resources and reference books to read independently, and listen to, or watch, news or excellent films and TV dramas in a planned way; and guide them to evaluate and reflect on their own learning process and results against their learning goals and improve learning efficiency.

The sixth suggestion is **"To promote the integrated design and implementation of teaching, learning, and evaluation"** . Teachers should understand that "teaching-learning-evaluation" is a holistic concept. "Teaching" is mainly reflected in the teaching objectives and activities designed. "Learning" is mainly reflected in a series of language practice activities which are based on teachers' instructions. "Evaluation" is mainly aimed at monitoring the process and effect of teaching and learning. Teachers should realize that the three aspects are interdependent, mutually influential in realizing the education goals. In the process of teaching and evaluating, teachers can collect evidence of students' learning through observations, questioning and other methods like testing to find out what the students have understood, what they can express, what they can do, and whether they have formed correct values. By diagnosing students' problems in the learning process in a timely manner, teachers can provide necessary support and timely feedback as needed, to ensure the promotion of learning and teaching through evaluation.

The last suggestion is **"To enhance efficiency in the use of IT"**. Teachers should fully realize that modern information technology provides not only multi-modal means, platforms and spaces for English teaching, but also rich resources and opportunities for language learning and language use across time and space. Therefore, It's important to follow closely the development and progress of the application of modern information technology in English teaching, striving to create an information-based teaching environment, develop and utilize rich and personalized high-quality course resources based on the Internet platform, and build independent learning platforms for students. To improve the efficiency of English learning, efforts should be made to integrate "Internet+" into teaching concepts, methods, and models, expand the use of information technology in English teaching, and facilitate the combination of online and offline learning. When using information technology to carry out teaching, teachers must ensure the safety and reliability of website information and guide students to pay attention to security issues involving the use of network resources. Modern information technology must be used in a reasonable and appropriate manner, avoiding its complete replacement of real and vivid interpersonal interactions or exceisively emotional communications through language activities in the classroom.

2.7 Summary: implications for the future

As we all know, English curriculum in China have gone through several stages of change over the past 30 years in order to meet the changing needs resulted from the rapid social, economic, technological, and educational change of the country and in the world. The 2022 Curriculum by the Ministry of Education, calls on developing students' core competencies through the English subject in order to implement the fundamental task of fostering students' Whole person development. The core competencies are composed of language ability, cultural awareness, thinking capacity and learning ability. Thus, how to help students develop the English core competencies has become the main concern for deepening curriculum reform. With these new goals and requirements, language learning is expected to reflect a theme-based, meaning-oriented exploratory process based on various written, oral, or multimodal texts.

[微课]
英语学习活动观的解读

Along with the change of goals, the content of English curriculum has been reorganized to provide a good basis for developing students' core competencies through the learning of English. It consists of six components: thematic contexts, types of texts, language knowledge, cultural knowledge, language skills and learning strategies. As we can see, the curriculum content of the 2022 Curriculum for nine-year compulsory education is very different from the content of the 2011 Curriculum, which consists of language knowledge, language skills, effects, cultural awareness, and learning strategies.

In order to achieve what is laid out as the overall goals of the 2022 curriculum, the learning activity-based approach is proposed to advocate that students learn English through a series of integrated, relevant and practical theme-based activities. When doing these activities, students use their existing knowledge, explore the meaning of texts of different types, and analyze and solve problems so as to develop multiple thinking skills, form positive values, and utilize learning strategies.

The changes in goals, content, and teaching approach in the 2022 Curriculum have important implications for future English teaching. Teaching should change from learning disconnected pieces of language knowledge or simply practice of skills or strategies, to designing integrated, relevant and practical learning activities so that students can participate in a variety of learning tasks such as learning and understanding, applying and practicing, and transferring and creating. Such way of learning is able to integrate language, culture and thinking aiming for cultivating language ability, cultural awareness, thinking capacity and learning ability. In the process of participating in these activities, students learn to understand various texts, express personal opinions, emotional attitudes and values, analyze similarities and differences between Chinese and foreign cultures, develop multiple and critical thinking skills, to improve the ability to learn and use English for life-long learning.

To conclude the chapter, highlights of the major changes in the 2022 Curriculum are summarised below:

(1) Change in goals. Students' core competencies are constructed indicating the change from subject teaching with a focus on language to a focus on students' development through English.

(2) Change in content. To develop students' core competencies, the content of teaching should change from language knowledge and skills to content on thematic exploration through various types of texts through which language knowledge and skills, cultural knowledge and strategies are developed and strengthened.

(3) Change in teaching approaches. To improve the effectiveness of English teaching and learning and promote the formation of students' core competencies through the learning of English, unit design aimed at developing Students' core competencies along with a series of learning activities named English Learning Activity-based Approach are recommended for classroom teaching which unifies language learning, culture understanding, thought development and learning skills development into one process with teachers as guides and students as main agents.

(4) The balance between teaching, learning and assessment. To promote key competencies-based learning, there is a need to find a balance between teaching, learning and assessment so as to practice assessment for learning.

(5) Narrowing the educational gap between regions. To balance the distribution of teacher personnel and educational resources among regions and to narrow the gap between regions, new course structures are proposed to lower the overall requirement for all senior middle school graduates. However to ensure the quality of teaching at all levels, modern information technology should play an important role in supporting key competencies-based education and enabling students' English competence at different levels to satisfy different needs.

(6) Teacher development To realize all of the above, teachers' professional development

is vital and teachers are required to continuously improve themselves and their language proficiency.

In fact, there has been changes in the teaching approach of the English language. The change of approaches has been following a gradual paradigm shift from grammar-translation to audio-lingual approaches and then to a more functional-structural based communication-oriented approach and now moving towards core competencies through language education. The changes in the 2022 Curriculum will exert a profound impact on the English language education in China.

Reading

Reading 2.1.1

Should a Child Learn a Second Language?

Much media attention has recently been focused on the importance of early learning experiences on brain development. *Newsweek* devoted a special edition to the critical first 3 years of a child's life and indicated that there is a "window of opportunity" for second language learning starting at 1 year of age. A February 1997 article in *Time* magazine suggested that foreign languages should be taught to children as early as possible. With so many demands already placed on children, parents might ask: Is it important that my child learns a second language at a young age? Why? What options are available?

What are the benefits of knowing another language?

In addition to developing a lifelong ability to communicate with more people, children may derive other benefits from early language instruction, including improved overall school performance and superior problem-solving skills. Knowing another language ultimately provides a competitive advantage in the workforce by opening up additional job opportunities. Students of foreign languages score statistically higher on standardized tests conducted in the native language. In its 1992 report, College Bound Seniors: The 1992 Profile of SAT and Achievement Test Takers, the College Entrance Examination Board reported that students who averaged 4 or more years of foreign language study scored higher on the verbal section of the Scholastic Aptitude Test (SAT) than those who had studied 4 or more years in any other subject area. In addition, the average mathematics score for individuals who had taken 4 or more years of foreign language study was identical to the average score of those who had studied 4 years of mathematics. These findings are consistent with College Board profiles for previous years.

Students of foreign languages have access to a greater number of career possibilities and develop a deeper understanding of their own and other cultures. Some evidence also suggests that children who receive second language instruction are more creative and better at solving complex problems. The benefits to society are many. Americans fluent in other languages enhance our economic competitiveness abroad, improve global communication, and maintain our political and security interests.

Why is it better for a child to learn a language in primary school?

Studies have shown—and experience has supported—that children who learn a language before the onset of adolescence are much more likely to have native-like pronunciation. A number of experts attribute this proficiency to physiological changes that occur in the maturing brain as a child enters puberty. Of course, as with any subject, the more years a child can devote to learning a language, the more competent he or she will become. In any case, introducing children to alternative ways of expressing themselves and to different cultures generally broadens their outlook and gives them the opportunity to communicate with many more people.

Will a second language interfere with the first language?

In most cases, learning another language enhances a child's native language ability. Children can learn much about their native language by learning the structure of other languages. Common vocabulary also helps children learn the meaning of new words in their native language. Experimental studies have shown that no long-term delay in native language development occurs in children participating in second language classes, even in full immersion programs.

In fact, children enrolled in foreign language programs score statistically higher on standardized tests conducted in their native language. A number of reports have demonstrated that children who have learned a second language earn higher SAT scores, particularly on the verbal section of the test. One study showed that by the fifth year of an immersion program, students outperformed all comparison groups and remained high academic achievers throughout their schooling.

Most importantly, we should encourage the child's interest in the language and in other cultures. Show him or her that you value the ability to speak another language. Attend cultural events that feature music, dance, or food from the country or countries where the language is spoken. If possible, provide some books, videos, or other materials in the new language. If you are familiar with the language yourself, read to your child.

Reading 2.2.2A

Objectives in the English Language Teaching Syllabi / Curriculum from 1978 to 2001

Syllabus/ curriculum	Overall objectives
1978	The emphasis was put on developing students' reading abilities, self-learning abilities and listening, speaking, writing and translating ability in order to prepare students for further study in college and using English after graduation.
1982	It aimed to provide students with basic practice in listening, speaking, reading, writing and translating. It put more emphasis on developing reading and self-learning ability so as to set a good foundation for further study and the use of English.
1986	It aimed to provide students with basic practice in listening, speaking, reading and writing and to develop students' basic ability in using English in spoken and written forms. It concentrated more on reading ability development and setting a good foundation for further study and the use of English.
1992 for junior middle schools	It aimed to help students acquire basic English knowledge and the ability to use English in simple communication through the training of listening, speaking, reading and writing; stimulate students' interest in studying; help them formulate good learning habits, provide a primary foundation for further study, educate them in aspects of virtues, patriotism and socialism, and develop students' ability of thinking and self-study.
2001 for 9-year compulsory education and senior high schools	The overall goal is to cultivate students' comprehensive language ability, which is based on the overall development of students' language skills, language knowledge, emotional attitudes, learning strategies and cultural awareness. Language knowledge and language skills are the basis of comprehensive use of language ability. Cultural awareness is the guarantee of proper language use. Emotional attitudes is an important factor affecting students' learning and development, and learning strategies are the guarantee to improve learning efficiency and develop autonomous learning ability. These five aspects jointly promote the formation of comprehensive language ability.

Reading 2.3.3A

Content requirements of the six elements for Level 1 and Level 2 (Table 1 to Table 6).

Table 1 Content requirements: thematic contexts

Thematic contexts	Thematic clusters	Sub-themes	
		Level 1	Level 2
Man and self	Life and learning Learning to be and learning to do	1. Things and environment around oneself; 2. Time management; 3. Self-care and hygiene habits; 4. Expressing personal preferences and emotions; 5. Family life and home life; 6. School and classes; school life and personal feelings; 7. Diet and health	1. Self-management of study and daily life; 2. Eagerness to learn; effective learning; frequent reflections, and learning to learn; 3. Well-mannered behaviors and healthy lifestyles; 4. Sports and games; safety and safeguarding; 5. Self-confidence and optimism, self-compassion and empathy; 6. Emotions and feelings, regulation and management of emotions and behaviors; 7. Challenges, issues and solutions in life and study; 8. Use of pocket money, responsible consumption, and awareness of cost saving; 9. Habits and skills of engaging in physical work; passion for participating in physical work
Man and society	Social services and interpersonal communication	1. Class and school rules, awareness of rules; 2. Team activities and communal living, sense of participation and collectivism;	1. Environmental protection on campus and in the community; voluntary work and public services;

continued

Thematic contexts	Thematic clusters	Sub-themes	
		Level 1	Level 2
Man and society	Literature, art, and sports History, society, and culture Science and technology	3. Campus and community environment and facilities, caring for public facilities; 4. Peer interaction, mutual respect, be friendly to each other and helping each other; 5. Respect for the elderly and love for the young, sense of gratitude; 6. Common sports, physical exercises, and staying healthy; 7. Traffic regulations and safety awareness; 8. Common occupations and people's lives; 9. Common festivals and cultural experiences	2. Self-respect and self-discipline, well-mannered behaviors, honesty and integrity, filial piety and respect for parents and the elderly; 3. Personal emotions and opinions, listening to and understanding others, being inclusive and forgiving; 4. Student clubs of sports, arts and culture; exploring personal talents and potentials; 5. Public figures with outstanding contributions to society, and their deeds; 6. Knowledge about and experience of visiting famous sites and places in China and other countries in the world; 7. Traditional festivals in major countries, cultural experiences; 8. Life-changing science and technology
Man and nature	Natural ecology Environmental protection	1. Weather and everyday life; 2. Characteristics and changes of seasons, seasons and life;	1. Geographical locations and natural environment of one's hometown and major cities in China; 2. Names, geographical locations, and natural landscapes of major countries in the world;

continued

Thematic contexts	Thematic clusters	Sub-themes	
		Level 1	Level 2
Man and nature	Disaster prevention Space exploration	3. Natural phenomena and ecological environment around oneself; 4. Common animals, and their physical features and living environments	3. The interdependence of man and nature, concept and practice of sustainable living; 4. Planting greens and breeding animals, showing love and kindness to all living creatures 5. Natural disasters and personal safety, general knowledge of disaster prevention; 6. Exploration of the Earth and the universe

Table 2 Content requirements: text types

Level 1	Level 2
1. Ballads, songs, and children's rhymes; 2. Monologs and short everyday dialogs; 3. Illustrated stories and narrative diaries; 4. Introduction to people, things, and places; 5. Letters, event notices, operating instructions, birthday and New Year cards, and invitation cards; 6. Other text types, such as signage, notice boards, restaurant menus, shopping lists, simple diagrams, pictures, and videos	1. Monologs and simple everyday dialogs; 2. Narrations, such as illustrated stories, narrative diaries, biographical stories, fables, humorous stories, and fairy tales; 3. Expositions, such as short explanation of things, short science introductory texts, short written instructions, and operating procedures; 4. Practical texts, such as greeting cards, invitation cards, letters, event notices, announcements, event arrangements and plans, promotional posters, rules, and questionnaires; 5. New media texts, such as simple social media messages, web pages, and E-mails; 6. Other text types, such as songs, rhymes, scripts, charts, diagrams, pictures, and videos

Table 3 Content requirements: language knowledge

Language knowledge	Level 1	Level 2
Phonetic knowledge	1. Identify and read the 26 letters in upper and lower cases; 2. Perceive the sounds of letters in words; 3. Perceive simple spelling rules, and use them to help spell words; 4. Perceive and imitate speaking English, and recognize word stress and the rising and falling tones of sentences	1. Spell words using the spelling rules; 2. Read aloud learned dialogs and short texts using correct pronunciation and intonation; 3. Express attitudes and emotions by stressing words in sentences; 4. Perceive and imitate speaking English, and recognize units of meaning, intonation, and rhythm; 5. Use correct phonetic features in speaking, and speak naturally and fluently
Vocabulary knowledge	1. Understand that words are made up of letters; 2. Understand the meaning of words with the help of pictures and realia; 3. Say words and phrases according to visual or auditory prompts, such as pictures, actions, animations, and sounds; 4. Learn vocabulary based on the sound, spelling, and meaning, and appreciate the meanings of words expressed in context	1. Understand the meaning of words in context, and gradually build up vocabulary by using the words; 2. Use vocabulary to describe things, behaviors, processes and features in specific contexts, and express key messages and ideas related to the theme; 3. Learn to use about 500 words (see Appendix III) as a start to communicate with others and express oneself related to a given theme. In addition, be exposed to and learn 100-300 Level 3 words found in related themes, as well as a certain number of idiomatic expressions and fixed collocations as needed

continued

Language knowledge	Level 1	Level 2
Grammar knowledge	1. Perceive and appreciate the meaning-expressing functions of common, simple sentences in context; 2. Understand the form, meaning, and use of present simple and present continuous tenses in context ; 3. Use learned grammar knowledge to describe people and things, and communicate in simple language in the context of relevant themes	1. Understand the basic structure and meaning-expressing functions of common, simple sentences in discourse; 2. Understand the form, meaning, and use of past simple and future simple tenses in context; 3. Use learned grammar knowledge to describe and compare people and things, describe the ins and outs of specific events, and describe time, place and location in context
Discourse knowledge	1. Recognize turn-taking in dialogs; 2. Be aware of different types of discourse, such as dialogs and illustrated stories; 3. Appreciate the relationship between pictures and texts in discourse	1. Identify the beginning, middle and end of story-like discourse, and identify time, place, and characters, as well as the ins and outs of events; 2. Identify the relationship between the topic sentence and the remaining content in a paragraph; 3. Use information such as headings and pictures to help comprehend the text
Pragmatic knowledge	1. Communicate appropriately with others when addressing people, greeting others, and bidding farewell; 2. Communicate with others using basic, polite language in context; 3. Respond appropriately to compliments, apologies, and acknowledgments from others	1. Start to use the learned language to express one's emotions, attitudes, and opinions appropriately according to the needs of specific contexts; 2. Communicate appropriately with others in specific contexts, such as shopping, seeking medical care, making phone calls, and asking for directions; 3. Respond appropriately to others' invitations, wishes, requests, and help

Table 4 Content requirements: cultural knowledge

Level 1	Level 2
1. Similarities and differences between the English and Chinese language in terms of expressions in interpersonal communication, such as names, titles, and greetings; 2. Similarities and differences in different countries or cultures in terms of school life, family life, dietary habits, and so on; 3. Basic information about typical cultural symbols and traditional festivals in both China and other countries	1. People's behaviors, customs, dietary habits, etiquette of receiving people, and taboo topics in conversations in different cultural backgrounds; 2. Names, dates, and celebrations of key Chinese and foreign festivals and their cultural connotations; 3. Simple outstanding English literary works (such as fairy tales, fables, and biographical stories) and the moral lessons or values they embody; 4. Figures (代表人物) from China and other countries who have made outstanding contributions to the development of human society and their life stories; 5. Mainstream sports activities and key sports events in China and other countries; outstanding athletes and their achievements; sportsmanship; 6. Acclaimed artists from China and other countries and their works; 7. Basic information about major countries in the world (such as capitals, flags, and languages), tourism culture (such as important cultural symbols), and customs; perception and experience of cultural diversity

Table 5 Content requirements: language skills

Language skills	Level 1	Level 2
Receptive skills	1. Understand and respond to simple classroom instructions; 2. Infer the theme, context, and key information of a text according to the title and picture(s); 3. Extract and sort out the required information purposefully while listening, reading, and viewing;	1. Understand simple classroom and life instructions, and complete tasks accordingly; 2. Comprehend texts of common themes using pictures, images, and so on, and extract, sort out, and summarize key information;

continued

Language skills	Level 1	Level 2
Receptive skills	4. Infer the meaning conveyed by pictures, images, sounds, colors, and so on in multimodal texts (e.g. animations, front and back covers of books and other printed materials, invitation cards, and greeting cards); 5. Infer the mood, emotions, attitudes, and intentions of the speaker with the help of tone, intonation, gestures, and facial expressions; 6. Carry out out-of-class listening and video-watching activities for at least 30 minutes per week; 7. Carry out out-of-class English reading of 1 500—2 000 words in total	3. Guess the meaning of words in a text and infer unknown information according to contextual clues and non-textual information in the process of listening and reading; 4. Summarize the ins and outs of the main plot in story-like texts; 5. Categorize information in a text; 6. Compare the similarities and differences between characters, things or opinions in a text, and try to observe and understand the world from different perspectives; 7. Summarize the main content of a text, and identify the connections between key messages; 8. Understand the meaning in multimodal texts (e.g. animations, posters, front and back covers of books and other printed materials), and extract key messages; 9. Carry out out-of-class listening and video-watching activities for at least 30 minutes per week; 10. Carry out out-of-class English reading of 4 000—5 000 words in total
		+ Read simple chaptered books with illustrations, understand the general idea, and give a simple oral summary and description of what is read

continued

Language skills	Level 1	Level 2
Productive skills	1. Exchange simple greetings or bid farewell with others in specific contexts; 2. Sing simple learned English songs; 3. Follow audio and video materials to read aloud, and correctly read out learned conversations, stories, and passages; 4. Communicate simple personal and family information, such as names and facts about family; 5. Express simple feelings and preferences, such as likes or dislikes, wants or don't wants; 6. Describe briefly one's daily routine and life, such as schedules, three meals, sports and exercises, and interests and hobbies; 7. Introduce briefly one's school and school life, such as school facilities, classes, activities, classmates, and teachers; 8. Introduce briefly one's favorite animal(s), such as their physical appearances and living environments; 9. Describe pictures or things in simple sentences; 10. Perform simple role-plays as guided by the teacher; 11. Write letters, words, and sentences correctly; 12. Model to write simple sentences according to pictures or the context	1. Use everyday language learned to engage in simple communications, such as asking for basic personal information; 2. Coherently read aloud learned texts in their entirety, and retell the gist of texts briefly as guided by the teacher or with the help of a language framework; 3. Give a short narration or communicate briefly about the relevant themes and the content, and express personal emotions, attitudes, and opinions; 4. Perform short stories or plays with the help of the teacher; 5. Briefly describe events or tell short, simple stories; 6. Write a few coherent sentences describing the content of a picture; 7. Write a few coherent sentences modeling the structure and content of an example text, and try to add details using descriptive words to make the content rich and vivid; 8. Use capital and small letters and common punctuation correctly, and spell words correctly; 9. Use diagrams, posters, and DIY picture books to express meaning creatively as needed

continued

Language skills	Level 1	Level 2
Productive skills	+1. Dub the learned segments of dialog, story or animation with prompts; +2. Narrate events or tell short stories orally	+1. Give short speeches on relevant themes with generally clear opinions, good coherence, correct pronunciation, and natural intonation; +2. Create stories orally with some plots and generally use correct language based on thematic pictures or comics

Table 6 Content requirements: learning strategies

Learning strategies	Level 1	Level 2
Metacognitive	1. Maintain concentration while studying; 2. Listen and think actively in communication; 3. Try to use a variety of ways to learn English, and take the initiative to seek help from the teacher or peers when encountering difficulties; 4. Make simple study plans as guided by the teacher, and act on them; 5. Be aware of progress and gaps in one's English learning, and make appropriate adjustments accordingly	1. Preview as needed, and take the initiative to review, organize, and summarize the learned content; 2. Develop simple study plans as guided by the teacher, and organize study time effectively; 3. Use libraries and related resources actively for extended learning; 4. Start to use simple reference books (e.g. dictionaries) to learn English; 5. Take the initiative in understanding English learning methods, and explore suitable methods for oneself; 6. Self-evaluate and reflect on the learning process and its effectiveness, adjust plans as needed, and actively seek advice when encountering difficulties

continued

Learning strategies	Level 1	Level 2
Cognitive strategies	1. Establish connections between words and corresponding things; 2. Establish connections between old and new language knowledge; 3. Learn vocabulary and grammar in context; 4. Strengthen understanding and memory of vocabulary using methods such as categorization; 5. Use the English language learned actively to express oneself and communicate with others; 6. Pay conscious attention to simple English used in everyday life and in mass media	1. Use existing language and life experience to complete new learning tasks; 2. Summarize and organize the learned content using tools such as charts and mind maps; 3. Spell words following spelling rules; 4. Establish meaningful connections between learned content and one's personal experiences; 5. Develop the habit of reading by units of meaning
Communication strategies	1. When failing to understand the speaker, ask the speaker to repeat more slowly; 2. When encountering difficulty in expressing meaning, use simple gestures, indicative pronouns, and other means to facilitate expressions	1. Understand the information expressed by using non-verbal information clues; 2. Be able to express meaning orally by using non-verbal means, such as eye contact, facial expressions, gestures, and actions
Affective strategies	1. Be interested in learning English, and keen to participate in learning activities; 2. Feel free to speak English without fear of making mistakes;	1. Maintain a positive attitude and self-confidence toward English learning, and take the initiative to participate in a variety of practice opportunities to learn and use the language;

continued

Learning strategies	Level 1	Level 2
Affective strategies	3. Have a desire to learn collaboratively with peers, and be keen to work with others to complete learning tasks	2. Actively engage in collaborative learning with peers, and be keen to share learning resources and strategies and methods with others; 3. Be able to adjust one's emotions effectively when encountering difficulties or making progress

Unit 3

Instructional Design

Aims of the unit

In this unit, we are going to focus on the following:

3.1 What is instructional design?

3.1.1 Is instructional design important?

3.1.2 What basic components should be included in an instructional design?

3.2 How to do text analysis

3.3 How to do student analysis

3.4 How to design lesson objectives

3.5 How to design lesson activities

3.6 How to do overall unit design

3.1 What is instructional design?

Teachers are generally more familiar with "lesson planning" rather than "instructional design" . An instructional design is, in fact, the planning of a lesson or a series of lessons within one unit with the purpose to support students' learning. An instructional design often indicates a more scientific and systematic view towards the preparation of teaching. An instructional design can be a long-term plan for a semester or a short-term plan for a unit or a particular lesson. In this section, we will focus on the short-term plan, planning for one lesson or one unit of lessons.

3.1.1 Is instructional design important?

A good instructional design is prerequisite for effective teaching no matter for novice or experienced teachers. Although preparation does not guarantee successful teaching as classroom teaching is often unpredictable, being unprepared is most likely to lead to failure. What is also very embarrassing for a teacher is that children can immediately notice that their teacher is not prepared.

TASK 3.1.1

Work in pairs and think about the reasons why we need to be well-prepared with an instructional design.

Reasons why we need to get prepared with an instructional design
• Make ourselves more confident.
• Feel more secure when teaching.
•
•
•
•

Discussion Point

There is always a misconception that experienced teachers do not need to plan their lessons and only new teachers do. This is simply not true. It is important for all teachers to prepare their lessons before teaching. This is because through careful preparation the teacher will think clearly about his or her principles for teaching and study the curriculum requirements carefully. And these will guide his or her selection of teaching content, the decision about lesson objectives, and the choice as well as organization of activities. Also, they will know clearly what kind of teaching aids are needed.

Moon (2000) also adds that good preparation will enable the teacher to monitor, assess, and improve his or her teaching. She identifies the following benefits for teachers to plan their lessons.

Planning one's lesson can:

(1) help the teacher become more confident in teaching.

(2) provide a systematic outline or guide for smooth and efficient teaching.

(3) help the teacher become more organized in teaching.

(4) help the teacher prepare for students' individual needs.

(5) enable the teacher to know whether he or she has achieved the lesson objectives.

(6) help the teacher identify which part of the lesson went well or did not go well.

(7) prove that the teacher has made a considerable amount of effort into his or her teaching.

(8) enable the teacher to meet administrative requirements.

(9) demonstrate the teacher's professional ethics.

(10) prove that the teacher has taken good responsibility for students' learning.

3.1.2 What basic components should be included in an instructional design?

TASK 3.1.2

Work in groups. Think about all the possible components that should be included in an instructional design. Take notes using the diagram below.

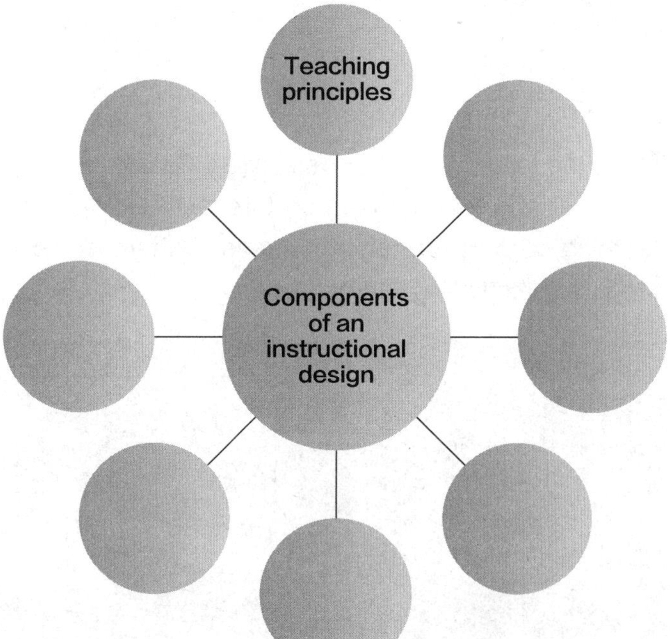

Discussion Point

An instructional design for a specific lesson generally contains eight components:

(1) teaching principles;

(2) analysis of learning content;

(3) students' analysis;

(4) unit or lesson objectives;

(5) main teaching focuses and students' potential difficulties;

(6) teaching procedures and activities;

(7) assessment of learning;

(8) teaching aid and board design.

There should be another component which is called "After the lesson reflections" .

Teaching reflections refer to the teacher's personal thoughts on the process and effectiveness of the lesson after teaching.

3.2 How to do text analysis

Analysis of the learning content can be done based on a unit or a single piece of text including oral texts such as dialog. Understanding the learning content is crucial for planning effective teaching. If a teacher does not know what to teach, how can he/she manage to teach well?

TASK 3.2.1

Read the following text— *Caterpillar, Caterpillar* (Figure 3.2.1 and Figure 3.2.2) What will you teach based on this text? On what basis will you decide on the learning content for beginning level students? Discuss in groups and list your ideas in the space given below:

Figure 3.2.1 *Caterpillar, Caterpillar*(1)

Figure 3.2.2 *Caterpillar, Caterpillar*(2)

My list of the teaching content for this text
(1)
(2)
(3)

Discussion Point

In the past, analyzing the learning content has been largely ignored by most teachers. The problem lies in our understanding of what composes the "content" of a lesson or a unit. For a long time, many teachers consider the knowledge of vocabulary and grammatical structures as the main teaching content, ignoring the theme, context and meaning of the text. In order to develop students' core competencies through English, cultivate students' cultural awareness and positive attitude towards self, others, society, and the world, teachers need to change the traditional ways of treating a text as a source for learning language only. Instead, teachers should pay more attention to both the language to be learned and the cultural meaning behind the language. Therefore, analyzing the learning content of a text thoroughly becomes a crucial ability of the teachers, because a teacher's understanding of the teaching content determines what he/she is to teach and how it will be taught.

TASK 3.2.2

Read the text *Caterpillar, Caterpillar* in TASK 3.2.1 carefully again. Try to analyze it from 3-5 dimensions. You may use the following questions as a guide to start your analysis.

(1) What is the theme of the book?

(2) What does the picture book specifically talk about?

(3) How is the story organized?

(4) How many parts can you see in the book?

(5) What is the relationship among the parts?

(6) What expressions are used in the book to support the theme?

(7) What does the writer want to express in the book?

(8) What educational values can be explored from the story for the students?

Discussion Point

Analysis of a text as learning content can include its main theme and the specific content. For example, the story lines and plots or/and the structural knowledge imbedded in the text, types of text or texts contained in the unit, typical language expressions such as vocabulary and grammatical structures to be learned, useful expressions for understanding and discussing the theme and content, as well as the unit's or lesson's educational values. A thorough analysis of a text is the foundation for designing unit/lesson objectives and activities. Therefore, text analysis decides learning outcomes to a great extent and teachers' ability to analyze the text affects students' learning experience and engagement.

Specifically, a text can be analyzed from three broad dimensions and five related sub-dimensions (Figure 3.2.3): What (theme and content), How(text structure and features of language), and Why (theme and value).

[What] in text analysis: It contains two sub-dimensions—theme and content which answer the questions of "What is the theme of the text?" and "What does the text mainly talk about?" Based on such analysis, teachers can summarize the key points or information of the text to decide upon the instructional focus of the lesson, create a context for learning and understanding, application and practice, and further to transforming and innovating. It can also help students locate the key problem to solve in this lesson so as to base one's instruction on exploring solutions to the problem and promote students' active engagement in learning activities.

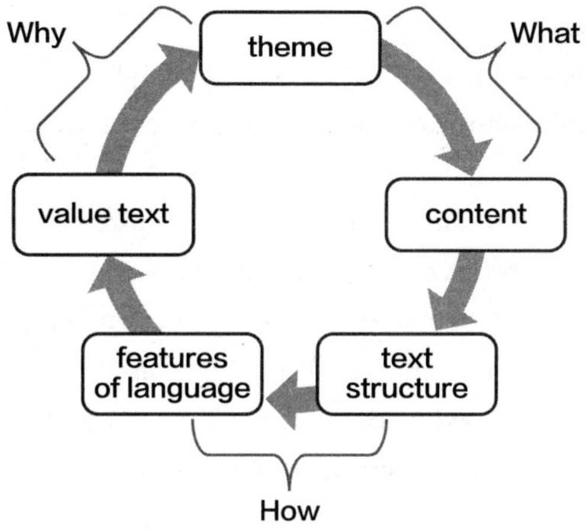

Figure 3.2.3 Text analysis framework

[How] in text analysis: It contains two sub-dimensions—text structure and the features of language which answer the questions of "How is the text organized?" and "How is it written?" Through such analysis, teachers can get to know how the information is presented around the theme, how logical connections are built in the text, what language, crafts, and styles are used to support the presentation of information or ideas.

[Why] in text analysis: It involves the educational value of the text and answers to the question of "Why does the author write the theme?" . By answering the question, teachers can notice the opinions or values the writer wants to express so as to formulate an objective in values education. It also helps students evaluate the text critically to converse with their prior knowledge so as to fully internalize and transfer what is learned and form new opinions and values about the main theme discussed.

TASK 3.2.3

Work in groups. Based on the above discussions on text analysis, use the text analysis framework as a guide to write your analysis of the text either in Chinese or English. Then share with the class what have you learned from doing this.

Your text analysis on *Caterpillar, Caterpillar:*

Discussion Point

The following is an example of text analysis of the text *Caterpillar, Caterpillar*. Read it and compare how this analysis is different from yours.

[What] *Caterpillar, Caterpillar* is a picture book with about 100 words. It talks about how a caterpillar deals with dangers skillfully. The main plot of the story is: A bird wanted to eat the caterpillar but the caterpillar saved itself by successfully finding an excuse, saying "I am too little." Later, it ate a lot of leaves, became a butterfly and finally avoided the fate of being eaten by the bird. The broad theme of the text is "human and society" and the specific theme can be "how to deal with dangers skillfully" .

[How] This book is a narrative. It can be divided into three parts. In the first part, the story setting, characters and the initiating event are given. A bird found a little caterpillar in the tree and wanted to eat it. The caterpillar persuaded the bird not to eat it by saying it was too little and asked the bird to eat it after it became bigger. The second part is the development of the story plot. In this part, the caterpillar kept its promise by eating leaves and changed into a cocoon. The bird looked for the caterpillar but did not find it so the bird asked the caterpillar to show itself. The last part is the ending of the story. The caterpillar became a butterfly and escaped the fate of being eaten by the bird. The story is told with simple past tense. Dialog between the bird and the caterpillar are immersed in the story. The language in the text is concise and vivid. For example, "No! No! I am too little.", "Yes, you are too little.", and "The caterpillar ate and ate." "It ate and ate and ate." . The story is also illustrated vividly with the images of the caterpillar gradually getting fatter and turning into the form of a butterfly.

[Why] The story has two logical lines: one explicit and one implicit. The explicit line follows the story plot, showing the process of how the caterpillar deals with the danger of being eaten skillfully. It teaches children how to calm down and solve a problem when facing danger. The implicit line reveals the process of how a caterpillar turns into a caterpillar by eating leaves: caterpillar → cocoon → butterfly. It helps children understand the life cycle of a caterpillar from a scientific perspective.

TASK 3.2.4

How to do text analysis. The ultimate goal of text analysis is to design effective lesson objectives and related activities. In order to achieve the goal, teachers can analyze the text following certain procedures. Work together and summarize a few important steps in doing text analysis based on your experiences with the text *Caterpillar, Caterpillar.*

The steps you have summarized or your tips for doing text analysis:

Discussion Point

The following are the steps we recommend. Read carefully and compare with yours.

1. Read the text carefully at least 3 – 4 times. Try to read it with a specific focus each time from students' perspectives. For example, read for the main idea first, then read for specific information, and finally read to retell. Try all the activities you may want your students to do later and test if they are appropriate and feasible.

2. Analyze the text structure and find out how many parts there are. Text types and genres play essential roles in this process. If it is a narrative, you may try to divide it into three (the beginning, the middle, and the ending) or five parts (the setting, the character, the problem, the development, and the ending). If it is non-fiction, you may try to explore the knowledge structure of the topic and work out the logical connection among the different aspects about that topic.

3. List the key expressions of each part. When doing so, you should pay more attention to repeated expressions that support the presentation of the key information or the theme. These expressions usually contain specific words especially nouns, verbs. Note that not all expressions are worth listing here and teaching later. Avoid listing unimportant expressions.

4. Draw a story map or concept map to figure out the logical connections of the text parts and related key expressions. A logical connection is useful when we make a connection between two things (or ideas) based on similarities, differences; parallel ideas, sequential ideas; chronological, spatial order, or causal relationships. The explicit and implicit story lines of *Caterpillar, Caterpillar* can be depicted as follows with the story map (Figure 3.2.4).

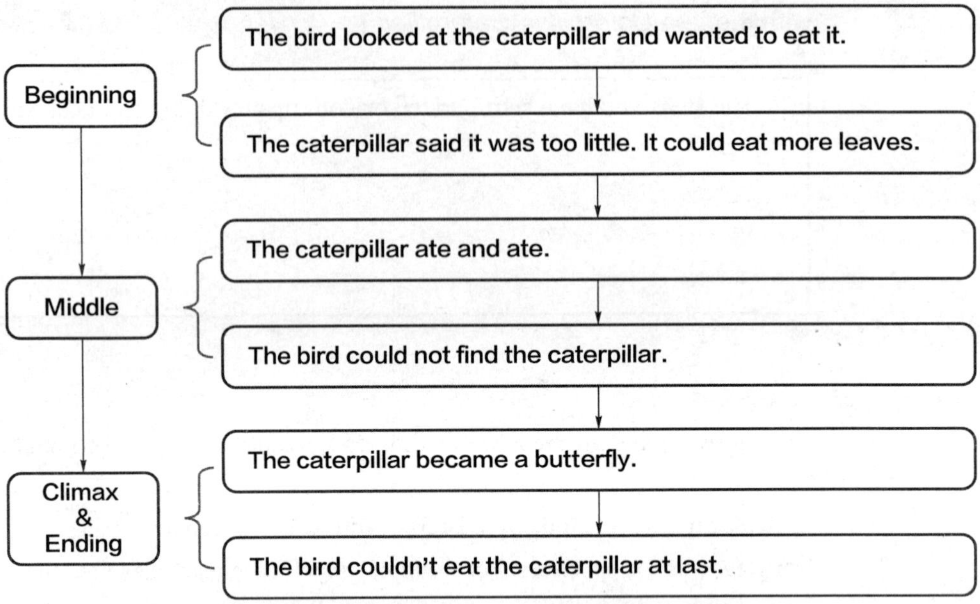

Figure 3.2.4 A story maps based on "*Caterpillar, Caterpillar*"

The Five parts of *Caterpillar, Caterpillar*:

(1) The setting: in the woods.
(2) Characters: a bird and a caterpillar.
(3) The plot: caterpillar → cocoon → butterfly.
(4) The ending: the caterpillar becomes a butterfly.
(5) The knowledge gained: life cycle of a caterpillar.

5. Summarize the writer's crafts or styles. Writers' crafts include specific figure of speech applied in the text, like tense, metaphor, simile, personification, etc. And every writer has his / her own style. For example, some writers like to use simple and concise expressions while some writers like to use "big" words. Analysis of these two dimensions help students understand the text critically from a writer's perspective and provide them scaffolding and modeling for their later writing.

6. Summarize the content and the theme of the text. Based on all the previous procedures, you may easily figure out what the text is mainly about. When summarizing the content, try using one sentence and when summarizing the theme, condense it into a phrase. Themes are harder to summarize than content. You may try to locate the text in three broad and commonly-used themes—human and nature, human and society, and human and self, and then figure out the specific theme in the text.

7. Summarize the educational values of the text. This has to do with what can students do after learning the text to help solve real-life problems. This requires teachers to have a good understanding of their students: what they are interested in and what problems they are facing at present.

8. Design lesson objectives and activities. At this point, you are quite clear about what your students can learn, apply and transfer after the lesson. So, you may try to design a draft version of your lesson objectives and activities and wait until you finish student analysis to finalize them.

3.3 How to do student analysis

Understanding the students is another prerequisite for effective instructional design. If teachers do not know their students well, they cannot determine what students need to know or do to foster the expected learning outcome.

TASK 3.3.1A

Try to analyze the following situations and offer possible solutions.

Situations	Student analysis	Possible solutions
After reading a story, the teacher asks students to discuss what they think of the story, but nobody responds.		
Students always make mistakes when reading the text aloud. Once they do so, the teacher will remind them and they can correct the mistakes soon. But without the teacher's help, they tend to make the same mistakes repeatedly.		
Students can understand the text very well but most of them often fail to retell it.		

Discussion Point

Teachers tend to rely on their own subjective understanding about their students to decide what to teach and how to teach. However, this can be partial or even wrong without systematic student analysis. When analyzing students, teachers should try to answer the following questions based on systematical reflections and observations:

1. What might the students know already? What can they do? These questions have to do with students' prior knowledge and related skills. Prior knowledge here refers to what students know about the topic and the linguistic knowledge supporting the topic expressions. Related skills involve students' listening, speaking, reading, writing, and viewing skills. By answering the two questions, teachers can know students' actual knowledge and language level to decide what to activate to promote knowledge acquisition and skill development.

2. What DON'T students know? What CAN'T students do? These questions involve students' potential developmental level, e.g. what they can't do alone but can do with the help of a more knowledgeable other. Here, the more knowledge others can be teachers, peers, or tools like textbooks or dictionaries. Answering the two questions can help teachers decide upon students' zone of proximal development (ZPD) so as to design effective, feasible and educational lesson objectives.

3. What do students want to know? What do students want to do? Answers to these questions reveal what motivates student learning. Students differ greatly and these differences often stem from age, gender, personal experience, habits, hobbies, and even social-economic status. By answering the two questions, teachers can know how to motivate students by selecting appropriate texts, designing interesting activities, offering a genuine learning purpose, etc.

4. How can teachers help students know what they want to know? How can teachers help students do what they want to do? In order to answer the two questions, teachers need to integrate answers to the previous six questions and come up with a possible "solution" . This will help teachers focus on their ultimate lesson objectives so as to keep a balance among lesson activities by avoiding the "urge" to design interesting but ineffective or inefficient lesson activities.

TASK 3.3.1B

Read the following two pieces of student analysis (Table 3.3.1). Which one is more useful for effective learning activity design? Why?

Table 3.3.1 Two pieces of student analysis

Student analysis A	Student analysis B
本节课的授课对象是小学三年级的学生，多数学生具有良好的语言基础，已学习了关于颜色的词汇和部分动词。学生思维活跃，善于思考，对英文阅读有一定的兴趣，但还有部分学生，语言基础薄弱，阅读能力弱，他们理解本篇故事有一定困难。大部分学生虽然乐于思考，但受到语言的限制，不能准确地表达个人的观点	本节课的授课对象是小学三年级的学生，多数学生乐于阅读英文小故事，对小动物及昆虫类主题的故事感兴趣。故事中学生不熟悉的词汇有 caterpillar、butterfly、leave、ate、looked for 等。虽然丰富的图片和语境可以帮助学生认识主人公并理解故事大意，但是学生可能无法清晰地提炼并表达自然界生命轮回的规律

Discussion Point

You may all agree that Student Analysis B is more useful for designing effective learning activities, because its analysis is based on what students are going to learn in this lesson. When the teacher is clear about the students' strengths, and weaknesses in learning this particular lesson, whether it is a story or a short text or dialog, they will know what to do to motivate and help the students. As the students may have difficulties recognizing some new words, and also have difficulties understanding or describing the life cycle concept, the teacher will design focused activities to help students overcome these difficulties. In comparison, Student Analysis A is based on general information of the students which is not directly related to what is to be learned. Therefore, it has not provided any useful information for the teacher to design purposeful activities to help students learn this particular story. Therefore, Student Analysis A is not helpful or useful.

Other ways of student analysis can be done using different kinds of methods.

1. Using a questionnaire. Teachers can design a simple questionnaire to do student analysis. The advantages of a questionnaire are: it can be anonymous, so the information collected is highly reliable; it covers the whole class, so the data collected are highly representative; it is easy to design and collect, so it saves time and energy for both teachers and students. Here is an example:

在学习本课之前，教师设计了前测题目，从学生兴趣、学习策略、知识背景等方面了解学生的情况。前测题目如下：

（1）你是否喜欢“X 计划”的系列故事？

A. 特别喜欢　B. 喜欢　C. 一般　D. 不喜欢　E. 特别不喜欢

如果喜欢，原因是：

____

如果不喜欢，原因是：

____

（2）你是否能根据题目推测故事情节？

A. 能　　B. 不能

（3）你是否能从封面寻找故事相关信息？

A. 能　　B. 不能

（4）你是否喜欢和老师一起观察图片讲故事？

A. 特别喜欢　　B. 喜欢　　C. 一般　　D. 不喜欢　　E. 特别不喜欢

（5）你是否参加过体育比赛，如跑步比赛、游泳比赛等？

A. 是　　B. 否

如果参加过，结果如何？感受如何？

____

（6）你是否阅读过《龟兔赛跑》的故事（包括中文故事）？

A. 是　　B. 否

如果读过，通过《龟兔赛跑》的故事你明白了什么道理？

____

This questionnaire consists of 6 simple questions. Question 1 aims to find out whether students like the book series and what the possible reasons are. Questions 2-4 involve the analysis of students' prior reading skills while Question 4 involves students' interest. Questions 5-6 try to reveal students' prior experience about the topic. By analyzing the questionnaire data, the teacher comes with the following conclusion:

本节课的教学对象是我校五年级三班的学生，共计 25 名学生参与问卷调查。问卷结果表明：72% 的学生表示特别喜欢，主要原因是故事中的人物变小后可以去探险；20% 的学生表示喜欢；不喜欢的学生有 8%，主要原因是有不认识的单词。可见，通过一年多的校本阅读课程“X 计划”系列故事的学习，大部分学生非常喜欢“X 计划”的系列故事，对于故事中 4 个小主人公的探险故事充满了好奇，学习兴趣较高。28% 的学生能根据题目推测故事内容，92% 的学生能通过封面寻找信息，84% 的学生喜欢和教师一起观察图片讲故事。可见，学生初步掌握了一定的阅读策略和阅读技能，能在教师的指导下进行师生互动，学习故事。学生在体育课和运动会上参加过跑步比赛，很多学生提到了获胜、兴奋、疲劳，可见学生对这一话题并不陌生。学生对于话题的意义、话题的相关语言结构有所了解，有利于师生互动学习故事。大部分学生表示阅读过《龟兔赛跑》的故事，很多学生提到不能像兔子一样过于骄傲，要像乌龟一样坚持到底。可见，学生能理解本课故事的意义，可以借助阅读过的中文故事推测英文词义，理解难点。

Although questionnaires can offer some useful information about the target students, it takes time and energy to analyze. Validity is also a problem as it depends on teachers' research ability in designing effective questionnaire items and asking students to cooperate by providing valid and reliable information.

2. Using an interview. Teachers can also interview students to get information. This can be done casually by talking with a specific number of students after class or formally by interviewing them with a set of questions. This can provide teachers with an in-depth understanding of the students. However, since teachers do not have enough time to ask everyone, how to select students for interviewing need to be carefully considered. For example, you need to consider that the selected students should be representative of both genders and different proficiency levels, for example, 2 high, 2 medium, and 2 low proficiency levels.

3. Keeping a teacher journal. Keeping a journal regularly is another way to analyze students. This can be done after each class by writing a journal. The content can include: the effectiveness of lesson design and possible reasons; students' behavior in class; critical incidents in classroom teaching; insights gained from reading and training workshops. The journal notes can not only provide teachers with plenty of information about students but also help them form a habit of multi-perspective thinking as a teacher researcher.

4. Videotaping. When there is no clue, videotaping a lesson can often reveal a lot. What we see is not always equivalent to what it is. Videotaping can offer teachers a vivid and direct way to analyze students and their learning outcomes. Teachers can choose a specific point (e.g. students' engagement) to analyze by transcribing the videotapes.

5. Observation. Asking colleagues or experts to observe a lesson is another effective way to analyze students. It offers a totally different perspective about students and the effectiveness of teachers' classroom teaching. Teachers can choose a focus point for observation and discuss with the invited observers to get in-depth information.

3.4 How to design lesson objectives

TASK 3.4.1

What are the main features of good lesson objectives? Read the following lesson objectives of *Caterpillar, Caterpillar*. Are they well designed? Why or why not? Discuss in groups and try to list features of good lesson objectives.

在本课学习结束时，学生能够：
（1）根据故事中的主人公、情境，梳理毛毛虫脱险的故事情节发展脉络；
（2）根据故事地图，尝试使用文本中的语言简单讲述毛毛虫脱险的故事；
（3）根据对话和图片，分析关于毛毛虫和小鸟关系变化的细节，有感情地朗读并表演故事；
（4）从自然科学的角度，总结、归纳毛毛虫的成长过程；
（5）评价故事角色，表达自己对毛毛虫巧妙摆脱困境的看法。

Discussion Point

Effective lesson objectives should have the following features:

1. Focus on students' performance. Good lesson objectives should specify what the students are able to do after learning the lesson, not what the teacher should teach. They usually start with this line: "By the end of this lesson, the students will be able to ..."

2. Use specific action verbs. Good lesson objectives should be specific, using action verbs. For many teachers, the objectives they set up for their lessons are often too general or vague with the use of verbs. The general description of verbs cannot be carried out nor can they be assessed, such as learn, master, etc. For more effective lesson objectives, we suggest that teachers avoid using the above mentioned verbs. Instead, try to replace them with specific action verbs like recognize, classify, describe, explain, compare, analyze, create, design, discuss and share, etc. In the example of Task 3.4.1, the teacher used the following verbs as lesson objectives: "梳理……（发展脉络）、使用……简单讲述、分析、有感情地朗读并表演、总结、归纳、评价、表达看法等". These verbs are very specific action verbs and they can be carried out by the students and assessed by the teacher.

Reading 3.4.1A 《英语学科能力及其表现研究》

3. Hierarchical. Lesson objectives should be layered. According to Wang and Hu (2017), English core abilities are hierarchical with three broad levels and nine sublevels (Table 3.4.1 and **Reading 3.4.1A**). Without Level A, students cannot reach Level B. When designing lesson objectives, teachers should consider the relationship among each objective. In Task 3.4.1, objective (1) belongs to Level A, objectives (2)-(4) are of Level B, and objective 5 is Level C, showing a gradual procession of ability development.

Table 3.4.1 Framework for English core abilities (Adapted)

能力要素		内涵及表现指标
A 学习理解能力	A-1 感知、注意	能有目的、有意识地关注主题和语境，以及与主题相关的英语语音、词法、句法等知识和现象，及其背后的本质
	A-2 记忆、检索	能结合即时性情境，对存储在长时记忆中的英语语言知识进行关联和检索
	A-3 提取、概括	能通过识别词语和句义，抓住英语信息，在目标范围内找到所需的信息；能在观察英语语言现象的基础上，归纳概括信息，建立关联，形成结构或语言规律
B 应用实践能力	B-1 描述、阐释	能用英语表达或叙述图表、程序 / 步骤、相关主题（如个人生活、工作）等；能用英语阐释词汇、语句以及图表的含义和用意
	B-2 分析、判断	能根据语言材料判断或用英语分析语句之间、事件之间的因果关系；能用英语结合事实和道理来判断和阐述论点。它反映出学习者具有用英语进行逻辑推理，得出合乎事理规律的能力
	B-3 整合、运用	能用英语系统地组织、合并及编排语言材料所提供的语境、篇章结构、逻辑关系等信息，能从零散的信息中梳理信息间的关联，并能综合地运用语言（如写作中的衔接手段、谋篇布局等）
C 迁移创新能力	C-1 推理、论证	能整合语言材料中的线索、逻辑、因果关系等多重复杂的信息，推导出未知内容，论证观点或结论，根据已知信息合理推断和论证人物关系、事件的后续发展、作者的情感态度等。能用英语表达自己的推理与结论
	C-2 批判、评价	能进行批判性思维，利用理论展开论证和评判，提出令他人信服的个人见解。该能力涉及英语学习者的认知立场、情感态度、是非观念等，是多种心智和多种能力的有机聚合，是综合素质的集中体现
	C-3 创造、想象	能基于已知信息发挥想象，衍生丰富、多样的创意，如创编对话、提出新的解决方案、表达个人观点和情感、为开放式故事续写结局等

4. Feasible. Lesson objectives should be set up according to what the students are able to achieve, which is also known to be within the students' zones of proximal development. That means, if students are able to do a certain activity with the help of a more knowledgeable other, its objective is feasible. If not, the objective is considered as unfeasible. Deciding whether lesson objectives are feasible or not relies on teachers' ability to analyze the target students.

5. Educational. When designing lesson objectives, the teacher should take into consideration the educational values of the lesson. That means what the students are supposed to learn and achieve should be beneficial for the students' life-long learning and for maintaining positive attitudes towards self and others, which will lead to right decision-making and value judgment. If the objectives do not foster good habits or correct attitudes, they are not educational.

6. Assessable. Learning objectives should be also assessable. In other words, they can be assessed by the teacher through classroom observations, questioning, activities that students do or tell whether they have learned or achieved the specific objectives the teacher set for them. If the objectives are not assessable, teachers cannot determine whether the lesson objectives are achieved, whether the lesson activities are effective, and whether learning has taken place. This feature is closely connected with the feature of "specific" . If a lesson objective is not specific enough, teachers will not be able to design relevant assessment activities. For a better understanding of the significance of designing assessment activities, go to **Reading 3.4.1 B**.

Reading 3.4.1B
教—学—评
一体化

TASK 3.4.2

Work in groups. Based on the above discussion, what do you think needs to be taken into consideration when designing lesson objectives? Summarize a few tips and discuss the procedures that can be followed.

Tips for designing lesson objectives
•
•
•

Discussion Point

For designing effective lesson objectives, more are suggested here.

1. Determine the skill type of the lesson. Common types of the lessons in primary schools include reading, listening and speaking, reading, or reading and writing lessons. Take *Caterpillar*, *Caterpillar* as an example. It can be taught as a reading lesson or a reading and speaking lesson. Then, the teacher can decide on the key learning objectives accordingly.

2. Determine the ultimate goal of the lesson. It is highly suggested that teachers should make clear the ultimate goal of the lesson first before going into specific lesson objectives. The ultimate goal usually embodies the overall objectives. It can be a real-life problem that students will try to solve after the lesson. It can also be a production activity (e.g. a drama performance or a writing activity) that the students need to do at the end of the lesson. It is usually Level C abilities according to the framework of English core competencies discussed in Section 3.4.

3. Work out lesson objectives that serve the ultimate goal of the lesson. After determining the ultimate goal of the lesson, teachers can try a backward design. That means, the teacher keeps the ultimate goal in mind and thinks about what specific activities are needed for achieving the goal and these specific tasks will then be used as specific objectives to be carried out. These objectives should enable the realization of the final goal. When doing so, remember the logical connection or progression of the objectives.

TASK 3.4.3

Work in groups. Go back to examine again the lesson objectives of *Caterpillar, Caterpillar*. What is its ultimate goal? Is there a logical connection or progression among the objectives? Give evidence to support your opinion.

Evidence:

3.5 How to design lesson activities

Once lesson objectives are set, the next step is to design activities that will ensure the achievement of the lesson objectives.

TASK 3.5.1A

What are some of the features of a good activity design? What activities will you design for *Caterpillar, Caterpillar*? Discuss in groups and write a few lesson activities next to each lesson objective. Make sure that the activities are aimed for the realization of the objectives.

Lesson objectives	Lesson activities
（1）根据故事中的主人公、情境，梳理毛毛虫脱险的故事发展脉络	
（2）根据故事导图，尝试使用文本中的语言简单讲述毛毛虫脱险的故事	
（3）根据对话和图片，分析关于毛毛虫和小鸟关系变化的细节，有感情地朗读并表演	
（4）从自然科学的角度，总结、归纳毛毛虫的成长过程	
（5）评价故事角色，表达自己对毛毛虫巧妙摆脱困境的看法	

Discussion Point

Good lesson activity design should have the following features:

1. Effective. Lesson activities should be designed to serve lesson objectives. In other words, they should enable the students to achieve the objectives after carrying out the activities. For a long time, many teachers tend to jump to the activities first before thinking about the lesson objectives. This can be misleading and ineffective. As teachers, we should bear in mind that activities should serve for the realization of lesson objectives and therefore they should match with each of the objectives.

2. Efficient. Lesson activities should also be efficient. It means they should be time-saving. Under one lesson objective, teachers can design more than one activity which should be closely connected with one another that help drive learning towards the particular objective. Teachers should choose the most time-saving one to allow for more space and time for student learning.

3. Engaging. Lesson activities should be motivating. It relies on how the teacher understands his or her students. "Engaging" is not equal to "interesting" or "fun" . Teachers should avoid "over-entertaining" in classroom teaching. Games, songs, and roles plays are interesting and fun, but it does not mean they are all engaging for developing students' culture awareness and thinking capacity. It is commonly found that in many primary classrooms activities are fun but not intellectually engaging or they are hands-on without being minds-on (Wiggins & McTighe, 2005).

TASK 3.5.1B

Read the following lesson activities(Figure 3.5.1). Are they effective, efficient and engaging? Discuss in groups.

绘本教学课例①

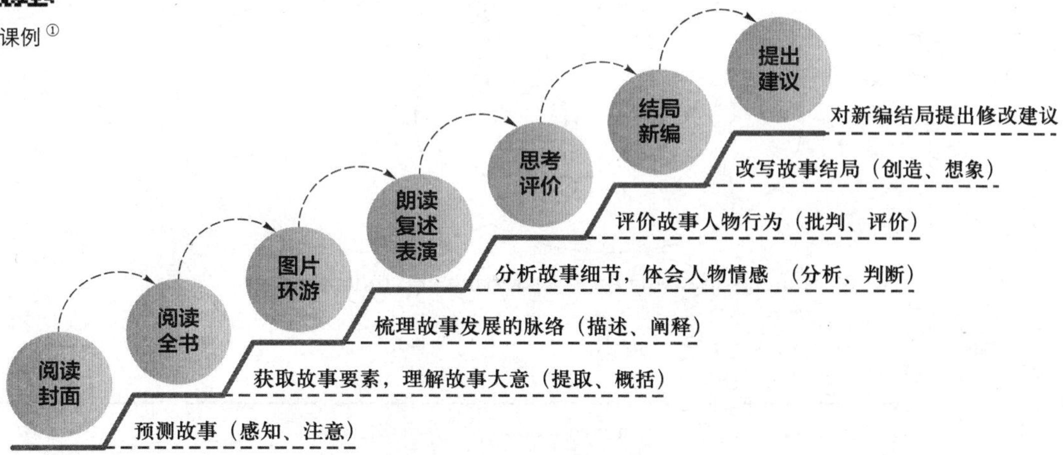

Figure 3.5.1 绘本的教学过程

Discussion Point

1. Worksheets design. Worksheets can be classified according to levels of lesson objectives. Some focus on Understanding and Learning, some on Applying and Practicing, and others on Transferring and Innovating. When designing Worksheets, teachers should pre-do them to make sure that students can finish them effectively and efficiently. Here are some examples:

① Helicopters Help由广东省东莞市长安镇第一小学许彤授课；Monkey Fun由广东省东莞市长南城阳光第二小学杨沛珊、许宇华提供。

1) Worksheets focusing on Understanding and Learning

2) Worksheets focusing on Applying and Practicing

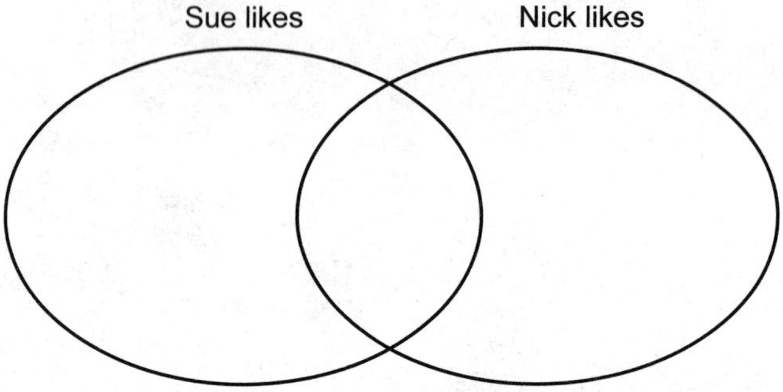

3) Worksheets focusing on Transferring and Innovating

My Friends

by________

I learned to ________ from my friend ________	I learned to ________ from my friend________
I learned to ________ from my friend ________	I learned to ________ from my friend ________

2. Board design. Board design offers students a visualized and concrete framework for understanding and analyzing the text, learning about language structure, summarizing and integrating information, and transforming and innovating. For primary school students, abstract thinking is quite hard, so board design should be as vivid as possible with pictures, flashcards and structured expressions. Mind maps or story maps are effective ways to design a board. Teachers can construct maps with students together while doing related activities or use posters to replace traditional board design. Here are some examples (Figure 3.5.2 and Figure 3.5.3).

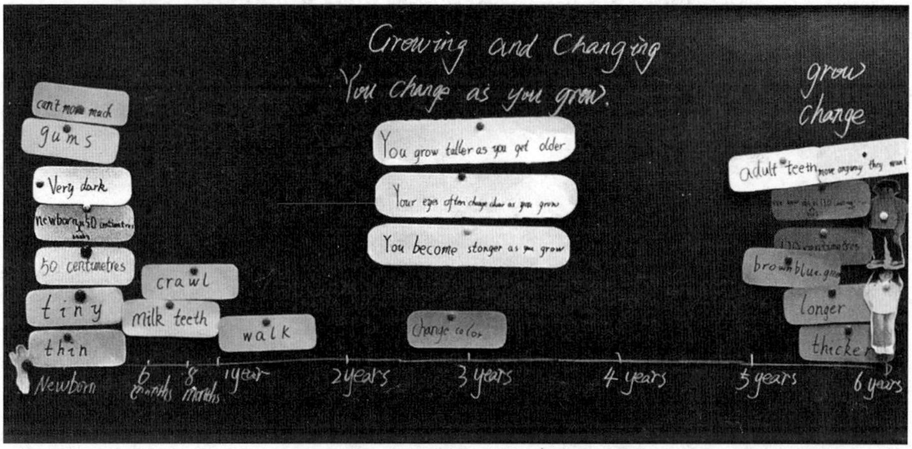

Figure 3.5.2 Board design sample A

Figure 3.5.3 Board design sample B

3. PowerPoint slide design. PowerPoint slides help teachers visualize information that is hard to present on the board. For example, when doing a shared reading activity, teachers can show the book on the slide. With careful design, they can also serve to attract students' attention. Colorful images, vivid videos, and animation effects are always eye-catching. However, using slides too often has negative effects. Students are easy to get bored with slides and sometimes get distracted by them. Therefore, teachers should use slides only when they are absolutely necessary.

3.6 How to do overall unit design

TASK 3.6

Read the lesson design in **Reading 3.6.1A and Reading 3.6.1B**. Summarize the procedures of the design based on a whole unit.

单元整体教学课例①

Step 1
Step 2
Step 3

Discussion Point

An overall unit design refers to an instructional design based on a whole unit instead of a single text or a part of the unit. It has many advantages. First, it sees one unit as a whole, so the learning content and activities of the unit is more closely connected. This can offer students a logical line for learning, helping them accumulate knowledge and skills gradually around a unified topic. Second, instructional design is more effective and efficient since unnecessary objectives and activities can be avoided. Finally, it is more structured so teachers can analyze the text more effectively to decide what to add and what to omit, leaving students more space for effective learning.

When doing overall unit design, teachers can follow the procedures below:

1. Analyze the texts in the whole unit. When analyzing a whole unit, it follows the same order as in analyzing a single text. Teachers should analyze the whole unit from "What", "Why", and "How". When doing so, an easy way is to figure out the logical connections among the texts by comparing and contrasting their content and functions in the unit.

2. Analyze students based on the whole unit. The dimension of student analysis should also be extended. Teachers should try to get more information by various approaches. However, a unit is often constructed with one topic. So after finding the topic,

① 广东省东莞市莞城教育管理中心罗羽授课。

it will be easier to proceed.

3. Determine the objectives and activities of the whole unit and each lesson. Objectives should be designed in two steps. First, objectives of the whole unit should be determined based on each text analysis of a unit and student analysis. After that, teachers can allocate the time and try to relate the unit objectives to those of single lessons. Corresponding lesson activities will then be designed with appropriate assessment activities, worksheets, board designs and PowerPoint slides.

Reading

Reading 3.6.1A

案例：Meet My Family 单元整体教学设计（4 课时）[1]

该主题属于“人与自我”和“人与社会”范畴，涉及“家庭与家庭生活”和“常见职业与人们的生活”。

一、单元内容分析

本单元内容围绕 Meet My Family 这一主题展开，涉及四个语篇，包括两组对话、一个配图故事和一篇配图短文。

语篇一是小学生日常生活对话。Amy 请同学陈洁到家里做客，翻看家庭相册，并向陈洁介绍自己的家庭成员。

语篇二也是小学生日常生活对话。张鹏和好朋友 Sarah 一起翻看家庭相册并交流，张鹏了解了 Sarah 叔叔和婶婶的职业。该语篇拓展和延伸了家庭主题。

语篇三是配图故事，标题是“June Sings”，讲述了主人公 June 与家人组织家庭音乐会的故事。June 因不擅长唱歌、被兄弟嘲笑而感到失落。父母通过和孩子们一起制订家庭规约，教育孩子们要彼此欣赏、互相帮助。该故事充满家庭温情，学生在阅读、理解故事的过程中，体会家人间需要相互理解、欣赏与爱护。

语篇四是配图短文。小学生 Mike 通过图文结合的小书向同学介绍他的家庭，包括家庭成员的职业以及每位成员在家庭中承担的责任：爸爸是非常忙碌的消防员，晚上帮妈妈做饭，陪 Mike 玩；妈妈是教师，常给家人做美食，周末陪 Mike 读书；爷爷、奶奶在家帮忙照看 Mike 和小弟弟；Mike 学习努力，经常帮助家长做事情。该语篇有助于引导学生感悟家庭成员对社会和家庭的责任与贡献，形成积极的情感体验，养成主动承担家庭责任的意识，并付诸行动。

表 1 为学生需要在本单元学习的核心要点。

表 1　单元主题：Meet My Family 教学的核心要点

语篇	核心词汇	核心句式	技能与策略学习要点
1. “Family Album”	家庭及家庭成员： family, parent, uncle, aunt, cousin, baby, brother, father, mother	询问、介绍家庭成员： How many people are there in your family? My family has ...	• 根据图片和标题，推测对话的主题、语境及主要信息； • 在语境中，根据单词的音、形、义学习词汇

① 中华人民共和国教育部. 义务教育英语课程标准：2022年版［M］. 北京：北京师范大学出版社，2022：143–148.（有调整）

continued

语篇	核心词汇	核心句式	技能与策略学习要点
2. “Jobs of Family Members”	职业： football player, doctor, nurse, teacher, cook, driver 外貌： tall, strong, short, beautiful, cute	询问、介绍家庭成员的职业： What’s his / her job? He / She is a ... Is your ... a ...?	• 询问和应答有关个人或他人家庭成员的信息
3. “June Sings”	家庭活动： play the drums, play the piano, play the violin, sing 情绪和行为： sad, mad, cry	描述家庭成员之间的相处方式： Don’t be rude. I am part of the family. Family Rules: 1. Work Hard 2. Be Kind 3. Say Sorry	• 根据图片和标题推测故事的主要信息； • 推断故事的画面、色彩、声音等传递的意义； • 借助图片和核心语言讲述故事的主要内容
4. “My Family”	职业及贡献： fires, put out fires, rescue people and animals, teacher, teach English 家庭活动： play, cook, read	描述家庭成员的活动： He plays with me. She reads books with me. My grandparents take care of my baby brother and me.	• 借助语言输出框架（总体介绍—父母职业—每位成员对家庭的贡献—小结）和语言提示，介绍自己的家庭

本单元的四个语篇从不同视角谈论家庭及家庭成员，单元内各语篇与单元主题之间、各语篇之间相互关联，构成三个子主题，即“认识家庭成员在家庭和社会中的不同角色”“感悟家庭成员间应彼此关爱，相互支持和鼓励”“主动承担家庭责任，表达对家人的爱”。各课时围绕单元主题和子主题展开，课时之间既相对独立，又紧密关联。语言学习渗透在对语篇主题意义的探究中，学习活动由浅入深，理解性技能与表达性技能协同发展，有效帮助学生形成基于主题的结构化知识（见图 1）。

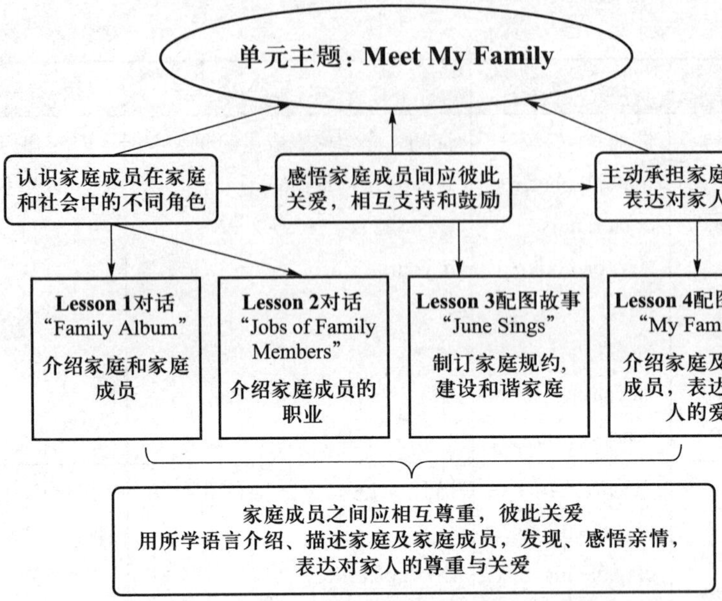

图1 Meet My Family单元主题及内容框架图

二、单元教学目标

表 2 为单元教学目标及其语篇。

表 2 单元教学目标

单元教学目标	语篇
1. 在语境中，与同伴交流并介绍自己的家庭和家庭成员，如外貌特征和从事的职业等	1. 对话 “Family Album” （1 课时）
	2. 对话 “Jobs of Family Members” （1 课时）
2. 独立或合作设计“和谐家庭建设提示卡”，介绍家庭成员之间应如何相处	3. 配图故事 “June Sings” （1 课时）
3. 仿照范例，以图文结合的方式介绍自己的家庭成员，包括外貌、职业、在家庭中承担的责任等，并表达自己对家人的情感	4. 配图短文 “My Family” （1 课时）

Reading 3.6.1B

案例：Clothes 单元整体教学设计（5 课时）[①]

单元主题：Clothes

教材：北京师范大学出版社的义务教育教科书《英语》（三年级起点）5 年级上册第 3 单元

服饰是我们生活中必不可少的部分，学生通过本单元的学习能够合理选择与购买适合自己的服饰，了解不同文化、不同时间或场合的着装要求，认识到旧衣可以新穿，形成健康的消费观。本单元围绕这一主题和育人价值，以培养学生核心素养为指引进行教学设计。教师要深入研读语篇，把握教学核心内容，建立内容间的有机关联，形成单元育人蓝图，设计单元教学目标，并在此基础上，践行英语学习活动观和“教—学—评”一体化的理念，精心设计学习活动和评价活动，助力核心素养目标落地课堂。

一、单元内容分析

1. 单元语篇分析

本单元以服饰为话题，讨论了如何选择服饰，讲述了如何利用旧衣、旧衣新穿的故事，属于“人与自我”中的“做人与做事”主题群，有助于学生形成健康的消费观和勤俭节约意识。本单元共包含七个语篇，见表 1。

表 1　单 元 语 篇

语篇类型及内容	主题意义	调整前的顺序
1. 配图对话故事 Enjoy the story 故事讲述了 Ken 和家人在服装店，从多个方面考虑、选择购买的衣物	多维度考虑购衣需求 学会选择适合的服饰	1
2. 对话 Talk together 通过对话的形式呈现主人公 Ken 购买服饰的情境，再次复习购衣考虑的三个维度	学会从不同维度挑选服饰	3
3. 韵文 Let’s chant 通过韵文，呈现小女孩买衣服考虑的三个维度：颜色、尺寸、价格	内化挑选衣物的不同维度	4
4. 配图对话故事 Uncle Booky’s storytime 小女孩为参加聚会活动选择合适的服装，妈妈改造了旧连衣裙，她收获了一条漂亮的裙子也收获了同学的赞誉	合理利用破旧衣物，形成勤俭节约的意识	7

① 案例设计者：林红，北京市昌平区教师进修学校；刘明，北京市昌平第二实验小学；苏祎，北京市昌平第二实验小学；王睿，北京师范大学昌平附属学校。

continued

语篇类型及内容	主题意义	调整前的顺序
5. 歌曲 Let's sing 通过韵律歌曲的方式，描述三个学生对待不同衣物问题的解决方案，呈现不同衣物问题的不同解决办法	思考生活中的衣物问题及解决方案	2
6. 阅读 Let's read 春节时，Li Jie 给 Jack 写了一封信，信中描写了三位主人公不同的着装	聚焦中国人春节做新衣、穿新衣的传统，渗透节日文化习俗	5
7. 拓展学习 Fact file 图片呈现了四种不同国家/地区的传统服饰的名称与样子	传递了节日、场合、文化等与服饰之间的关系	6

2. 单元顺序调整

本单元的七个语篇中，Enjoy the story、Talk together、Let's chant 呈现了购买衣物的过程，具有连贯性；Let's sing 和 Uncle Booky's storytime 呈现衣服的护理及再利用的内容，体现了勤俭节约的理念，是对购物内容的深入探讨与补充；Let's read 和 Fact file 呈现了中国及其他国家节日穿衣习俗，是对衣物话题的延伸。因此，在进行单元整体规划及设计时，教师依据子主题的逻辑对主要语篇的顺序做了必要调整。

3. 学情分析

从学生语言基础来看，本单元学习前，学生在四年级学习过购物的相关话题，对购物话题并不陌生；在语言知识方面，学生能够使用已学语言描述尺寸、价格、颜色及购物的交际用语，这些都为本单元的学习奠定了语言基础（图 1）。

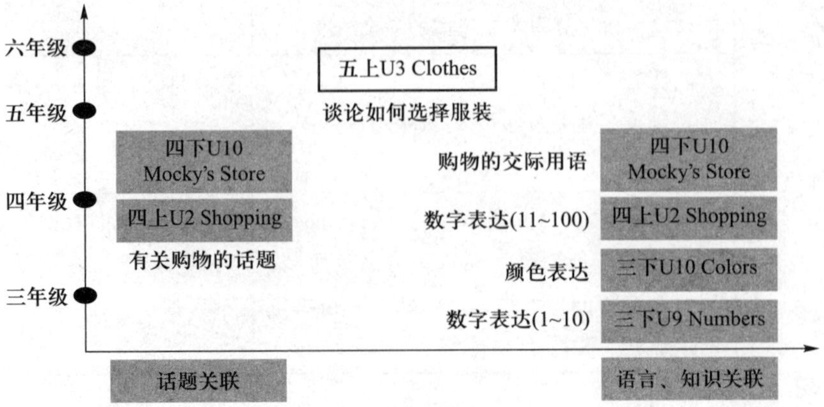

图1 学情分析

4. 单元育人蓝图

基于以上分析，结合单元主要内容，教师提炼出本单元三个子主题，即学会购物、勤俭节约、节日与服饰。根据这三个子主题，形成单元大主题：Smart Buying、Smart Clothes。

根据各个课时的具体内容，教师结合子主题进一步分析语言活动，梳理、提炼出支撑子主题构建的语言学习内容，使学生能在完成本单元学习后形成结构化知识（图 2）。

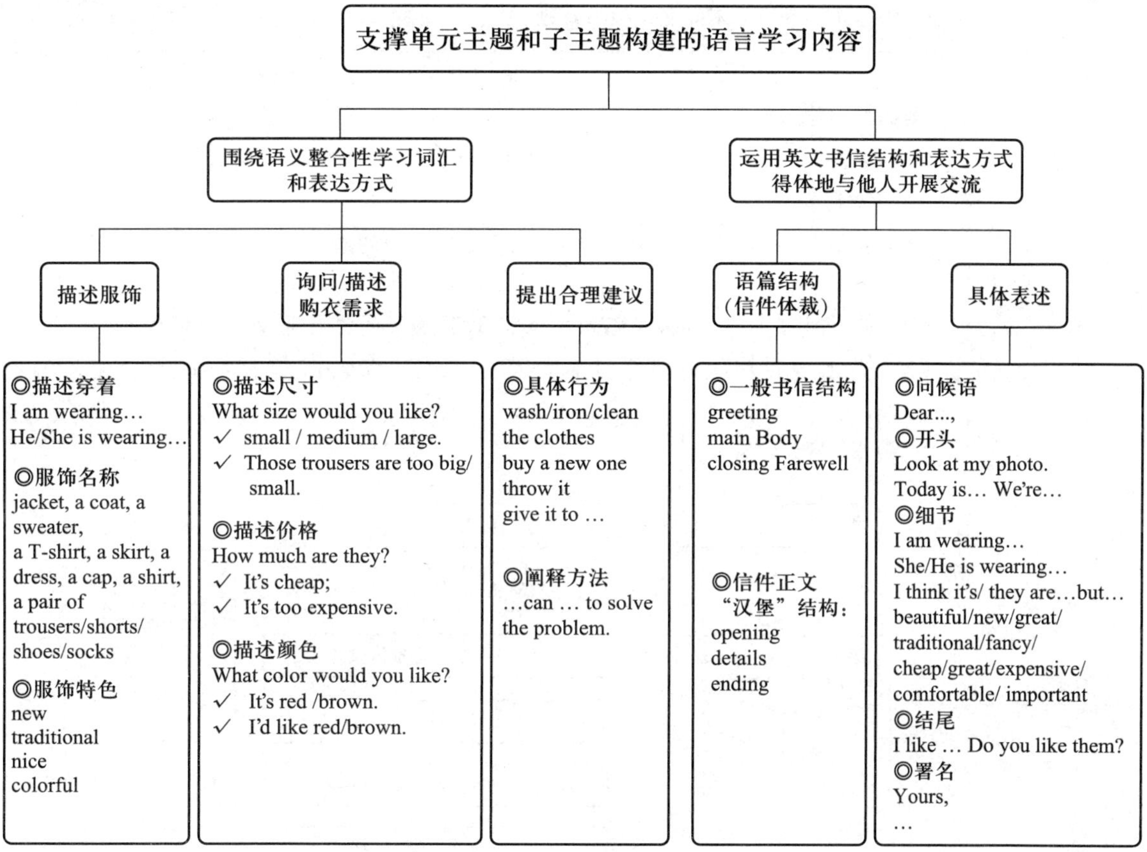

图2　语言学习内容

二、单元目标设计

单元目标	课时内容安排
1. 基于所挑选衣物的尺寸、价格、颜色等，运用语言知识和信息，模拟购物情境	第 1 课时　故事教学 Enjoy the story、Match and say、Show time
	第 2 课时　对话交际 Talk together、Learn to say、Let's chant
	第 3 课时　综合运用 Listen and check、Listen and number、Let's find out、Choose and write

continued

单元目标	课时内容安排
2. 针对他人再利用衣物的做法进行观察、分析与评价，思考并阐述生活中合理消费、旧物利用的行为与方法	第 4 课时　阅读教学 Uncle Booky's Storytime、Let's sing
3. 观察、描述、分析与评价不同场合下的着装，介绍不同场合、不同文化中的着装	第 5 课时　读写教学 Let's read、Fact file

三、课时教学设计

第 1 课时

1. 教学目标

（1）获取和梳理 Ken 一家去服装店购买的服饰的颜色、尺寸和价格，师生共建板书。

（2）表演故事片段并描述 Ken 或 Ann 购买衣服的过程，语音、语调自然。

（3）提炼购买衣服时需考虑的维度，尝试续编 Ann 带着 Mocky 换帽子的新故事。

2. 教学流程（图 3）

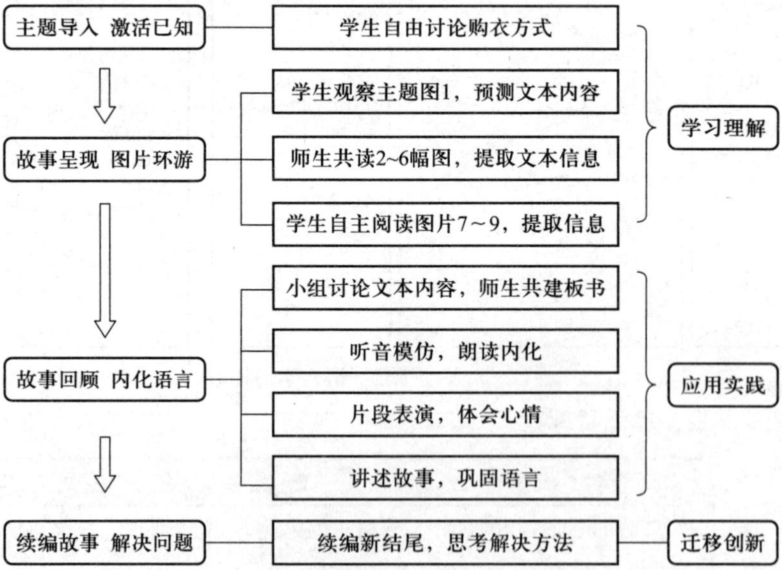

图3　第1课时教学流程

第 2 课时

1. 教学目标

（1）在对话中梳理服装的相关词汇：shorts、shoes、shirts、sweaters、skirts、dresses、socks，并针对价格进行问答。

（2）熟练使用“Do you have any...? What color/size would you like? How much is/are...?”等句型。

（3）正确流利地朗读韵文，创造性使用购物用语进行韵文的创编。

2. 教学流程（图 4）

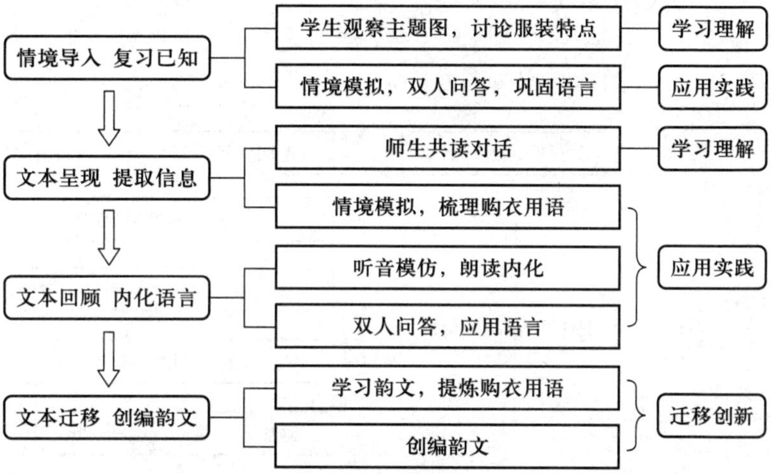

图4　第2课时教学流程

第 3 课时

1. 教学目标

（1）批判性评价 Mike 的服装店，并补充开业宣传单。

（2）分组设计开业宣传单，总结购买服饰用语。

（3）模拟购买服饰的游戏，针对尺寸、价格、颜色等进行问答，根据需求购买合适的服饰。

2. 教学流程（图 5）

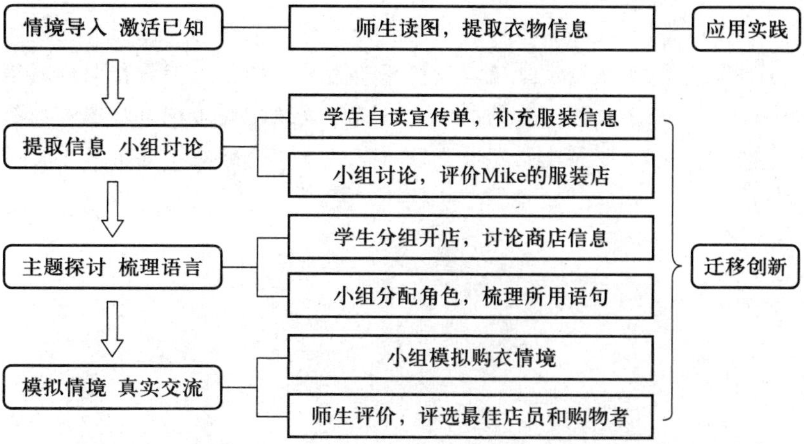

图5　第3课时教学流程

第 4 课时

1. 教学目标

（1）获取小女孩找衣服、买衣服、改造衣服的过程，师生共建故事思维导图。

（2）分析小女孩的心情变化过程，有感情朗读或表演故事。

（3）对小女孩选择和处理衣物的行为做出简单的评价。

（4）思考并阐述生活中合理消费、旧物利用的行为与方法。

2. 教学流程（图 6）

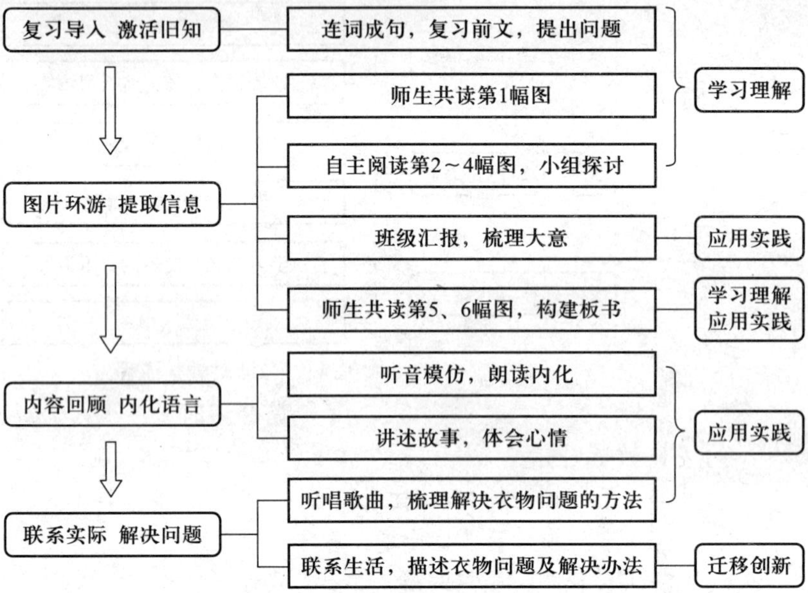

图6 第4课时教学流程

第 5 课时

1. 教学目标

（1）提取和梳理人物的服饰信息，依据图片匹配相应人物名字。

（2）批判性地梳理并提炼书信写作的相关要素，明确写信的基本结构。

（3）描述人物的服饰，分析与阐述中国传统节日服饰的特点。

（4）联系生活实际，以写信的方式介绍在不同节日中自己的服饰及其特点。

2. 教学流程（图 7）

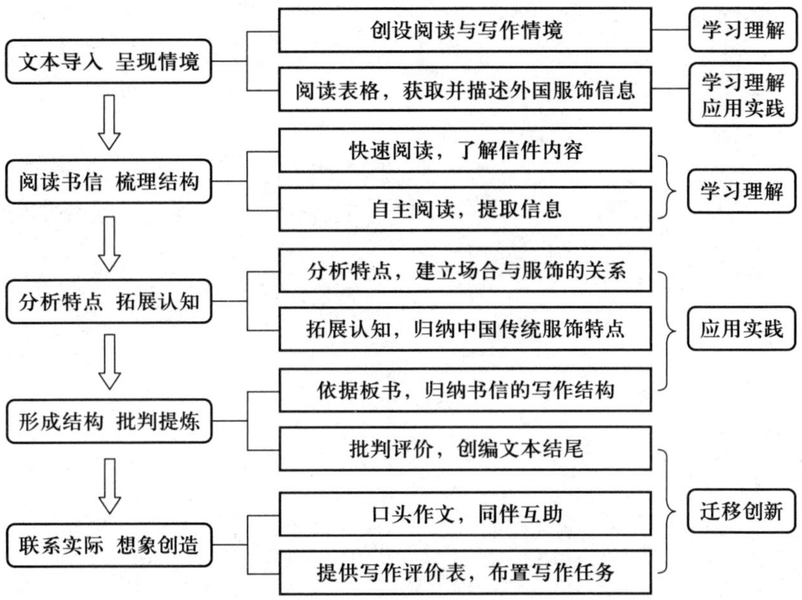

图7　第5课时教学流程

Unit 4

Classroom Management

Aims of the unit

In this unit, we are going to focus on the following:

4.1 How to motivate children to learn English

4.1.1 What influence children's motivation?

4.1.2 How can we motivate children in learning English?

4.2 How to give effective classroom instructions

4.2.1 What functions do teacher's instructions have?

4.2.2 Why should teachers use English instructions?

4.2.3 How to give clear instructions

4.3 How to ask effective questions

4.3.1 Why do teachers ask questions?

4.3.2 What kind of questions do we ask?

4.3.3 How can we engage learners in asking questions?

4.4 How to set up classroom discipline

4.4.1 Why is there a discipline problem in the classroom?

4.4.2 How to create a good learning atmosphere

4.4.3 How to keep discipline in the classroom

4.5 What should teachers do when teaching large classes?

4.5.1 What are the problems of large classes?

4.5.2 How to teach large classes effectively

4.6 How to manage classroom interaction

4.6.1 What are the most commonly used classroom activities?

4.6.2 What kind of grouping is suitable for certain activities?

4.6.3 What are the problems of different grouping?

4.7 How to organize activities in a lesson

4.7.1 How to start a lesson

4.7.2 What are stirring and setting activities?

4.7.3 What are physically engaged and mentally engaged activities?

4.7.4 How to organize activities effectively

4.8 How to treat children's errors in the classroom

4.8.1 Do we need to correct errors?

4.8.2 What is the difference between a mistake and an error?

4.8.3 How do we correct errors?

Classroom management refers to the way teachers organize what happens in the classroom. It plays a very important role in a primary school classroom, for even the most effective activities cannot reach their objectives without the guarantee of good classroom atmosphere. So in this unit, we are going to discuss some aspects of classroom management. We hope teachers will teach more effectively and efficiently with the help of these skills.

4.1 How to motivate children to learn English

4.1.1 What influences children's motivation?

Attitudes and motivation have been regarded as the most important factors affecting learning. As far as adult learners are concerned, it is relatively easy to find out what factors influence their attitude and motivation because they usually have clear goals or reasons for learning the language. However, it is often difficult to know exactly what influences children's attitude and motivation.

TASK 4.1.1A

Read the following comments made by children and try to find out the factors that may influence children's attitude and motivation.

(1) What we do in class is very interesting.
(2) I like to speak English.
(3) I like group competitions best.
(4) I've got 5 red flowers this week for my English.
(5) I like it. It's fun to have our English class.
(6) I like to sing songs and play games.
(7) I can sing English songs for my parents.
(8) I really like my teacher. She's nice.
(9) I don't like English. It's difficult.
(10) I can't remember the words and often fail in my spelling tests.
(11) I feel nervous when I speak English. I can't say things well.
(12) I don't like my English teacher. She's very strict and rarely smiles.

(13) I don't like to do my English homework, always copying and copying.
(14) My teacher thinks that I'm stupid and she seldom asks me to answer questions.
(15) I want to be praised by my teacher, so I work very hard on English.

Discussion Point

There are two kinds of motivation, namely, intrinsic motivation and extrinsic motivation. Intrinsic motivation in language learning is defined as "the extent to which the individual works or strives to learn the language because of a desire to do so and the satisfaction experienced in this activity" (Gardner, 1985). Students are motivated to learn the language for its own sake and enjoy the learning activity and completion of a task. Extrinsic motivation,on the other hand, "comes from outside the individual. Students are extrinsically motivated when learning is done for the sake of rewards (such as grades or praise) that are not inherently associated with the learning itself" (Ehrman, Leaver & Oxford, 2003). In other words, all the effort put into learning is not for learning itself but for the purpose of gaining those rewards.

TASK 4.1.1B

Now look at children's comments in Task 4.1.1A, which of these belong to intrinsic motivation and which belong to extrinsic motivation? Discuss with your partners.

Motivation	1	2	3	4	5	6	7	8	9	10	11	12	13	14	15
Intrinsic motivation															
Extrinsic motivation															

4.1.2 How can we motivate children in learning English?

Now that you have known what motivation is and you must be wondering what you, as a teacher, can do to motivate your pupils. This is a popular topic and many other teachers are struggling with this.

TASK 4.1.2A

Reading 4.1.2A is taken from a mini-conference. Participants are discussing how to motivate young children to speak English more in class. Read them and discuss with your group members and work out your own list. The list can be about the same theme or you may choose a different issue you are interested in exploring, e.g. how to involve children in learning more actively or how to motivate children to be more autonomous. You may wish to contribute to the mini-conference by posting your list to classmates. It could be fun!

TASK 4.1.2B

Read the following situations and the teacher's behavior. Are the teachers motivating learners or demotivating them? What are the reasons behind these behaviors? If you do not like any of these, can you improve them? Discuss in groups.

Situation 1

The teacher is showing a very exciting cartoon and the purpose is to ask children to pick up what is being said in the cartoon. The children get so excited that they stand up and move with the music. The teacher gets very angry and she says:

— 再有一个人起来我就关掉，不看了。

Situation 2

The teacher is trying to organize an activity and one of the pupils continuously fights with others sitting around him and the teacher has to stop him doing so for several times. Finally she says to him:

— 你怎么总是影响我？

Situation 3

The teacher is going to start a game. Pupils get very excited and they put up their hands high and start shouting "me, me". The teacher stops this by saying:

— 谁叫呢？再叫，5 轮都不叫你。好的，开始，大家不许说话，只许做动作。

Situation 4

Some pupils are making a lot of noise and some are playing with each other. The teacher suddenly stops talking and the games she is organizing. She waits silently and says:

— 我还在等一个人。

Situation 5

Pupils are listening to the tape, each word is read twice and they have to tell the teacher what they hear. Many of them shout out the answer after listening to it once only. The teacher tries to change this so she says:

— 等他说完两遍你再说，好吗？因为有的同学还没有听清楚呢！我看谁做得最棒。

Discussion Point

Moon (2000) states that, young children tend to be influenced by their feeling for their teacher, the general learning atmosphere in the classroom, the method used, and their parents' opinions. Do you agree with her?

Children are different from adults who often have clear personal goals and objectives for learning a foreign language, e.g. finding good jobs, going abroad, making more money, talking to foreigners, etc. For children, a foreign language is simply another school subject they have to do in school. Children do things that interest them and make them feel good about themselves. It should be easy and enjoyable to learn with attainable targets. Children are active, creative and imaginative. They like to act and play games. And they need the opportunity to exercise their imaginations and creativity. They will not like to be lectured to but to be involved in actions and presentations. They need to be recognized for what they do and praised for their efforts and participation. Therefore, their experience of learning the language is very important for shaping their attitude and motivation. Participation, enjoyment, and success are three keys that will make all the difference to children in building up their attitude and motivation towards learning English.

It is obvious that the teacher and the teaching method are playing crucial roles in shaping and fostering children's interest in learning. A lot of children like to learn the language simply because they like the teacher or they enjoy the classroom activities in which they can demonstrate their capability and gain success. Similarly, children can develop a negative attitude towards the language simply because they do not like their teacher or the classroom activities. Bearing in mind the theory of multiple intelligences, we need to design a variety of activities that cater for different needs and provide different opportunities for children to exercise their different intelligences.

Understanding the importance of motivation doesn't mean that you'll be good at this. A number of educators (Stevick, 1976; Littlewood, 1981, and Rivers, 1992, cited in Senior, 2002) refer to "the importance of developing non-threatening classroom atmospheres, in which pupils feel comfortable enough to interact readily with others in the target language". In task 4.1.2B, we see some irritating behaviors of the learners and teachers' responses. Some criticize pupils' behaviors when they get excited in trying to gain the chance to participate in language games. Some choose a more skillful way to deal with this. Keeping a good discipline when teaching young learners is undoubtedly important and it is a way to guarantee effective learning but teachers also need to protect learners' enthusiasm and try to create a nice and encouraging learning environment for learners to enjoy the class.

So how to motivate young language learners then? There are some strategies that teachers can adopt in their teaching to motivate children. **Reading 4.1.2B** introduces some good ideas for motivating children in learning English. Harris also has some ideas:

(1) Explain.

Teachers should spend more time explaining why we teach, what we do, and why the topic or approach or activity is important and interesting and worthwhile (how you do this with young learners needs to be discussed).

(2) Reward.

Rather than criticizing unwanted behaviors or answers, reward correct behavior and answers.

(3) Care.

Pupils will attend to teachers who care about them and not just authority figures.

(4) Have pupils participate.

Pupils love to be needed so getting them involved in activities and problem-solving exercises and even making decisions are good ways to motivate them.

(5) Teach inductively.

Create opportunities for pupils to explore so that they can have the joy of discovery.

(6) Satisfy pupils' needs.

Attending to need satisfaction is a useful way to keep pupils interested and happy.

(7) Make learning visual.

It was recognized that memory is often connected to visual images, so use drawings, diagrams, pictures, charts, graphs, etc to gain pupils' attention.

(8) Use positive emotions to enhance learning and motivation.

Teachers can try to make something fun, exciting, happy, loving in their class so that pupils can learn better and the memory lasts longer.

(9) Remember that energy sells.

Being energetic in one's teaching is a motivating factor in itself.

If we compare Harris' idea and Vernon's idea (in Reading 4.1.2B), it is not difficult to identify that both attach importance to teacher's attitude and behavior in the classroom and learners' involvement in activities. Teachers need to be enthusiastic about the things they teach and be excited about the games to be played and need to take care of their pupils. They also need to think of ways to involve pupils more and train pupils to be active and take responsibility for their own learning. Rewarding is a good way but teachers also need to think about how they can improve pupils' intrinsic motivation so that they do not learn just for rewards.

4.2 How to give effective classroom instructions

Classroom instructions refer to the type of language teachers use in the classroom to organize or guide learning. They include giving directions to tasks or activities, providing explanations to a concept or language structure, setting requirements, checking comprehension,drawing attention, motivating learners, giving feedback, and assigning homework, etc. Generally, they include all classroom language that teachers may use for teaching purposes as well as for managing teaching.

It is generally easier to give instructions to advanced and adult learners, but with young learners, it is something that teachers need to pay much attention to.

4.2.1 What functions do teacher's instructions have?

TASK 4.2.1

In the process of teaching in the classroom, besides giving instructions to children, teachers talk to children for many other purposes. Can you make a list of the functions of teacher's talk? What type of language do teachers normally use and why?

Functions of your talk	Any examples?	English or Chinese?	Any reasons?
Classroom language			
Controlling discipline		Chinese	Show more authority
Getting pupils' attention	Is everybody listening to me?	English	
Correcting errors			
Grouping pupils			

Discussion Point

As a teacher, we talk for various purposes. We give instructions, control discipline, praise good behaviors, ask questions, set up tasks, provide information, tell stories, explain things, demonstrate, provide examples, check understanding, give feedback and assign homework, etc. Obviously, you may talk sometimes in Chinese and sometimes in English. Teachers vary widely in how much English they use in their classrooms. There are no right or wrong answers concerning when and how much Chinese or English should be used in the language classroom. It depends on the pupils' level of English and it also depends on how comfortable teachers feel in using the language, as well as on the level of the language involved in setting up the task (Moon, 2000). We need to keep in mind that the purpose of using Chinese or English is to enable effective teaching and learning.

It is important that we always have a reason for what we do. L1 does have a role to play in an L2 classroom as sometimes it can be very time-consuming to try to explain things in the target language and possibly cause more confusion. Atkinson (1993) suggests a careful, limited use of L1 to help pupils get the maximum benefit from activities which in other respects will be carried out in the target language. The mother tongue may be useful in the management stages of a class, for example:

- setting up pair and group work.
- sorting out an activity that is clearly not working.
- checking comprehension.

Moon (2000) also makes an important point with regard to the use of the mother tongue. She says, " both languages are a resource. It may be most helpful to view pupils' use of L1 as a useful strategy for communicating at a stage when they do not have enough English to express their own ideas." However, we also need to be aware that in fact, classroom language is one of the most realistic communicative situations for children to learn English as a foreign language and the teachers are the main source of input. We believe that it will help our learners if we teach them in the target language because they need to experience the target language as a real means of communication. Also, if we teach them in the language they are learning, we give them more chances to be exposed to the language. By teaching through the target language, we are offering them the opportunity to see how the language they learned is used so as to bridge the gap between classroom-based controlled practice with the real language used outside the classroom (Halliwell and Jones, 1991).

4.2.2 *Why should teachers use English instructions?*

TASK 4.2.2

When you learned English in school, did your teacher use English or Chinese in the classroom? Can you think of some possible reasons for them to do so? What are the advantages and disadvantages of using each language? Write down your reasons in the table given and then compare and discuss them with your partner.

Situations	Reasons	Advantages	Disadvantages
My teacher used Chinese most of the time.			
My teacher used English most of the time.			
My teacher used both languages equally.			

Discussion Point

We understand that many teachers may use more Chinese to teach children, especially when teaching beginners because they worry that:

- children will not be able to understand and won't know what to do.
- children without understanding will be discouraged to continue.
- children without understanding will misbehave.
- they are not able to speak very fluent English themselves.

We understand these worries very well. Because at the beginning children have no experience of English, how can we teach them all in English? However, we would like to make two points here. First, one does not have to understand meaning just from words of a language, for example, one can understand a message from body language (Figure 4.2.1), nodding for agreeing and waving the hand for goodbye, etc. Second, on many occasions, meaning can be understood with very limited language, sometimes just one word, for example, "good" with your thumb raised.

Even for very young children, intonation, gesture, facial expressions, actions and context all help them "guess and understand the unknown words and phrases uttered by the adults" (Halliwell, 1992). Also, Moon (2000) points out that because many teachers do not think that children will be able to understand without any English yet, they tend not to use English at the beginning stage. She says that if this is the case, in fact, they have lost the opportunity to create a communicative environment, provide authentic input, and set up routines at the beginning. Therefore, we suggest that for everyday organization and running of the lessons, with the kind of simple instructions that you will possibly be using in every English class later, you can try to use them at the very beginning.

Figure 4.2.1 Body language

However, it is necessary to establish a classroom routine from the very first lesson. Use gestures and contexts to demonstrate the meaning, especially for instructions, which will be repeatedly used later. Gradually you can reduce the use of the mother tongue once the routines are established. Sometimes you may feel that it is time-saving to use Chinese for explaining complicated steps for an activity, especially when you are doing the activity for the first time. The second time you do the activity, you can give your instructions in simple English and then check if children understand your English by asking them to tell you in Chinese how to do the activity.

One way of encouraging the use of English in the classroom is to write the most commonly used phrases in speech bubbles and stick them on the walls where children can see them clearly. Day by day, children will be familiar with these instructions. Such as:

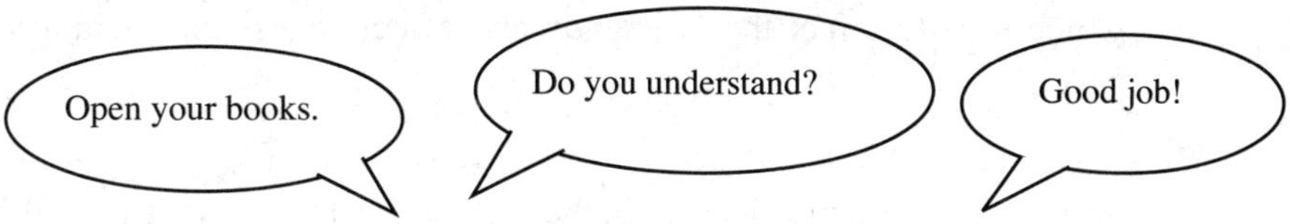

4.2.3 *How to give clear instructions*

TASK 4.2.3A

Look at the picture (Figure 4.2.2) and read the classroom instructions from a novice English teacher. Discuss what problems there are.

Figure 4.2.2 A novice English teacher in class

Problem 1	She uses adult language, such as “准确率高”
Problem 2	
Problem 3	
Problem 4	

Discussion Point

Novice teachers often have problems giving clear instructions. This is not because their language proficiency is low. On the contrary, they are very competent in the language because they have been teaching since graduating from the university. The problem for these teachers is that they are not able to adapt their instructions to the level of the learners. Their instructions are often long and rather complicated for pupils to follow, which greatly affect the efficiency and effectiveness of teaching and learning (Wang, 2006).

As we can see that the teacher in the picture was trying to organize the activity of "Passing the Message" with children and she was explaining everything in Chinese, but most of the children did not understand her. She repeated the instructions three times, but still could not make all the children work. What is the problem? Here we are not concerned about the complexity of the activity itself, but just the way the classroom instruction is given. We can see that the teacher uses most adult-like language instead of children's language. We can also see that the language she uses was long, plain, quite distant and without any friendly feeling. That is why most children could not understand what to do. The third problem is that she does not try to use body language or invite any children to work with her to demonstrate the activity but merely uses verbal language to explain.

Giving clear instructions is not an easy job, Scrivener (1994) proposed five steps towards better instructions:

(1) Become aware of your own instruction-giving (e.g. listen to yourself, record yourself, ask others to watch you and give feedback).

(2) For a while, pre-plan instructions. Analyze the instruction beforehand so as to include only the essential information in simple, clear language. Sequence the information in a sensible order. Use short sentences—one sentence for each key piece of information. Don't say things that are visible or obvious. Don't give instructions that they don't need to know at this point.

(3) In class, separate instructions clearly from the other chit-chat, telling off, joking, etc. that goes on. Create silence beforehand, make eye-contact with as many children as possible, find an authoritative tone, make sure they are listening before you start. Use silence and gestures to pace the instructions and clarify their meaning.

(4) Demonstrate rather than explain wherever possible.

(5) Check that they have understood what to do—don't assume that everyone will automatically understand what you have said. Get concrete evidence from the children that they know what to do. Getting one child or two children to tell you what they are going to do is one very simple way of doing this.

Compared with the steps Scrivener proposed, we can see that the teacher needs to improve her classroom instructions in many aspects. No one is born to know how to give instructions. It needs constant practice and training.

TASK 4.2.3B

Look at the instructions in the left column and discuss how you would demonstrate your meaning with body language. You can describe it in words or draw a sketch to illustrate your demonstration. Or you can work in groups to demonstrate to each other.

What you say as instructions	How you support your meaning
1. Look at this picture, here.	
2. Turn to page 10, please.	
3. Come to the front, please.	
4. Listen again.	
5. Repeat after me.	
6. Say it again, please.	
7. Who wants to have a try?	
8. Who'd like to answer this question?	
9. Be quiet.	
10. Close your books now.	
11. Take out your colored pens.	
12. Take out your word cards, please.	
13. Put up your hand if you know the answer.	
14. Hands up when you hear "duck" in the song.	
15. Now you are going to do this in pairs.	
16. I need two helpers. Who'd like to help?	
17. You must not show your card to anyone else.	

Discussion Point

We can understand meaning from a variety of sources besides language. Language can be understood through context, body language, facial expressions of the speaker and the tone of the language even if the children do not know the words and structures.

Also, the teacher's language does not have to sound like a native speaker. The important thing is that the use of the target language is meaningful, real and has a clear purpose. In fact, even limited language can carry quite complex messages (Figure 4.2.3).

Figure 4.2.3 The effective instruction

Therefore, we can conclude that the target language should be used as much as possible even with beginners, but we should use very short and simple words, phrases and sentences and always put them in a context or use body language to demonstrate their meaning. If teachers use certain words and phrases persistently and consistently at the beginning, children will gradually know their meanings. If you are not confident about the English you are going to use in class, write out the most important words and practice them before class. Of course, you can always find a lot of excuses not to use the target language from time to time as long as you have good reasons for it. Just remember that instructions can be very simple at the beginning, and with the proper demonstration with body language, children will be able to understand your instructions.

Since our aim of teaching is to help pupils develop their language and mind, we should create opportunities for maximal pupil participation from the very start of a lesson. When teaching, teachers should invite pupils to model activities and use pupils' responses as basis for further questions, create contexts for pupils to ask questions, make pupils rehearse roles, and get all the class involved by giving them different roles. Teachers should try to avoid lengthy explanations since demonstration is usually more effective than words.

4.3 How to ask effective questions

4.3.1 Why do teachers ask questions?

TASK 4.3.1

We all know that teachers ask many questions in teaching. What are questions for? Work in groups and discuss the functions or purposes of questions in teaching. Make a list. When you finish, share your list with another group.

e.g. Teachers ask questions to focus children's attention.

Discussion Point

Questioning is a very important skill for teachers because it is the most common form of interaction between the teacher and the pupils in the classroom. It is an element that can be found in any type of lesson, no matter in reading or listening, writing or speaking, grammar or vocabulary learning. Teachers use questions to focus pupils' attention, to invite thinking and imaginations, to check understanding, to stimulate recall of information, to challenge pupils, and to assess learning. It is such a common form of teaching that almost all primary English teachers use everyday. In addition, proper questioning can extend pupils' thinking from the concrete and factual to the analytical and evaluative; can lead pupils through a planned sequence which progressively establishes key understandings; can promote reasoning, problem-solving, evaluation; and can promote pupils' thinking about the way of their own learning.

Though asking questions is important for learning, it does not mean that the more questions, the better. Questions should be wise and purposeful, contributing to the overall objectives of the lesson, stimulating the development of knowledge and thinking, as well as helping to maintain effective interaction.

4.3.2 What kind of questions do we ask?

TASK 4.3.2A

Let us look at the two classroom interaction episodes at the beginner level and discuss the differences in teachers' questioning strategies.

After the teacher presented the new structure "How many... are there?"

(T=Teacher S=Student Ss=Students)

T : Now, look! Oh, what are these? (T shows a picture with mushrooms.)

Ss : They are mushrooms.

T : Now listen to me. How many mushrooms are there?(twice) Ok, Lucy.

S : There are two mushrooms.

T : There are two mushrooms! Yes or no?

Ss: Yes.

T : Who can answer again?

S : There are two mushrooms.

T : Very good. Who can? Again? Next, please.

S : There are two mushrooms.

T : Ok. Now. Let's ask and answer. Ask and answer (pointing at two halves of the children).

T : How many mushrooms are there, begin!

Ss (one half) : How many mushrooms are there?

Ss (another half) : There are two mushrooms.

T : Ok. Change. Understand? How many... once again!

(Two halves ask and answer again.)

T : Ok, now, next one. What are these? (T shows a picture of eggplants.)

Ss: They are eggplants.

T : Yes. They are eggplants. Now, in two parts, ask. How many..., one, two begin!

Ss: How many eggplants are there?

T : Are there?

Ss: Are there?

T : How many eggplants are there?

Ss: How many eggplants are there?

T : There are...(pause)

Ss: Three eggplants.

Adapted from Wang Qiang, 2005.

After the teacher presented the new language—names of 12 months:

(T=teacher S=Student Ss=Students)

T : What's your favorite month, Jacky?

S : My favorite month is June.

T : Why?

S : Because it's Children's Day.

T : Oh, because Children's day is in June.

T : What is your favorite month, Larry?

S : My favorite month is January.

T : Why?

S : Because my father's birthday is in January.

T : Oh, your father's birthday is in January.
T : You know what is my favorite month? Guess.
S : January?
T : January? No.
S : May?
T : May? No.
S : April?
T : Yes, of course. My favorite month is April.
Ss: Why? (Children start to imitate the same question T has asked them.)
T : Do you know why?
S : It's your birthday!
T : Yes. My birthday is in April so I like April very much.

Adapted from Wang Qiang, 2005.

Discussion Point

Questions have been classified using different criteria, mainly based on the level of thinking involved in answering the questions. For example, one type of classification makes a distinction between closed and open questions. Closed questions refer to those with only a single correct answer while open questions may invite many different answers. Another classification makes a distinction between display questions and genuine questions. Display questions are those that the answers are already known to the teacher and they are used for checking if pupils know the answers, too. Conversely, genuine questions are questions which are used to find out new information. They often reflect real contexts and are, therefore, more communicative (Ur, 1996). A third classification makes a distinction between lower-order and higher-order questions. Lower-order questions refer to those questions that simply require recalling of information or memorization of facts while higher-order questions require more reasoning, analysis, and evaluation. Please refer to **Reading 4.3.2A** for examples of higher-order questions.

Reading 4.3.2A 《李老师是如何讲〈灰姑娘〉的故事的》

We used to observe a class in which the teacher asked more than 80 questions in a 30-minutes lesson. When we examined those questions, we found that most of the questions asked are closed questions which means the answers are already known to the teacher and many of them are simple "yes/no questions" among which very few are genuine questions. In most language classrooms, questions mostly involve lower-order thinking rather than higher-order thinking.

TASK 4.3.2B

Work in groups. Look at the following questions based on a non-fiction story about sharks. Read and classify them into lower-order thinking (LOT) and higher-order thinking (HOT) questions.

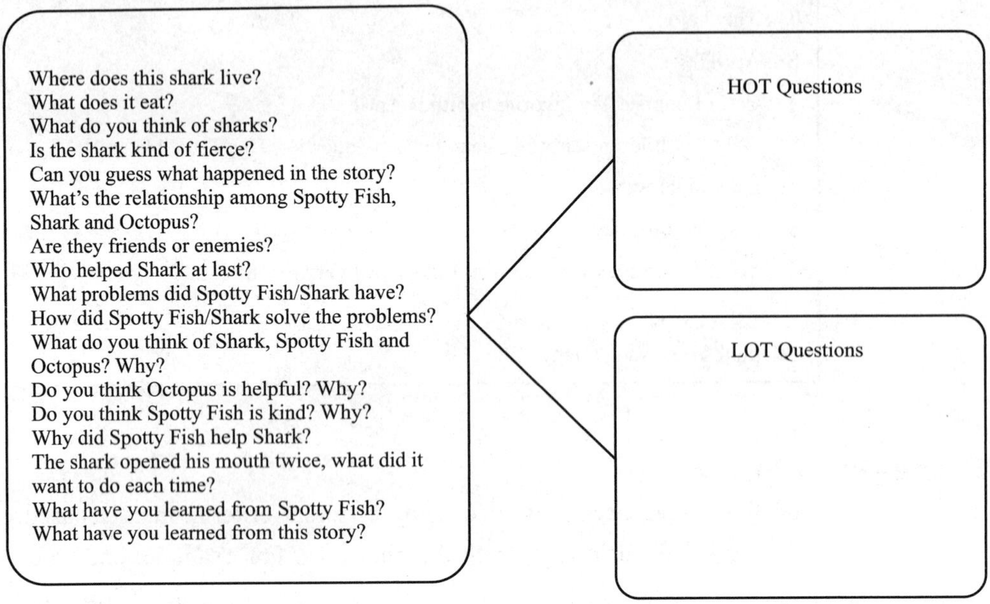

Reading 4.3.2B 《小学英语阅读教学中的批判性思维培养》（陈则航，王蔷）

What have you found from the above task? Can you add 2–3 higher-order questions to the HOT list? Then, go to **Reading 4.3.2B**.

Discussion point

You may have found that most questions asked regarding the non-fiction story about sharks are LOT questions. Although they are necessary for checking students' comprehension of facts about sharks, they are not enough for developing students' HOT skills. According to Bloom's Revised Taxonomy of Educational Objectives, there are six levels of thinking skills (Figure 4.3.1).

The six levels of thinking skills include, from lower to higher-order, remembering, understanding, applying, analyzing, evaluating and creating. As the diagram shows, each level involves some typical cognitive activities that reflect the level of thinking skills involved at that level. For example, at the level of remembering, typical cognitive activities include: recalling, listing, retrieving, finding, naming, recognizing, identifying, locating, describing. If we ask students to do these activities in the language classroom, we will mostly engage students at the lowest level of thinking.

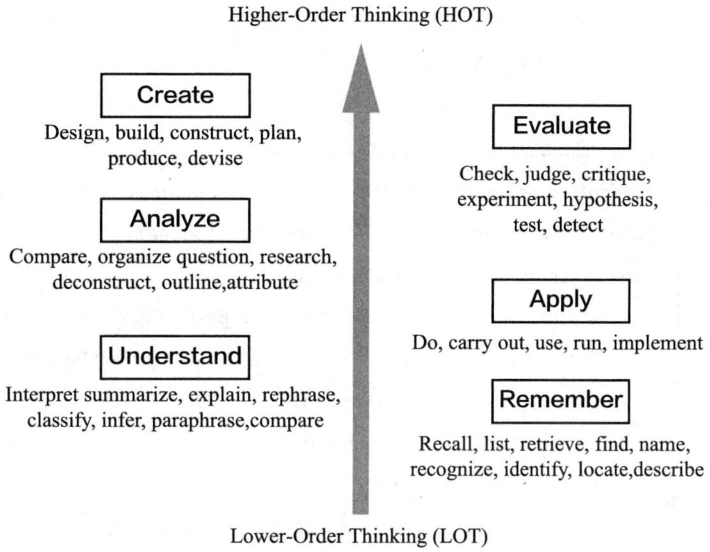

Figure 4.3.1 Bloom's Revised Taxonomy of Educational Objectives

The key thinking skills include making choices, making decisions, problem-solving, making plans, selecting strategies, and analyzing reasons, etc. referred to as critical and creative thinking skills.

How we can engage students in higher order thinking? What can we do as teachers? The following are some ways you may invite students to do:

- make predictions based on what is found as clues from the cover-page, pictures or personal experiences;
- make comparisons and contrasts between things or pictures;
- provide reasons or respond with emotional reactions;
- make a connection among things or ideas so as to establish relations;
- think from two sides;
- make a list to illustrate the feature of what they have read;
- analyze any possible factors that may have led to the results;
- think of alternative solutions;
- make an evaluation about a person, an event, a decision or an idea with facts and reasons.

4.3.3 How can we engage learners in asking questions?

TASK 4.3.3

Read the following classroom episode carefully. What have you found from it?

What kind of questions did the teacher ask? Did pupils ask questions? Share your views in groups.

Students have just learned the past tense and in today's class they are learning the new structure: "Did they have...then?" and some new vocabulary.

(T=teacher S=student Ss=Students)

T : We are going to talk about life in the past, 805 years ago. Now, let's look at the castle (There is a big picture of an old castle on the blackboard). Do you have any questions about life then? Any questions? Harry.

S : How did they cook? (T repeats the question and nominates a student who raised his hand)

S : They cooked by open fire.

T : Oh, they cooked by open fire. Any more questions?

S : How did they have a bathroom?

T : Have a bath. OK. Now look carefully. Do they have any water? On the top of the castle, we can see a wooden tub. Do we use a wooden tub?

Ss: No.

T : Today we use a bathtub. Now, where do we put our bathtub? In our washroom, right? (The whole class repeats after the T, bathtub three times). Any more questions?

S : How did they travel?

S : They travel by horse.

T : Yes, very good! Any more questions?

S : How did they write?

S : They write with a feather.

S : Why they didn't have a bath in the bathtub?

T : Maybe they (not clear). Any more questions?

S : How did they eat?

S : They ate by hand.

S : Why do they use candles?

S : Because they had no electric light.

T : Very good. Now, say it after me, "electric light" . (The class repeats after the T together a few times).

T : Now, boys and girls, I have some questions. Did people have refrigerators?

Ss: No.

T : Did people have refrigerators? Kelly.

S : No, they didn't.

T : They didn't. They didn't have...

Ss : Refrigerators.

T : They didn't have refrigerators. Refrigerators can help us keep the food fresh and ...

Ss : Cold.

T : How did they keep their food fresh?

S : They put their food in the water.

T : In water? In cold water? Anyone?

S : They kept their food in a box.

S : Maybe they are... they put... en... in very cold place.

T : In a very cold place, far away from the fire.

T : Next question. How did people cook?

S : They cooked by open fire.

T : How do we cook today? We cook by electric stoves. (T writes on the blackboard "electric stove". Ss repeat the words after the T several times.) (T now writes on the blackboard the main structure: Did people have... then? No, they didn't.) Now, can you ask more questions using this structure on the blackboard?)

S : Did they have electric stoves then?

S : Did people have refrigerators then?

...

T asks children to repeat the sentences on the blackboard after her. Did people have (electric light, electric stoves, bathtubs, refrigerators) then? No, they didn't.

T : Now, can you ask more questions?

S : Did people have telephones then?

S : Did people have airplanes then?

S : Did people have televisions then?

S : Did people have computers then?

S : Did people have washing machines then?

S : Did people have... then?

T : OK. Please ask and answer questions about the castle in pairs.

Source from a classroom observation by Wang Qiang, 2005.

Discussion Point

Another issue related to questioning is the opportunity for pupils to ask questions. In most classrooms, it is common for teachers to ask questions and pupils are only expected to answer questions raised by the teacher. As a result, many pupils are used to answering questions but are incapable of asking questions. How to make pupils ask more questions is a skill. Teachers need to create a meaningful context and motivate pupils to ask genuine questions on the basis of the limited language available to them.

Here are some tips for engaging pupils to ask questions in class:

(1) Invite a visitor or create a character. For example, the teacher can bring a puppet to the classroom and encourage pupils to ask him/her questions like "What's your name?" and "How old are you?".

(2) Create a context with the need to ask questions. Teachers can organize a shopping activity in which children have to ask questions to find out about the prices, other colors, or sizes, etc.

(3) A guessing game. Teachers can integrate vocabulary learning with questioning. When the child is asked to guess the name of an object he/she cannot see, he/she has to ask: "Is it an apple?"

(4) Question time. Teachers can set aside a three-minute question time from time to time to give pupils opportunities to ask any questions they are interested in finding answers from their fellow classmates. In such situations, pupils are also encouraged to use the language they have recently learned for meaningful communication.

(5) Activities such as a role-play, an interview, or a press conference can also provide excellent opportunities for pupils to ask and answer questions. But before the activity begins, teachers may need to prepare pupils with some questions or give some help.

Effective questioning is not only a matter of planning for what questions to ask but also to stage or sequence the questions so that they guide pupils towards achieving lesson objectives. In other words, effective questioning also depends on how questions are asked. Here are some tips for making questioning more effective:

(1) Questions should be closely linked to the learning objectives in the lesson.

(2) Questions should be staged so that the level of challenge increases as the lesson proceeds.

(3) There should be a balance between closed and open, lower-order and higher-order questions;

(4) Wait time is important to allow pupils to think their answers through;

(5) Pupils should be provided opportunities to ask their own questions and seek their own answers.

(6) A secure and relaxed atmosphere of trust is needed and pupils' opinions and ideas are valued.

Questioning is not without limitations. Asking questions to the whole class, you will not get a personalized answer. Asking questions to individual pupils, you simply have not enough time for every pupil. Very often, when a question is asked to one pupil, the other pupils may feel neglected and their minds will wander away. Therefore, although questions are important teaching strategies, we need to be aware that there are other strategies which might prove to be more effective than questioning.

4.4 How to set up classroom discipline

Discipline is crucial in a primary classroom. In many circumstances, teachers cannot implement what they planned because they cannot maintain good discipline in the classroom. Children are too noisy or they do not listen to the teacher. Some teachers complain about the naughty pupils, we think it is useful to find the cause of the problems first.

4.4.1 Why is there a discipline problem in the classroom?

TASK 4.4.1

Discuss Figure 4.4.1 with your partner: what was the cause(s)?

- Children were over-excited.
-
-
-
-
-
-
-
-
-
-
-

Figure 4.4.1 A discipline problem

Discussion Point

There are different reasons for children to misbehave in the classroom. These may include:

(1) Children are too young to sit for a long time.

(2) The contents are too difficult and some children could not understand them.

(3) The contents are too easy and some children know them already.

(4) The teacher is talking all the time, paying no attention to the children.

(5) The lesson is very boring, and children feel tired.

(6) The activities are too stirring and children are overexcited.

(7) The teacher pays attention to only active pupils, and those ignored children want to do something to attract the teacher's attention.

(8) The children just finished an exciting (e.g. P.E.) class and could not shift the mood into an English class yet.

The last note we would like to make is that quite often children misbehave because of a variety of reasons. One of the most widespread reasons, however, is usually a pupil's inability to cope with the tasks or to catch up with the speed. The noisiest pupils will demonstrate their frustration by loud outbursts, and disruptive behavior, while the rest of the class may remain passive. Sometimes they misbehave because the task is rather boring or mechanical, sometimes because the task is too easy or they may have done it before (Brewster, Ellis, and Girard, 1992), and of course, sometimes because they simply want to get attention from the teacher or the class. As teachers, we need to move around the class while teaching to check whether our pupils are attentive so that we can modify our teaching accordingly. For those who try to get attention, we may satisfy this need by giving them the opportunity to do the right thing and praise them when they perform well. Remember that behaviors receiving positive comments are likely to be repeated while behaviors receiving negative comments tend to disappear only for a short while (Dean, 2001). To a child who seems to be doing wrong things, we simply need to look for something positive to say to him/her if proper behavior is to be achieved.

4.4.2 How to create a good learning atmosphere

TASK 4.4.2

Think back again and recall lessons you have ever taken, what kind of classroom atmosphere is the best for learning? What kind of teacher is the most welcome? Is he/she the strictest, or the most patient? Read the comments from three children below and discuss the above questions with your partner.

I remember my English teacher was very strict. I felt scared each time she called my name. I could not even speak when I stood up and I never liked learning English. . .

Our English class was the noisiest one at school. My teacher never seems to care very much what we were doing in class. We chatted, played cards and had lots of fun. She was just so good-tempered and talked to herself all the time. . .

Our English teacher really listened to us and treated us as friends. She smiled all the time and we all liked her. We sang songs and did lots of interesting activities in her class. . .

Discussion Point

Teachers vary in teaching styles and they hold different attitudes toward discipline. For example, in some classrooms, pupils may be allowed to walk around during an activity or give answers without always putting up their hands. Teachers will just have to think carefully and decide for themselves what is acceptable and let children know.

At the same time, children need to feel secure and relaxed before they start to learn. So creating a friendly and relaxing classroom atmosphere is more important in keeping discipline. The first teacher in the picture is very strict and we can imagine that she should have no problem keeping her pupils disciplined. But the pupils would feel scared and could not concentrate on learning in her class. We could sense the tension in her class and feel sorry for her pupils. The second teacher totally lost control in her classroom. She gave up all her efforts as well. The chaotic classroom cannot guarantee that any learning may happen. The last teacher is friendly and treats children as human beings. Obviously, children have great interest in learning English. The classroom atmosphere is relaxing and active.

Anyway, in solving the problem of discipline, establishing good relationships with children in the class is vital. As teachers, we need to spend time knowing as much as possible about our pupils—try to learn their names, get to know their interests and attitudes towards English, their likes and dislikes, etc. All these will help us know the children better and help us establish good relations with our pupils. All these will contribute positively to resolving the problem of discipline.

Moon (2000) gives some suggestions on creating good learning atmosphere:

(1) Showing genuine interest in and responding positively to pupils' answers so as to motivate them to want to speak, e.g.Yes? with an encouraging smile.

(2) Encouraging attention to language accuracy but in a constructive way.

(3) Using English at a level that pupils can understand so that pupils are getting more input.

(4) Helping pupils express their messages by prompting or cueing pupils to say more so that they are "pushed" to use the language to communicate.

(5) Relating talk to familiar contexts which are meaningful to pupils and so encourage them to want to talk, e.g. pupils' own news.

(6) Working in partnership with pupils to achieve a common goal.

Obviously, all the above strategies emphasize that creating a supportive, motivating, encouraging and involving learning atmosphere is the key to tackling the discipline problem.

4.4.3 How to keep discipline in the classroom

TASK 4.4.3

Write individually on how you would keep discipline in the classroom. Compare with a partner and write down the useful points you find from your partner. Then,join another pair and compare all your lists. Finally, produce one list that you all agree with and would like to recommend to others.

1.
2.
3.
4.

Discussion Point

Every teacher has his/her own way of keeping classroom discipline. Some methods may work well for one class or one teacher, but may not for another. It is important for a teacher to work out his/her own list and find out his/her effective way. Although following others' ideas may not help, it is useful to share and exchange ideas and give advice to each other.

It is wise to begin some courses in a fairly formal or even strict way, and relax little by little as you gain the co-operation of the group. So when teachers plan their lessons, try to take the following into consideration (Davies & Pearse, 2000):

(1) Plan the lessons, and include varied activities and interactions that keep the learners busy.
(2) Use topics and activities that you think will be interesting and enjoyable for the learners.
(3) Motivate the learners by focusing on what they do satisfactorily or well more than on what they do badly.
(4) Try to create a sense of community in the group.
(5) Be fair to all the learners, never favoring some over others.
(6) Show that you respect and are interested in all the learners as people, irrespective of how good they are at English.

In spite of every precaution and effort on your part, there is occasionally a learner or a group of learners in a class who seem determined to make trouble. If you have most of the learners on your side, it is much easier to handle such situations. Harmer (2007) suggests the following measures for indisciplined acts and badly behaving pupils:

(1) Act immediately. If possible, indisciplined acts should be immediately stopped so that less damage is made. The longer a discipline problem is left unchecked, the more difficult it is to take action.

(2) Stop the class. If the indiscipline is so disruptive as to hinder the progress of the whole class, the teacher should stop the class and make it clear what is wrong.

(3) Rearrange the seats. If troublesome pupils are sitting together, the teacher should separate them. Besides, if pupils are moved to the front of the class they will behave better.

(4) Change the activity. If the class seems to be getting out of control, or if discipline occurs due to inappropriacy of the activity, a change of activity will often restore the class.

(5) Talk to pupils after class. If a pupil is continually making trouble, the teacher should talk to that pupil after class. The pupil should be given a chance to explain why he/she behaves in this way.

(6) Create a code of behavior. This means that the teacher and learners can work together to create some basic rules for the class during activities. For example, they have to work quietly during group work.

As for the problem-making pupils, teachers need also to be more considerate since the "trouble makers" are not necessarily bad boys, and sometimes they are not aware of their indisciplined acts. So when the teacher is trying to stop the indisciplined pupils, he/she should be careful not to hurt the pupils. Ur (1996) gives the following advice about problem-makers in class:

(1) Deal with it quietly. If the problem involves only one pupil, the teacher's action should be a quiet response so that it will avoid other pupils' attention.

(2) Don't take things personally. When something happens, the teacher should try to address the problem rather than the pupil as the object. Besides, the teacher should relate to the problem impersonally even if the criticism is meant personally.

(3) Don't use threats. Threats are never constructive measures against indiscipline. In most cases, threats cause a negative affective state and resistance to cooperation.

As for the very noisy classroom, Vale and Feunteun (1995) have proposed the following to get the children's attention (adapted):

(1) Establish an attention-getting code, e.g. When you clap your hands, everybody should stop what they are doing and look at you.

(2) Give a short series of action game instructions, e.g. Everyone raises your right hand, Put down your right hand. Raise your left hand. Put down your left hand. Close your eyes and stand up. Sit down. Open your eyes.

(3) Cough or fold your arms and give a heavy look at the class.

(4) Walking up to a noisy child or group and start talking to them quietly.

(5) Always speak quietly. Do not raise your voice above the noise in order to get quietness in the room. Instead, you may make eye contact with noise-offenders, or call their names in a normal voice. Children will hear their names even in a noisy room.

(6) Use flashcards or symbols to help you.

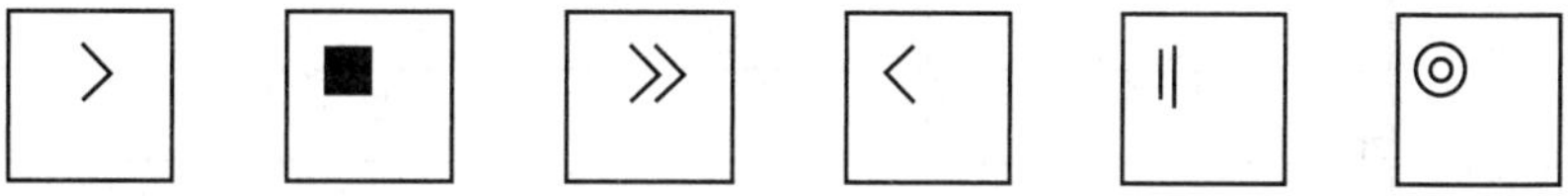

PLAY STOP FORWARD REPEAT VOLUME MUTE

(7) Ask all the children to rest their arms and heads on the desks with eyes closed in complete quietness for one minute.

(8) Stop the activity when it gets too noisy and introduce a new activity which settles children down a bit. (See later discussions on stirring and settling.)

(9) Discuss with the children and write an agreed contract with the whole class.

(10) Observe closely, when children are being good, praise good children and also praise the disruptive child for his minor good behavior. Focus on their good behavior rather than bad.

(11) Always speak in a normal voice. "Remember that the noisier the teacher is, the noisier the children will become" (Brewster, Ellis & Girard, 1992).

Discipline plays a vital role in the primary classroom. Teachers need to be cautious when dealing with problems. Find the reasons first and try to understand why children misbehave that way, and then see if you can find certain solutions to solve the problems, after that, implement the solutions accordingly.

4.5 What should teachers do when teaching large classes?

Large classes are a reality in many primary schools in China, both in rural and urban areas. Normal class size is between 30 and 40, but in some areas it may be well over 60, or even 80. O'Sullivan (2006) defines a "large class" by the class size of 25 to 30 in the U.K., and 35 in the U.S.A. He also points out that a large class in some developing countries is more than 60, or even more than 100. Compared with the teachers in developed countries, teachers in developing countries are faced with more challenges.

4.5.1 What are the problems of large classes?

TASK 4.5.1

Work in groups of 4. Recall your own learning experience in primary schools. What was the normal class size in your schools? Was it a large class? What problems did it create for both teachers and pupils?

Name	Class size	Problems of learning (pupils)	Problems of teaching (teachers)

Discussion Point

Large classes can create quite a lot of problems for both teachers and pupils. Problems related to pupils' learning may include:

- There are not enough resources for each pupil.
- Pupils do not have much opportunity to practice in class.
- Individual pupils cannot get enough attention from teachers.
- Pupils sitting at the back may not be able to hear what the teacher says or unable to see the blackboard clearly.
- ...

Problems related to teachers' teaching may include:

- It's difficult to keep good discipline in a large class.
- Pupils may be noisy, so teachers have to raise voice in class.
- There are more papers to grade after class.
- Teachers cannot monitor every pupil's learning.
- Teachers cannot remember pupils' names easily so that they cannot address them correctly.
- ...

As we can see from the above points, there are two major problems with large classes. One is the discipline problem and the other is lack of resources. At the same time, teachers need to be aware that it is impossible for a large class to achieve the same teaching objectives as a small class. Teachers do not have to feel discouraged when teaching large classes because some practical and flexible teaching techniques can help maximize learning in large classes.

4.5.2 How to teach large classes effectively

TASK 4.5.2

Work in groups of four, and think about some realistic solutions to the problems of large classes.

1.
2.
3.
4.

Discussion Point

Almost all teachers agree that when teaching large classes, careful and detailed lesson planning in advance do contribute greatly to less chaotic situation in the classroom. No matter how many times a teacher has been teaching a unit or a textbook, teachers always need to prepare it again to make it suitable for this particular class. As for the discipline problems, establishing a code of behavior that is created by teachers and learners together will help save a lot of time in class. It should state clear basic rules at the beginning of the semester, such as:

- we have to work quietly;
- we may talk, but not loudly;
- when hearing three rhythmic claps, everyone stops talking or working.

Teachers can also appoint responsible group leaders or class monitors to maintain discipline. When designing activities, teachers need to be more careful. For example, teachers need to reduce the ratio of "stirring activities" and "physically engaged activities". Some experienced teachers use "group discipline competition" to award those groups who maintain good discipline by giving them extra stickers or small red flowers. Teachers can also use more peer assessment to direct pupils to monitor their own learning.

Organizing more whole class activities can help maintain classroom discipline. Making good use of the blackboard and other visual aids can attract pupils' attention, too. However, sometimes, group work can help make good use of limited resources. For example, teachers can organize mixed-ability groups so that the more able learners in the group can help the others. Teachers can also organize same-ability groups so they can leave the groups of faster learners to get on with the work on their own and give extra help to individual learners in the slower groups. Teachers can also use group leaders to assign different roles in one group and to help slower learners. No matter what kind of groups teachers organize, teachers all need to move around the classroom to monitor the progress and to solve problems.

Every coin has two sides, so do large classes. They have advantages too. Such as when there are many children in a class they can share many different ideas and interesting life experiences. The most important thing is how we teachers make good use of it.

4.6 How to manage classroom interaction

Classroom interaction refers to the patterns of interaction taking place in the classroom. They can be whole class work where the teacher talks to the whole class, group work, pair work or individual work.

Wang (2006) gave the following definition for the four forms of interactions:

(1) Whole class work is where all the children are under the control of the teacher. They are all doing the same activities at the same rhythm and pace.

(2) Pair work is where the children work in pairs. It could be a competition over a game or cooperation in a task or project between the two children. They could also do certain exercises together or oral practice.

(3) Group work is where the children work in small groups. Each group has 3, 4, or 5 children, depending on the activity. What children do in group work is similar to pair work, only there are more members in the group.

(4) Individual study is the stage during the class where the children are left to work on their own and at their own speed. Usually they are doing the same task, but the teacher may give them a choice of tasks. Some activities cannot be done in pairs or groups, for instance,reading and writing.

4.6.1 What are the most commonly used classroom activities?

TASK 4.6.1

Work in groups and discuss the most commonly used classroom activities you have experienced as a student either in middle school or in university/college. Make a list of the activities and identify the kinds of classroom interaction patterns they involve. Discuss the advantages of each type of interaction patterns.

Most commonly used activities	Classroom interaction patterns	Advantages
• Dictation • • • • • •	• Whole class work • • • • •	• Easy to organize • • • • • •

Discussion Point

Different interaction patterns have their own advantages and disadvantages. There are no definite rules for teachers to follow.

Whole class work is the most commonly used interaction pattern in our everyday teaching, especially for large classes. It has lots of advantages, for example, it is good for teachers to give instructions and explanations together and it is an ideal way to show materials and do presentations together and it can also reinforce the sense of team (Harmer, 2007). But it has lots of problems too. Everyone is forced to do the same thing at the same time and at the same pace. Some pupils feel nervous and anxious when they are asked to present in front of the class. The class favours the transmission of knowledge from teacher to students rather than students discovering things by themselves. Pupils have little chance to experience real communication.

Compared to whole class work, group work and pair work can solve lots of problems that whole class work brings. First, it dramatically increases pupils' speaking time in each class. While working with classmates, nervous pupils feel easier to express themselves in small groups than in the class. It also creates a good opportunity for pupils to work and cooperate with each other. However, group/pair work brings lots of problems at the same time too. The most obvious problem it brings is that the classroom is noisy and the children are more difficult to control. Another problem is that some children may talk in native language or talk about other things when doing group work and pair work, so teachers' monitor becomes vitally important.

Individual work is less employed by teachers because teachers have the assumption that class time should be used to "teach" rather than "self-study". However, individual work becomes more and more important in English classes. It can develop learner autonomy and form good learning habit. It allows pupils free time, style and pace to learn on their own. But it may be much more difficult for teachers to monitor and it does not benefit communication.

The four kinds of interaction patterns can go hand in hand. After a session of group work, a whole class feedback phase will give cohesion to the learning process. Having "rehearsed" in small groups beforehand, pupils may face the whole class with more confidence in their ability to handle the target language. During the reading or writing study, individual work may best serve the purpose.

4.6.2 What kind of grouping is suitable for certain activities?

TASK 4.6.2A

The following are different types of classroom activities. Read them and decide which activities are best done with the whole class, which are with pair work and group work and which are with individual work.

1) reading aloud
2) story-telling
3) listening and doing
4) information gap
5) listening to the tape and repeating after it
6) copying
7) presenting a new language
8) giving instructions
9) gap filling writing exercises
10) singing songs
11) question and answer practice
12) guessing games
13) watching videos
14) paired reading
15) checking understanding
16) role-playing
17) drama performance
18) project work
19) reading silently

Pair work	Individual work

Discussion Point

There is no strict rule for a certain activity to be done in a certain way. And some activities can be done in both whole class form or in group form depending on the class size and the level of the learners. The following only gives a rough idea of which type of activities are best done in which forms, but definitely these are not the only ways of doing them.

A. For whole class work

1) reading aloud
2) story-telling
3) listening and doing
4) listening to the tape and repeating after it
5) presenting a new language
6) giving instructions
7) singing songs
8) watching videos
9) checking understanding

It is worth noting that when presenting a new language, it is best to ask questions to the whole class first, then to groups and finally to individuals. Also, when doing repetitions, to avoid the boring part of repetitions, we can vary the repetitions by asking children to say things loudly, quietly, quickly or slowly. Moreover, repetitions can be made meaningful by creating a context. For example, when practicing the structure of "Where is..." and "Is it in the box?" "No, it isn't.", you can have one pupil standing in front of the class. Behind him, you have a ball and put it in different positions for the pupil to guess where it is. The whole class watches you putting it in a place and the teacher asks the question to the pupil: "Where is the ball?" The pupil guesses by asking "Is it on/in/behind/beside/under the box...?" The whole class will be the judge by saying "yes" or "no". In such an activity, there will be a lot of repetitions of the same questions but they are meaningful rather than mechanical.

B. For pair or group work

1) information gap
2) question and answer practice
3) paired reading
4) role-playing
5) drama performance
6) project work

To make group work successful, you can have each group produce something different from the rest of the class so that you are creating a genuine reason for sharing activities and information upon finishing the work. For example, you can ask each group to make a dictionary of people's names with different focuses. One group is to make a dictionary of famous footballers, another of pop stars, another of world leaders, and so on. So by the time the activity finishes, each group will have a dictionary of names arranged in alphabetical order and other groups can add new information to it. Also, you can ask each group to think of a famous story and draw the main characters to make a poster.

C. For individual work

1) reading aloud
2) copying
3) gap filling writing exercise
4) reading silently

While pair work and group work are encouraged in language classrooms to provide more practice opportunities, individual study should not be forgotten. This is because learners need some quiet time of their own to engage in thinking and to internalize the language they have just learned.

TASK 4.6.2B

Figure 4.6.1 is a page from a primary English textbook. Work with your partner and decide on three activities—one with whole class work, one with pair work or group work and one with individual work. Explain your purposes and reasons for your decisions.

Figure 4.6.1 A page from a primary English textbook①

Discussion Point

This is a page cited from a primary textbook. It is a story adapted from the famous Chinese novel *Journey to the West*. There may be different ways to organize the activities, and

① 选自北京师范大学出版社的义务教育教科书《英语》（三年级起点）四年级上册 Unit1。

what we provide is only one option for teachers.

For whole-class works, teachers can first organize some pre-reading activities, such as asking children if they know the figures in the story or if they like them. Then they can also tell the story to children in the whole class. For group works, teachers can ask children to work in groups to read the story in different roles and role-play the story. They can also ask children to retell the story in small groups before presenting it in front of the whole class. For individual work, teachers can ask them to read the story by themselves or to create a surprising ending for the existent story.

4.6.3 What are the problems of different grouping?

TASK 4.6.3

Work in groups and discuss what potential problems there are in organizing children's group work and pair work. Do you think teachers need to take risks in organizing it and why? What are the possible solutions to these problems? Can you work out some suggestions?

Discussion Point

There is no doubt that group work and pair work are not as easy to manage as the whole classwork. It is no use telling children that a particular activity is good for them to learn the new language. Children only work when they know what to do and how to do it. So clear task-setting instruction is critical in organizing this activity. Often in such cases, demonstration and modeling may help. Besides, motivation also affects children's participation. Moon (2000) provides some solutions (Table 4.6.1) when organizing pair and group work.

Table 4.6.1 Some solutions

Problems	Solutions
The desks may be fixed so pupils cannot move around.	Do activities in the playground, the school hall or use the limited space you have at the sides of the desks.
Some pupils may dominate pair- or group work.	Plan the composition of groups more carefully.
	Put the dominating pupils together or swap them around.

continued

Problems	Solutions
The school may not allow pupils to make a lot of noise.	Discuss the purpose of the activities with the teachers next door to you and the headteacher.
	Agree on a suitable time.
	Train the pupils to keep their voices down.
Pupils may be unused to pair/group activities and use them as an excuse for misbehaving.	With older pupils (nine upwards) discuss why you want to do pair work or group work.
	Establish clear rules / procedures with them.
	With younger children, create a purpose for doing pair work or group work that makes sense to them.
Pupils may use L1.	Try to choose activities which ensure that all or at least some part of them has to be done in English, e.g., reporting back to the class.
	If pupils are old enough, discuss with them the reason for talking in English or develop imaginative reasons for group work, e.g. as part of a story or game.

Classroom interaction plays a very important role in language learning. Teachers need to keep in mind that no matter what kinds of interaction patterns they use, the purpose is to support children's learning. And varying interaction patterns can help activate children's interests and improve their concentration in learning.

4.7 How to organize activities in a lesson

4.7.1 How to start a lesson

When organizing an English lesson, teachers need to consider lots of factors which contribute to successful lessons or lead to failures. To start a lesson appropriately is the most important thing teachers need to consider. We can begin our lessons in many different ways. Some teachers begin their lessons by calling the rolls first. Some teachers begin by asking children to say a rhyme they have just learned. Some teachers begin by doing Total Physical Response (TPR) activities. Some begin by reviewing the words they learned before or reviewing the story told in the last lesson. One can also begin a lesson by doing some copying activities or a listening activity. Different starting of a lesson may create a different classroom atmosphere. The following are some possible ways teachers use to start a lesson, or warm-up activities called by many teachers:

- sing a song
- say a rhyme
- give duty report
- review words learned last time
- do a guessing game
- daily exchange questions and answers
- make self-introduction
- watch a cartoon
- do a TPR activity
- act out a play

TASK 4.7.1

Suppose you are going to teach a song (Figure 4.7.1 and Figure 4.7.2) to a group of Grade one pupils today. Discuss in groups of four: what warm-up activities will you organize? Why?

③ **Let's Sing**

My mother, my mother,
This is my mother.
Please say, "Hello."
This is my mother.

My father, my father,
This is my father.
Please say, "Hello."
This is my father.

My sister, my sister,
This is my sister.
Please say, "Hello."
This is my sister.

53

Figure 4.7.1 A song from a primary English textbook[①]

① 选自北京师范大学出版社的义务教育教科书《英语》（三年级起点）三年级上册 Unit 5。

Figure 4.7.2 A song from a primary English textbook[①]

Discussion Point

There are quite a few warm-up activities teachers can do in this lesson:

- Review words of family members.
- Sing family songs, for example, *Family Members Song.*
- Review animals.
- Sing animal songs, for example, *Old MacDonald.*

Warm-up activities not only arouse pupils' interest in learning, but also function as preparation for an English class. For example, reviewing family numbers and animals they learned can activate what children have already known and thus make it easier for children to learn something new.

A good beginning means half success. Making the beginning a bit more interesting and unpredictable can also make pupils look forward to your lessons. For example, instead of asking the same questions in every class, "What day is today?" and "What's the weather like today?" etc., you may ask the children to listen to what you say and then decide whether you are right or wrong by clapping their hands once for "YES", and twice for "NO". If you say "Today is Monday." and in fact it is Tuesday, children should clap their hands twice to indicate that it is not right. And when you say "it is raining" which is not true, children will again clap their hands to show their opinions.

① 选自北京师范大学出版社的义务教育教科书《英语》（三年级起点）三年级上册 Unit 2。

4.7.2 What are stirring and settling activities?

Besides a good start, there are some other factors teachers need to consider. Halliwell (1992) has proposed some ideas to help us think about how we can adjust the classroom atmosphere by using different activities. She points out that it is important for primary school teachers to understand which activities "stir" a class, which activities "settle" it. "Stirring activities", in a positive way, can wake the children up and stimulate them, but in the negative aspects, they may make the children over-excited and restless. "Settling activities", on the other hand, can make the children calm down when they are over-excited but they can also bore the children as well.

TASK 4.7.2A

Look at the following activities and decide which is a "settler" and which is a "stirrer". Share your answers with your partner.

Activities	Your comments
1. Ask the whole class to copy a list of food words onto a piece of paper from the board.	
2. Stick a list of flashcards on the board with numbers given to each card. Ask the pupils to listen and write down the number of the picture they hear.	
3. The teacher puts the cards together and takes away one of them and asks the pupils to guess what she has got on her flashcard by saying to the children: "Guess what I have got on my flashcard."	
4. Children take out their cards and do paired practice on "Guess what I have got on my flashcard".	
5. Teacher writes "May I have ...?" on the board. Ask the class the question and children show their cards.	
6. One child asks the class questions.	
7. Children practice in pairs using their cards.	
8. Children copy the sentence about requesting for food on their book with a chosen answer.	
9. Children open the book and practice the dialog and prepare for an acting out.	

Adapted from Halliwell, 1991.

Discussion Point

Activities 1, 2 , 8 and 9 in task 4.7.2A are comparatively settling activities, and the others are more stirring ones. Teachers need to be aware of the different functions of these activities and plan them before class. However, in classroom teaching, teachers need to adjust the use of these activities according to the situations. One thing is clear that varying the activity types can not only help maintain good classroom discipline, but also motivate the pupils and keep them interested in learning. However, too much shifting from one activity to another requires clear instructions or otherwise causes confusion.

TASK 4.7.2B

Work with your partner and make a list of activities that stir a class and activities that settle a class. An example is provided.

Activities that stir a class	Activities that settle a class
1. Competitions	1. Copying the words 10 times
2.	2. Reading aloud together
3.	3.
4.	4.
5.	5.
6.	6.

Discussion Point

According to Halliwell (1991), activities that usually stir a class include paired oral work, competitions, role-plays, guessing games, TPR activities, singing songs, drama acting, etc. Activities that settle a class include copying, coloring, listening, drawing, dictation, and other writing tasks. With a basically lively class you can use a settling activity to begin your class while with a relatively quiet class you can start by using a stirring activity (Halliwell,1991).

Usually, after a long presentation or some individual work, such as copying or listening, children will feel bored and may not be able to concentrate on the same activity. The teacher, at this point, may vary his/her activities by using some stirring activities. But if the class is already very active and excited, the teacher may think about a more settling activity. As we can see in the above two cases, the children may be either too tired or too excited to learn. There is no strict rule for using which kind of activities as long as the teacher feels necessary and comfortable using them.

4.7.3 What are physically engaged and mentally engaged activities?

Halliwell (1992) points out that some activities require children to think hard while doing them, such as guessing games. These activities are classified as "mentally engaged activities". There are also activities which require children to do things with their hands, such as copying or coloring. When doing these activities, children do not need to think as hard as mentally engaged activities. So these activities are called "physically engaged activities".

Like stirring and settling activities, both mentally and physically engaged activities are necessary in a language classroom. We cannot ask children to do one kind of activity for a long time. So we need to change the activity type once in a while and children will feel less bored.

TASK 4.7.3

Work with your partners and make a list of activities that engage children's mind and another list of activities that require children to do things with their hands. Examples are given below.

Mentally engaged activities	Physically engaged activities
1. Puzzles	1. Copying the words 10 times.
2. Imagination	2. Reading aloud together.
3.	3.
4.	4.
5.	5.
6.	6.

Discussion Point

Mentally engaged activities usually include activities like guessing games, solving problems, imaginations, telling one's own experiences, etc. Physically engaged activities include reading aloud, copying, coloring, repeating, drawing, etc. When teachers are aware of such differences, they can design better activities or arrange them in a more logical order.

4.7.4 How to organize activities effectively

TASK 4.7.4A

Think about a specific activity you want to use for your class. When designing the activity, what factors do you need to consider? Try to write them down in the spaces provided.

- Is it stirring or settling?
- Is it mentally engaged or physically engaged?
-
-
-

Discussion Point

The questions you need to consider may include: Does it need a lot of space to do the activity?What language preparation is needed to carry out the activity? Does it make a lot of noise? Which skills does it practice? Does it help develop children's imagination and creativity? How long will it take? Will it be too difficult for my pupils? Will children use Chinese?

The above questions are all very practical. Once these questions are answered, you can move into the details for designing the activity. For the actual designing of an activity, we suggest that you start by thinking about three phases of an activity: the **preparation phase,** the **main activity phase,** the **follow-up phase** or **consolidation phase.** During the preparation phase, you need to get children into the right mood for learning. You may start with a song or a rhyme and followed by a TPR activity to review what is learned in the previous lesson. Getting pupils motivated and interested in what is to be learned is the most important purpose of this phase. Entering the main activity phase, you will need to get children to complete a main task with enough language and social support from you. A clear context and a clear purpose are necessary for presentation and practice. At this stage, children will continue developing interest and motivation as well as confidence in learning and practicing. In the follow-up phase, the teacher uses confidence and experiences developed from the previous practice to encourage children to speak, to write, to draw, and to act out. The follow-up activity should be made personal whenever possible. The focus will be on the use of specific language points for the purpose of using the language in communication.

Besides, during class time, teachers need to monitor pupils' mood carefully and adjust it by using stirring/settling activities and mentally/physically engaged activities. In order to maximize participation and communication, teachers need to use a variety of groupings including whole class-work, pair/group work, and individual work.

No matter how we plan our lessons, we need to always remember in the process of teaching that children need confidence, interest and a sense of success for effective learning. They need to be engaged linguistically, physically, mentally, and affectively.

TASK 4.7.4B

Study the following teaching procedures proposed by Halliwell (1991). Work in groups of four and try to teach the colors according to this procedure. Discuss the order of the activities and connections between each activity.

(1) Children listen to the teacher saying the colors by looking at the color cards shown by the teacher one by one.

(2) The teacher sticks each colored card on the board and repeats each color for children to listen to.

(3) The teacher says the colors and asks one child to come to the board to point at the right card.

(4) The teacher writes numbers on the side of each colored card.

(5) The teacher says one color and writes its number on the other side of the board. Do the same with all the colors.

(6) The teacher says a color randomly, and gets a pupil to write the number down. Do the same with other colors.

(7) The teacher says a number and a color, and lets children judge whether they match by saying "Yes" or "No".

(8) Children close their eyes, the teacher takes away one color and says a color and a number, children should be able to remember whether the color and number match.

(9) The teacher says the match and children stand up if it is correct.

(10) Children say and repeat the color words after the teacher. (Note until this step, children have been doing listening without being forced to say the colors.)

(11) Children say the colors and the teacher takes away the colors one by one.

(12) The teacher puts the cards together, face down, and takes away one from them. Then shows them to the children. Let the children guess which one is missing by asking "Is it green?"

(13) The teacher introduces the words of colors and sticks the word cards one by one on the board.

(14) Let children do the matching.

(15) At the end of the class, let children copy the words.

If you were the teacher, how would you teach colors, and what are your considerations in designing the lesson?

Discussion Point

As we can see from the above, there are many different ways of organizing activities around one topic and you do not need to jump from one to another which makes no connections. The teacher intends to teach colors and she designs various ways to do it.

First, the teacher did not ask the children to repeat or say the words until the tenth step. From the first to the ninth step, all that the children need to do is to recognize the sound and match the sound either with flashcards or with numbers. At the 13th step, the teacher introduces the words and children relate the sounds and cards with the words. At the last step, children are asked to write. We think the sequence of the activities is from easy to difficult. Children are very well prepared when they are asked to produce language at that stage.

Second, the teacher integrates the number with the color. There are two purposes of using numbers here. On the one hand, we can take this opportunity to review what we learned before and children are more confident when they meet something they know already. On the other hand, when using numbers in a guessing game, the children really need to think before they point or do actions. It is real communication rather than mechanical memorization. When children just repeat after the teacher, they may not use their mind at all.

Third, when learning colors, the teacher tries to make children involved as much as possible, both physically and mentally. Children are asked to do actions (pointing, matching, standing up after a judgment, etc.) as well as listen, speak, read and write. The teacher controls and organizes the class well.

We do not want to say this is a perfect lesson or a perfect way to teach "colours". Any forms of teaching have rooms for improvement, so does this lesson. For example, the teacher does not use any songs or rhymes in this lesson to consolidate the words. The interaction patterns are not rich enough. The whole lesson focuses entirely on the learning of individual words, no communicative context for using the words learned is created. Therefore, if the teacher could have designed an activity that enables the children to use language in a real context, it would be more meaningful and it can help children develop their communicative ability.

Organizing effective and efficient lessons needs teachers' tremendous work. Experience does play an important role in this aspect. New teachers do not need to feel worried if they cannot organize the lesson in a very smooth way. We are sure you will be more skillful and autonomous when you gain some teaching experience.

4.8 How to treat children's errors in the classroom

It is important for both teachers and learners to accept the fact that errors are an inevitable part of the learning process. It is through learners' errors that "we can see what they are struggling to master, what concepts they have misunderstood and what extra work they might need" (Lavery, 2001). However, teachers' behaviors in dealing with errors in the classroom vary from one to another and it reflects different attitudes they hold towards errors. Some teachers tend to correct all the errors while others tend to be more tolerant and there are still some who do not correct at all.

4.8.1 Do we need to correct errors?

How to correct and what to correct largely depends on the objectives of teaching. For example, some program aims to train children to pass a certain test which contains mostly grammatical questions. In this case, the teacher may need to correct every error that children make in their production. But what are the aims of teaching English to children?

TASK 4.8.1

The following are some of the important aims of teaching English to children during the first few years of learning. Check the boxes that you agree with and then compare and discuss them with another teacher.

- ☐ Building confidence.
- ☐ Providing motivation to learn.
- ☐ Showing children that English is fun.
- ☐ Making sure that children speak accurately in both pronunciation and grammar.
- ☐ Encouraging children to communicate with their limited language.
- ☐ Teaching children to be active and brave in using the language.
- ☐ Stimulating the children's interest of learning a new language.
- ☐ Teaching them the alphabets and phonetic symbols.

- ☐ Making sure that they can read and write a certain number of vocabularies.
- ☐ Making sure they can master certain grammar rules and structures.
- ☐ Making sure that they can understand and respond to the teachers' instructions.

Discussion Point

Vale and Feunteun (1995) point out that the long-term aim of teaching English to children is to enable learners to use English confidently, correctly, and fluently. However, it is not reasonable nor desirable to expect children to achieve such a goal at the beginning of a language program. The Basic Requirements for Primary English has also stated that the important aim of teaching English to children at the beginning is to build up their confidence, to provide motivation, to show them that English is fun and to encourage them to use just whatever English they have learned to communicate. It is important to build a non-threatening learning environment for the children to experience the language and take risks in using the language. Vale and Feunteun (1995) further point out that the correction of errors in the early stages of a language course may have negative effects, making children lose confidence from fear of making mistakes, making them reluctant to take risks and they are likely to become dependent on the teacher to correct their errors. When they pay too much attention to accuracy, they will not be willing to speak freely without being 100% sure.

4.8.2 What is the difference between a mistake and an error?

However, does it mean that we should not correct our pupils' language errors at all? This is not what we are trying to say. To discuss this issue, we need to, first of all, make a distinction between an error and a mistake. According to Brown (2000), language mistakes and language errors are two different phenomena in language learning. "A **mistake** refers to a performance error that is either a random guess or a 'slip of tongue', and it is a failure performance to a known system" . Everyone makes mistakes, no matter in a native language or in a foreign language. As we can see that a mistake has nothing to do with language competence, but is a result from a temporary breakdown. When a mistake is challenged or given enough attention, it can be self-corrected. An **error**, on the other hand, has direct relation with the learners' language competence. Errors do not result from carelessness nor hesitation, but a lack of knowledge in the target language. Language errors cannot be self-corrected no matter how much attention is given.

TASK 4.8.2

Work with your group members and try to think of examples of mistakes and errors.

Discussion Point

After we distinguish the difference, we are clearer about the question—what to correct. But then here comes another question, how to correct? There are times when correction may be necessary. The point is we need to create a meaningful context for the form to be used correctly, meaningfully and appropriately. And we need to judge when and how to correct children's errors in order not to discourage them.

Another point we would like to mention is that at this stage, we teachers are children's coaches rather than judges. The purpose of correcting their errors is to help them to develop their language proficiency and to build up their confidence to learn.

4.8.3 How do we correct errors?

TASK 4.8.3

Below are some extracts from English teaching classes when teachers are trying to correct their children's errors. Work in groups and discuss: Which is the way you favor? And which is the way you dislike most? Can you think of some other ways to correct pupils' errors?

A.

T: What's your name?

S: My name Tom.

T: Oh, good. Your name is Tom?

S: Yes, my name is Tom.

T: Hello, Tom.

B.

T: What's your mother's job?

S: He is...

T: Oh, not he, your mother is a woman. You should use she.

S: She is a ...

C.

T: Make a sentence with "have"!

S: He have a car.

T: There is a big mistake in your sentence. Can you correct it?

S: Mmmm... No, I don't know.

T: Who can correct him?

D.

T: What did you do last Saturday, Mary?

S: I watch TV, and do homework.

T: Oh, great! How about you, John?

E.

T: Make a sentence with "have"!

S: He have a car.

T: He HAVE a car?

S: He <u>HAS</u> a car.

T: Great.

F.

T: Can you tell us something about your father,Tom?

S: My father is 40 years old. He is very high. He is a doctor. He works in our city hospital...

T: Oh, good. Very good, Tom. You said your father is very high? What word can we use instead of high?

S: Yes, <u>tall</u>. He is tall.

T: Very good, Tom.

Discussion Point

There are different ways and techniques for correcting errors, such as direct teacher correction, indirect teacher correction, self-correction, peer correction, whole class correction, etc. As a general rule, indirect teacher correction is encouraged rather than direct teacher correction to avoid damaging pupils' self-esteem and confidence. Indirect techniques include repeating the problem sentence with an emphasis on the problem in a rising tone, asking a question to invite the pupils to say it again with a hint of a problem, a simple repetition of a correct sentence as a model, and using facial expression or gesture to indicate a problem, etc. In practice, self-correction is encouraged before teacher correction or peer correction because if it is a mistake, the pupil himself/herself will be able to correct it. If he/she cannot self-correct, it means there is a lack of competence and the teacher can help with the correction or may ask other pupils to help correct it. Sometimes, the whole class can be invited to correct as well. For example, you can select the main error types. Write four or five errors on the blackboard. Put pupils in pairs for a few minutes to discuss and correct the errors. Then the whole class can do the correction together. The focus can be the choice of vocabulary, the use of grammar, or pronunciation.

The teacher in example A corrects the pupil's error by repeating his sentences. He/She cares about the pupil's feelings and does not want to embarrass him. Actually the pupil realizes his errors and says the correct sentence by himself.

The teacher in example B is not as tolerant as the first one. He/She corrects the pupil's error right after hearing his utterance. Obviously he/she is concerned more about accuracy than fluency. But the pupil is very nervous and probably he could not speak out what he plans to say later.

The teacher in example C has similar beliefs with teacher B. The only difference is he/she does not correct the error himself / herself but asks the pupil to correct it. When the pupil cannot, he/she turns to other pupils and elicits the correction language from other pupils. The advantage of doing this is that it helps raise the pupils' awareness of this kind of error. The disadvantage is that the pupil's confidence may be hurt and he may not want to answer any questions later.

The teacher in example D is the most tolerant to errors among the six teachers here. He/She cares about only fluency and meaning. He/She does not correct the error at all as it do not affect any understanding and communication.

The teacher in example E repeats the wrong sentence after the pupil answers the questions. He/She does not say it is wrong, but he/she uses a rising tone and expects the pupil to correct the error himself. Most of the time, the pupil could realize the problems and could repair them himself.

The teacher in example F is similar to the fifth one. He/She does not say it is an error, but asks the pupil if there are other options for saying so. The pupil realizes there is a better word to say this.

When we correct pupils' errors, we have to remember the objectives of correction: (Scrivener, 1994)

- building pupils' confidence;
- raising awareness;
- acknowledging achievement and progress;
- helping pupils to become more accurate in their use of language.

Reading

Reading 4.1.2A

What can an EFL Teacher Do to Motivate Young Students to Speak English in Class?

By Lida Baker & Maria Spelleri

Lida Baker worked with a group of teacher trainees from Hong Kong for six weeks. One of the questions they struggled to discuss was "What can an EFL (English as a Foreign Language) teacher do to motivate young students to speak English in class?" They came up with the following list:

(1) As much as possible, use materials and teaching contexts that are relevant to the students' ages and life experiences.

(2) Do not punish or shame students for making errors. Try to create a classroom environment where errors are accepted, even welcomed. Encourage risk-taking and reward effort.

(3) Incorporate movement, sound, color, visuals, and realia whenever possible.

(4) Work hard to match the learning materials and tasks to students' abilities.

(5) Use a system of rewards.

(6) Use your voice and body effectively.

(7) Use yourself as a role model of a successful English language learner. After all, you learned English under the same circumstances as your students. If you could do it, so can they!

Maria Spelleri saw the above list and she would like to add a few more points.

(1) Drama and role-play, especially if costumes and props are involved.

(2) Using a ball to pass around, or an egg timer to turn even the most dreary grammar drills into games or "competitions".

(3) Doing a project that raises children's awareness of other children around the world—E-mail pals, video conferencing, exchanging art or photos with another class of same aged kids on another continent, etc. How about a gift box of little things that the kids make and/or collect along with English explanations of each that the kids prepare to exchange with another group?

(4) Give kids some "power" and choices. Let the kids take attendance, call the class to order, dismiss the class, sometimes choose between lesson alternatives, etc. Make it an honor to be chosen to "help the teacher", by giving them a badge for the day, or putting their name in a special frame for the day. Some of the kids were much stricter than I would have been! (Doesn't work after around 8 years old!)

Reading 4.1.2B

How to Motivate Children to Learn English
By Shelley Vernon

There are many other ways to motivate your students and you do not have to keep a stock of "prizes" in your classroom.

Be more than just a teacher

No matter what kind of a class you have, there is one sure way to motivate your class into participating: get them interested in you as their teacher and the interest in your subject matter and class activities will soon follow. You're not just a teacher, you're a person too. Sometimes children tend to have the mentality that teachers are just teachers. They exist in school and nowhere else. However, if you let them see you as a person and not just a teacher, you might see a change in how they react to your class and class activities. If they respect you, they will respect the class and be motivated to participate in whatever it is you have for them to do. Of course, that is so much easier said than done. Here are some things you should think about when trying to figure out how to show your human side:

(1) Keep yourself motivated.

Think back to what classes you like best and why. If the teacher was bored and didn't make the subject interesting, then the children often didn't like the class either. To keep yourself motivated, change your activities to things that you are excited about. If you're not excited and motivated about the activities you have planned for your students, it's time to get some new ones.

(2) Be an individual.

Don't be afraid to talk about your interests outside of school. Look for commonalities between you and your students and capitalize on them. For example, if you like the same types of music as a lot of your students, bring in some CDs and let them listen to music when they are working on projects. Make sure the words are in English so that the children can take in some English language into their subconscious.

(3) Have fun and be silly.

Talk in a crazy voice or be daft and make them wonder what you'll be up to next. Some teachers frown upon the idea of playing the clown and having fun, because they think it is time-wasting and that it is not their role to be an entertainer. If it is not in your personality to be a big kid, then you cannot fake it, and that is OK. If you use fun games and ideas, your classes will still be enjoyable. However, if you are a big kid at heart then you will find that joining in, playing with the children and generally acting up and being enthusiastic will come naturally to you and is all part of the fun of teaching. It is not clowning around for the sake of it, it serves to keep a fun and happy learning environment, and this alone can motivate your students. If your children can laugh with you, and if they LIKE you, they'll be interested in what you're doing up there in front of the class.

(4) Encourage

When you're frustrated with your class, because they don't seem interested in participating, it's quite easy to forget that even when they do something small, you need to keep encouraging and to stay positive. The number one way to demotivate children is to have a negative or neutral attitude. If the children do not feel encouraged and good about learning, then they will not feel motivated to learn.

Make your students active learners

Think back to when you were in school. Did you like to sit at a desk and listen to the teacher drone on and on. This type of passive learning is BORING and demotivating. Active learning doesn't mean the children need to be physically active throughout the class period—it just means that you design your class period around having them actively participate in the learning process. There are lots of things you can do:

(1) Play games.

Implement games that have the same outcome that you might have them reach by doing a worksheet. You may access free samples of fun classroom games in the resource box. When you play games, you can use points and competition as a motivator, but not for kids under six who may find the competition too stressful. For them, just playing the game is motivating enough. You can also sometimes award extra credit, but use it sparingly so that it remains "extra" and a special reward. Also if you use it too much, children can have so much extra credit that it sways the actual grades too much.

(2) Get them moving.

Movement is a vital component to motivating children. The best way to prevent children from zoning out is to get them up out of their seats at least once each class period. Even if you just require them to come up to you instead of you going to them for help, the movement can help get them out of the trance that they sometimes get from sitting in one spot too long. Grouping the children for study projects and activities helps as well. If you can, let them move the desks around or sit on the floor to change things up as well. Many games involve movement without the children needing to leave their seats, such as miming, moving certain body parts and passing things around as part of a game or race. Therefore, even teachers with large classes and no space to move can use this technique, albeit to a more limited degree.

(3) Get their hands "drty" .

Well, not literally, but the more hands-on activities you can do the better they will learn and the more likely they will stay interested in the activity. It is much more motivating and effective to be handling real objects, or learning with pictures than copying down lists of words from the board. If you are discussing how to put a sentence together, have them construct their own sentences (alone or with a partner) and write them on the blackboard. You can also intentionally make mistakes to encourage them to look for the "right" way. If you do this you should warn the children so that they are on the look out for your deliberate errors, otherwise you could do more harm than good.

(4) Stick to a schedule.

Creating a schedule for your students helps them know what to expect in the class and will help them stay organized as well which will lower the frustration level for children who sometimes struggle in school. It is very difficult for frustrated children to stay motivated. If they know that every Friday is a vocabulary quiz, then they won't have to wonder on Thursday if they were supposed to study that night. If they have weekly assignments due on every Wednesday, then you don't have to spend the majority of the class time reminding them that the weekly assignment is due. This schedule should be clearly explained to the children as well as posted in the classroom.

(5) Variety is the spice of life.

With that all said, it's also important to change things up within the schedule. For example, if you spend the first 10 or 15 minutes each day doing vocabulary activities, make sure you vary these activities so they don't get bored and stay motivated. If you see that the children of one class don't respond to an activity, avoid it in the future and stick to the ones they like. It's also important to realize that some groups of children will be motivated by certain activities that the next group of children will literally detest. Another way to create variety is to keep changing the pace. Play a game that wakes the children up and follow it with a calm game so that the students do not get too excited. Then play a fast game so the children do not become so calm that they start to become restless and misbehave or drift off.

(6) Give them options.

If you spend long periods of time with your class, or if you have a mixed ability class and have to split your teaching time between groups, then the following ideas may help when the children have some free or unsupervised time in your class. Having a collection of fun learning activities for them can motivate children that like to pass time and be a time-filler for children that like to make trouble. Get a variety of activities for the children such as educational board games, crossword puzzles, art projects...anything that they can learn something from what they would also find fun. For older kids, you can make a competition to complete a packet of activities to get extra credit points or put them on a team to be the first to complete a series of tasks. If discipline is a problem then the children will have to work individually at their desks in silence, but at least they will be engaged in the activity.

One last idea... This really motivates younger classes of children up to age 12, but it can work with all ages. Plan an end of the term so the children can show off what they've learned to their parents and other teachers. You can do it right in the classroom and have the children play games, recite poems, whatever you can come up with to have them showcase what they've learned to their parents.

So, there you have it. There are lots of ways you can motivate your students to learn and to pay attention without bribing them with tangible gifts that become more important to them than learning the material.

Unit 5

Teaching Vocabulary, Grammar and Pronunciation

Aims of the unit

In this unit, we are going to discuss how language teachers teach vocabulary, grammar and pronunciation effectively. We will focus on the following:

5.1 How to teach vocabulary to young learners

5.1.1 What does it mean to learn a word?

5.1.2 What methods can be used to present new words?

5.1.3 What activities can be used to practice vocabulary?

5.2 How to teach grammar to young learners

5.2.1 Should grammar be taught in the primary school?

5.2.2 How should grammar be presented—deductive or inductive?

5.2.3 How should grammar be practiced—mechanical or meaningful?

5.3 How to teach pronunciation to young learners

5.3.1 What is your attitude towards the teaching of pronunciation?

5.3.2 Should we teach phonetic alphabet as a starting point for teaching English to children in order to help them get correct pronunciation?

5.3.3 Can pronunciation help with reading and writing?

5.3.4 How to help children improve their pronunciation

5.1 How to teach vocabulary to young Learners

As we all had the experience of being English language learners, we have rich experience in learning its vocabulary. This experience can be helpful for us to understand the teaching of vocabulary. Vocabulary has been recognized as one of the most important elements contributing to successful language learning. However, many learners find vocabulary very difficult to learn even with enormous time and effort put into it. It is also recognized that vocabulary is more vital than grammar for learners, because one can express ideas with a combination of words, but cannot do so simply with grammar. As Harmer (2007) states "If language structures make up the skeleton of language, then it is vocabulary that provides the vital organs and the flesh. An ability to manipulate grammatical structure does not have any potential for expressing meaning unless words are used". However, what vocabulary to teach and how to teach them remain to be crucial questions worth probing into.

In most beginning level primary English textbooks, vocabulary is often presented with pictures or illustrations. This is because vocabulary for beginners consists of words that are generally concrete in meaning and easy to be illustrated with pictures. This way of presenting new words can help children establish a direct relationship between a word and its meaning, which, in turn, can help children develop the ability and habit of thinking in English from the very beginning. However, when children move to higher grades, they will encounter more abstract words and the teaching of vocabulary should involve more than just knowing the word and its meaning.

5.1.1 What does it mean to learn a word?

TASK 5.1.1

What does it involve to learn a word? Study the sample below (Figure 5.1.1). Discuss with a partner what should be involved in teaching those words to children.

Figure 5.1.1 A sample[①]

① 选自北京师范大学出版社的义务教育教科书《英语》（三年级起点）四年级上册 Unit 7。

Discussion Point

As we can see from the diagram (Figure 5.1.2), knowing a word is more than just knowing its meaning, its spelling, and its pronunciation. Knowing a word also involves using it in a grammatically correct way, (e.g. *They acted very well* not *They acted very good*), knowing its grammatical connections with other words (e.g. *Thank you very much* not *Very much thank you*), knowing which words can be used together with it, which is also called collocations (*dark clouds* not *black clouds*; *heavy smoker* not *serious smoker*), knowing its positive and negative associations (*slim* is positive and *skinny* is negative) and most importantly knowing how to use the word in the right situation (*Would you like some drink?* is more formal than *Can I get you a drink*?).

What does knowing a word involve?

Words
- Word meaning
  - Meaning in context
  - Some relations
- Word use
  - Metaphor and idiom
  - Collocation
  - Style and register
- Word information
  - Parts of speech
  - Prefixes and suffixes
  - Spelling and pronunciation
- Word grammar
  - Noun:countable/uncountable
  - Verb complementation/phrasal verbs, etc.
  - Adjectives and adverbs;
  - Position, etc.

Figure 5.1.2 What does knowing a word involve?

Based on such an understanding, we should re-consider the ways we teach vocabulary. Obviously, the teaching of vocabulary should not only focus on spelling, meaning, and pronunciation but on word grammar, word relations, word groups, and word collocations. For example, words related to the same topic (e.g. *fruit—apple, banana, peach, etc.; vegetables—eggplant, cabbage, cucumber, etc.*) can be presented together as a group. Words can also be grouped into the same grammatical forms (e.g. *verbs describing daily routines, adjectives describing a person or personality*). Synonyms or antonyms (e.g. *good & fine, big & small*) can be another example.

The use of words in the right situation is another important aspect which should be given more attention. We are all aware of the fact that even if children can write the word correctly, it does not necessarily mean they can use it appropriately in communication. Therefore, teachers need to help learners develop their awareness about the formal and informal use of words when there is an opportunity and with more practice they can gradually become more capable in their use of words for the right context.

5.1.2 What methods can be used to present new words?

TASK 5.1.2

课例示范：词汇教学①

The following are some ways of presenting new words. Read them and match each with an example provided below. What other methods or ways can be used? Please give your examples.

☐ Using cards.
☐ Using pictures or illustrations.
☐ Using questions.
☐ Involving learners in actions.

Example 1

Teacher : OK, let's do some exercises. Listen and follow my instructions. Let's jump. (*Teacher jumps*)
Students : Jump. (*Students jump*)
Teacher : OK, now let's walk. Walk. OK, walk like this. (*Teacher walks*)
Students : Walk. (*Students walk*)

Example 2

Teacher : (*Finished story telling*) OK. ...Whose birthday is it in the story?
Students : It's Bobby's.
Teacher : Yes. It's Bobby's birthday. So, his mother gives him... (*Expecting children to answer*)
Student A : A box?
Student B : (*In Chinese*) 一份生日礼物。
Teacher : Ah, yes, a gift. His mother gives him a birthday gift. 一份礼物，A gift.
Students : A gift.
Teacher : Do you get a birthday gift for your birthday? ...

Example 3

Teacher : Now look at the picture of a zoo. What can you see in the zoo?
Students : Monkeys! Pandas!
Teacher : What else? What are these animals? (*Pointing to the giraffes in the picture.*)
Student A : Giraffe.
Teacher : Yes. They are giraffes.

① 上海工商外国语职业学院附属小学黄佳丽授课。

Students : Giraffes.

Example 4

The teacher gave out some vegetable cards to some pupils in the class before the lesson began.

Teacher : I have some vegetable here. Look, what are they? (*Showing several mushrooms*)

Students : They are...

Teacher : Listen, mushrooms. Listen carefully, They're mushrooms (The teacher writes the words along with a picture on the blackboard). Read after me, mushrooms.

Students : Mushrooms.

Teacher : OK. Now, who has mushrooms? Show your card to the class, please. "I have..."

Students : (Those who have the word cards of mushrooms stand up) I have mushrooms.

Teacher : Excellent, thank you. Sit down, please.

Other ways for presenting new words:

Using moving images from the websites or videos.

____

____

____

Discussion Point

From the examples shown above and with more options you may have added, we can see that there are different ways of presenting new words. An important principle we should all bear in mind is that "students need to see words in context to see how they are used". In other words, they need to "see or hear those words in action" (Harmer, 2007). Therefore, the best way to present new words is to provide a meaningful context and give children the chance to observe, to think, to act, and to activate their prior knowledge as done by the teachers in the above examples.

Presenting new words is only the first step of vocabulary teaching. We cannot expect our pupils to remember all the new words without helping them practice, restore, recall and use them later in the lesson or in the lessons that come after. Therefore, we will need to find out what activities can be used for practicing vocabulary.

5.1.3 What activities can be used to practice vocabulary?

TASK 5.1.3

Look at the following activities and deicide what their focuses are. How can you adapt them for your pupils in a specific teaching situation? What activities do you know for teaching and learning vocabulary? Add your activity in the space provided below.

Name: Look and match.

Target students: Beginning level.

Procedures/steps: Put pictures on the blackboard in one column, and then write the names on the next column in a random order. Have children look at the pictures and match them with the names.

Purpose or function: Practices recognition of word form and meaning.

Making it simpler or more challenging: ____________________.

Name: Listen and point.

Target students: Beginning and intermediate levels.

Procedures/steps: Put four or five pictures on the blackboard and number them. The teacher says a word, and children shout out the number that matches the right picture.

Purpose or function: ____________________.

Making it simpler or more challenging: ____________________.

Name: The odd one out / Which is different?

Target students: Beginning and intermediate learners.

Procedures/steps: Put four or five pictures on the blackboard. Children need to point at the one that does not belong to the group.

Purpose or function: ____________________.

Making it simpler or more challenging: To make it more challenging, have children explain the reason why acertain picture is different.

Name: Put the words into boxes.

Target students: Beginning and intermediate learners.

Procedures/steps: In this game, children need to put words into correct groups. Children are given several words and they need to put words into groups, for example, groups of fruit, vegetable, or verbs, nouns and adjectives.

Purpose or function: ____________________.

Make it simpler or more challenging: ____________________.

Name: A tape recorder.

Procedures/steps: In the classroom, teaching, it is often children who repeat after the teacher, but in this game, it goes the other way around with the purpose of increasing children's pronunciation awareness. The teacher acts as a tape recorder which can "record and play" what children say. Each time children say a word, the "recorder" repeats it with correct pronunciation and stress. Children can repeat the word as many times as they like until they think they get the pronunciation correct.

Purpose or function: ______________________________ .

Making it simpler or more challenging: ____________________ .

Name: Bingo game.

Target students: Beginners.

Procedures/steps: In this game, children need to listen and write words. Children need to prepare a diagram with 3 × 3 boxes (shown on the right). The teacher list nine words and children copy them into their boxes in whatever order they like. Then the teacher chooses a word one time and reads it out,children need to find it in their boxes and cross it out. When the crossed words form a line, vertical, diagonal, or horizontal, they say Bingo.

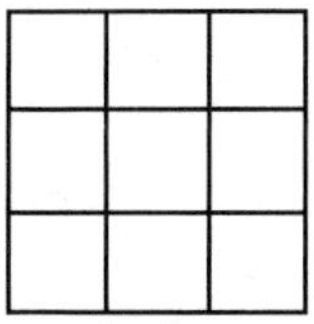

Purpose or function: ______________________________ .

Making it simpler or more challenging: To make it more challenging, you can choose to dictate the words instead of having them copied from the board for higher graders.

Other vocabulary activities/games I know

Name: ______________________________________ .

Target students: ________________________________ .

Procedures/steps: ______________________________

____

____ .

Purpose or function: ______________________________ .

Making it simpler or more challenging: __________________

____ .

Work in groups of four and choose a vocabulary learning page in a textbook. Work out a 20-minute lesson plan of vocabulary teaching, individually. Then share it in your group. What can you learn from each others' lesson plans?

Discussion Point

After presenting the new words, children need to use what they more or less know in various ways in order to remember the words. We need to provoke them into using the words or getting them to think about word meaning in more ways and in more contexts.

The examples we looked at have covered most of the areas we discussed regarding teaching vocabulary: word meaning, word recognition, word pronunciation, word category, etc. They practice not only language skills, some of them also involve higher-order thinking, such as reasoning, comparing, categorizing and other cognitive skills that are important for children's development. You can decide if they can be used directly in your teaching situations, or they may need adaptations to meet the needs of the children that you teach and the context where teaching takes place.

It is suggested by Cameron (2001) that vocabulary needs to be met and recycled from time to time in different activities, with new knowledge and new connections practiced each time when the same word is met again. Nation (1990) suggests that a word needs to be met five or six times before it has any chance of being remembered. This indicates that when we teach vocabulary, we should not expect our learners to remember them at once. We need to provide different interesting and meaningful contexts for the newly presented words to be practiced through a variety of activities, such as listening, speaking, drawing, ordering, classifying, reading, acting, and writing, etc. Cameron (2001) also points out that the best and most efficient way for young learners to actually learn and remember words is when they are involved in thinking and in constructing meaning. She believes that the amount of mental work done by learners affects how well a word is learned. In other words, "the more the learner has to think about a word and its meaning, the more likely they are to remember". Therefore, simple repetition of words which does not encourage much thinking should not be overused.

As children learn more words in English, vocabulary strategy instruction should be introduced in the teaching of vocabulary. Some useful strategies may include classifying words into different categories, guessing meaning from the context, spelling and memory strategies, and using word spiders or diagrams to organize certain topical words, etc. Figure 5.1.3 shows an example of a word spider. Pupils are at first given a simple and incomplete diagram of a group of words in the form of a word spider and then they can work in pairs and add more words they know to it. Each pair can then talk about "their house" using the diagram. The word spiders can also be shown on the class wall after the lesson for pupils to share their diagrams.

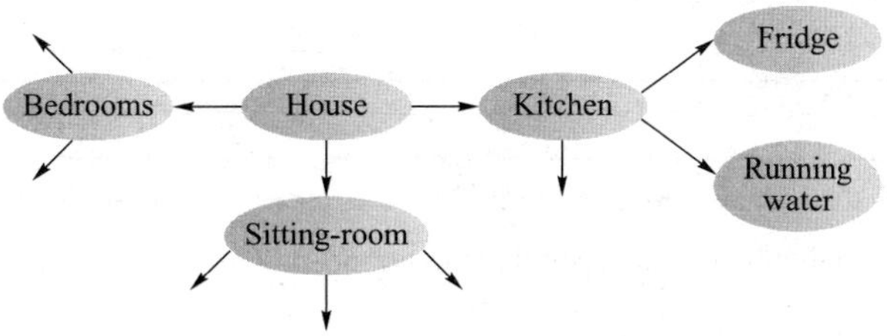

Figure 5.1.3 A word spider of house

Besides, young learners can also be helped and guided to reflect on their learning process by evaluating their learning results. For example, at the end of a lesson, they can be asked how many words they have learned and which are easy to remember and which need more practice. With frequent guided practice, children will understand more about their own learning in terms of what they are learning and how they should learn.

One more thing worth noting is that a pile of interesting activities and fun games does not automatically make a good lesson. Each activity or game should have its own function and purpose. As a teacher, it is our responsibility to decide when and where to use which activity, how the activities are related to one another, and for what purposes. Only in this way, will the activities we use be useful and practical for promoting children's language development.

5.2 How to teach grammar to young learners

The teaching of grammar plays an important role in language learning. It has also aroused a lot of discussions and debates. Some teachers and language educators argue that grammar should be taught at the primary level, while others may disagree. Thus, the teaching of grammar has been the most controversial issue in language teaching.

5.2.1 Should grammar be taught in the primary school?

TASK 5.2.1

Below are 10 assumptions about grammar teaching in the primary school. Discuss with your partner and decide if you agree or disagree with him. Why?

Assumptions	Your attitude
1. Pupils need to be given detailed grammar rules if they want to learn a foreign language successfully.	

continued

Assumptions	Your attitude
2. Children do not need to learn grammar rules when they acquire their first language, so they do not need them either when learning a foreign language.	
3. If pupils get enough chance to practice using a foreign language, they do not need to learn grammar.	
4. Making children understand the grammar rules should be a very important teaching objective.	
5. Grammar should be taught to help children analyze difficult structures in texts and dialogs.	
6. It's OK for children to make grammatical mistakes, because communication in a foreign language without errors is something most people will never achieve.	
7. Pupils in lower grades do not need to learn grammar, but when they move to upper levels, grammar should be taught explicitly.	
8. Knowing grammar is not enough for real communication.	
9. Helping children summarize the grammar rules from the examples is a very good way to teach grammar in primary schools.	
10. Children don't like grammar. They get bored with it.	

Discussion Point

In fact, there are different views regarding the issue of teaching grammar to young learners. Some educators (e.g. Larsen-Freeman and Long, 1991) strongly believe that grammar should be taught and grammar can improve communication, while others, (e.g. Celce-Murcia, 1991) believe that grammar is less important for children than for adults, and it is less important in listening and reading than in writing.

When talking about the importance of teaching grammar to children, the term "grammar" may mean different things to different people. Some people regard grammar as a list of rules in its technical forms. In this sense, we would say that grammar should not be taught to young learners. However, Cameron (2001) believes that grammar should not be viewed in this narrow sense. Grammar is important for children to learn a foreign language because in real communication, grammar is necessary for expressing precise meaning in discourse. For her, talking about something meaningful with children can be a useful way to introduce new grammar instead of explicitly teaching the rules. She suggests that as grammar ties closely to vocabulary in learning and using the foreign language, the teaching of grammar can start from chunks and texts. She believes that "grammar grows like a plant, perhaps, watered by meaningful language use, and pushing out new shoots while older stems are strengthened".

However, the ways how grammar is taught need to be carefully considered. Giving children detailed grammatical rules will not help them acquire the language, particularly for young learners. But for older children in grade five or six in primary schools, learning some grammar rules may help them produce more accurate sentences. What is more, grammar teaching does not need to be boring all the time. Sometimes, it can be fun.

As the goals of teaching grammar are not for the rule to be remembered for better use of the language in communication, we should follow the principles in teaching:

- teach learners to *express themselves* as clearly as possible with confidence;
- *strengthen* grammatical *accuracy* in a fun and purposeful way;
- *increase* grammar *awareness* among young learners;
- *meet learning styles* wherever possible.

5.2.2 How should grammar be presented—deductive or inductive?

TASK 5.2.2A

Compare the approaches used by two teachers when presenting grammar. Which one do you think is more suitable for children, and why?

A

我们用IS和动词的-ING形式表示正在进行的动作。比如：

He is singing.

She is dancing.

Tom is running.

Amy is reading.

B

Look at the picture. Who are in the pictures? Right, Lisa, Jenny, Amy and Tom. What's Lisa doing? She's singing. What's Jenny doing? Listen, she's dancing. Now, look at Tom. What's Tom doing? Yes, Tom's running. And how about Amy? Great. Amy's reading. (Teacher then writes the sentences on the blackboard.)

Obviously, teacher A and teacher B used different approaches to present the present continuous tense. The first teacher introduces the rule first and then gives pupils some examples. This kind of grammar presentation method is called the **deductive method**. After the presentation of the rules with examples, the teacher would provide some practice for pupils to apply the rule to produce sentences with given prompts.

When teachers teach grammar following the deductive method, he/she will most probably take the following steps.

(1) Explain the rules, most probably in Chinese. For example, the teacher explains that the superlative form of an adjective is made of an adjective plus *-est*: *clean* → *cleanest*, *tall* → *tallest*.

(2) Give one or two examples, e.g. *Mrs. Green has* <u>*the largest house*</u> *in town*.

(3) Ask pupils to make sentences based on prompts. Usually a substitute exercise.

For example: Change the underlined part with the proper forms of the given words.

Mrs. Green has <u>the largest house</u> in town.
clean house, green garden, nice flowers
Mrs. Green has the cleanest house in town.
Mrs. Green has the greenest garden in town.
Mrs. Green has the nicest flowers in town.

Teacher B, on the other hand, shows the pupils a picture first and tried to invite children to participate in speaking English. The teacher uses present continuous tense in context without telling her pupils the rules. This kind of grammar presentation is called the **inductive method**. In the inductive method, the teacher provides learners with authentic language data and induces the learners to notice grammar rules without any form of explicit explanation. It is believed that the rules will become evident if the pupils are given enough appropriate examples in a context. After presenting the rules, pupils can then be invited to apply the newly presented structure to produce new sentences with more pictures and verbal prompts. During the practice time, the teacher provides help for those who have difficulties. Finally, optionally, the teacher may ask pupils to summarize the grammar rule.

For example, the teacher intends to teach students to learn the structure: *someone will do something*. She/He may start by having children review some verb phrases using some pictures, such as *go swimming*, *do housework*, *visit one's grandma*, etc. Then she will ask children to look at the picture (Figure 5.2.1) and say:

It's Friday afternoon. What will Ben do this weekend?
Ben will help his mother with cooking.
Ben will visit his grandma.
Ben will go shopping with his father.
Ben will do his homework.

Figure 5.2.1 Ben's weekend

Then the teacher will ask students: What will you do this weekend?

Students are expected to answer:

I will go to the cinema.

I will play table tennis.

I will do my homework.

…

TASK 5.2.2B

Work in group and discuss: What are the advantages and disadvantages of these two methods respectively? What did your teachers use when you were learning grammar? Under what circumstances should the deductive method be used and when to use the inductive method?

	The deductive method	The inductive method
Advantages		
Disadvantages		

Discussion Point

The deductive method is often criticized because: 1) it teaches grammar in an isolated way; 2) little attention is paid to meaning; 3) practice is often mechanical. However, this method also has some advantages. First, it could be very successful with selected and motivated students. Second, it could save time when students are confronted with a grammar rule which is complex but has to be learned. Third, it may help students increase confidence in those examinations which are written with accuracy as the main criterion of success. For young learners, we think it may not be a good idea to use the deductive method to teach grammar as they are not strong in abstract thinking.

The inductive method, on the other hand, is more suitable for young learners. Though some people thought it is very time-consuming, it does provide children with more authentic situations. Children do not need to know the grammar rules explicitly. They can imitate teachers and learn to use the grammar rule gradually. For higher grade children,teachers may draw their attention to the rules after presenting and practicing the rules inductively, but for lower level children, it is not necessary.

5.2.3 How should grammar be practiced—mechanical or meaningful?

TASK 5.2.3A

课例示范：语法教学[1]

Work in groups of four and reflect on your own grammar learning experience. What kind of grammar practice methods did your teachers use to consolidate your grammar learning? Are they mechanical drilling or meaningful practice? List them in the following table.

Mechanical practice	Meaningful practice
1. Filling in the blanks.	1. Describing pictures.
2. Doing substitution drills.	2. Telling stories.
3.	3.
4.	4.
5.	5.
6.	6.
7.	7.

① 上海市愚园路第一小学蔡卓云授课。

Discussion Point

Mechanical practices are largely used in language classrooms both for grammar and vocabulary practice. This kind of activities can reinforce pupils' accuracy in using certain grammatical items. Pupils can remember the rules easily after lots of practice. But this kind of practice cannot enhance the use of grammar in real situations. So if we want children to use a certain grammar rule naturally in real life, only mechanical practice is not enough. We need to create situations that are similar in real life and involve children to use grammar rules for communicative purposes. Mechanical practice can be used as a preparation stage for meaningful practice.

For mechanical practice, teachers can ask pupils to do the following:

(1) Filling in the blanks.

(2) Doing substitution drills.

(3) Changing the sentence structure.

(4) Translating sentences.

(5) Repeating after the teacher.

…

For meaningful practice, we suggest the following activities:

(1) Identifying pictures with descriptions/paragraphs.

(2) Discovering identical pairs.

(3) Finding and describing differences.

(4) Following directions.

(5) Using rhymes and songs (Figure 5.2.2).

Figure 5.2.2 *RUN, RUN, RUN, YOUR RACE*①

① 选自北京师范大学出版社的义务教育教科书《英语》（三年级起点）六年级上册 Unit 3。

(6) Retelling stories.
(7) Role-playing.
(8) Listening and speaking.

The activity below is a practice activity on prepositions. The teacher reads out some sentences and children are to check the proper boxes according to what they hear. For example, the teacher says, "*The cup is on the table. The cat is under the chair. The girl is in front of the tree. Children should tick the three boxes based on what they hear.*" (Figure 5.2.3) Alternatively, the teacher can also tick a box for children to describe the situation.

In fact, both mechanical and meaningful activities are needed for effective learning of grammar. However, we should all remember that the purpose of learning a language is for communication. Therefore, in the classroom, teachers should design more meaningful activities so that children can acquire the language by using it in real contexts. Only mechanical drilling cannot meet the needs.

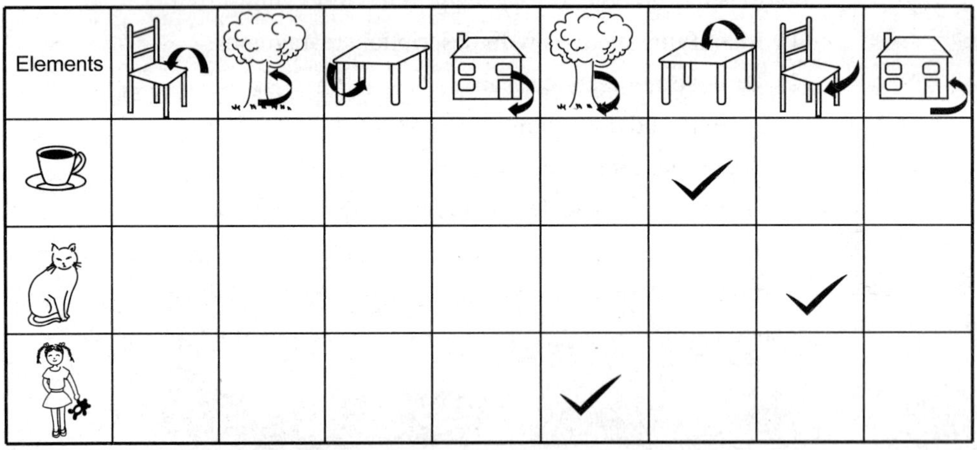

Figure 5.2.3 A practice activity on prepositions

TASK 5.2.3B

Work in groups of four and discuss how to teach the following grammatical items to children. Design your activities. Try to use both mechanical and meaningful practices.

(1) Present continuous tense.
(2) Comparatives of adjectives.
(3) Prepositions.

Discussion Point

Let's take the first one as an example. By mechanical practice, teachers can write a list of verbs on the blackboard for pupils to make sentences using the present continuous tense. Next, teachers can use some pictures to encourage pupils to describe them using the present continuous tense following an example given. Then teachers will move to more meaningful activities by involving children in actions and descriptions. For example, one is doing an action and another guesses. Or two children role-play a telephone call. One is asking about his/her family members' actions, the other is answering.

What activities have you come up with to practice these grammar items?

It is believed that grammar does not have to be the most boring bit of teaching or learning. It does not have to be something difficult and abstract. It can be learned as something in which social skills, physical activity, intellectual thinking skills, and personalization are combined to improve the learner's communicative performance. Meaning should always be the main focus in language learning, and grammar is a system that helps make meaning more precise.

5.3 How to teach pronunciation to young learners

课例示范：语音教学①

In language teaching, pronunciation is less emphasized than other language knowledge, such as grammar and vocabulary. Yet, it is in fact a very important element for learning a foreign language. In this session, we are going to discuss different views about teaching pronunciation and introduce some principles as well as ways for teaching pronunciation to children.

5.3.1 What is your attitude towards the teaching of pronunciation?

TASK 5.3.1

Do you agree with the following statements? Work in groups of four. Discuss with your group members.

- ☐ 1. It is easier for children to develop good pronunciation than adults.
- ☐ 2. Children do not have to learn phonetic symbols.
- ☐ 3. Children need to be able to distinguish the individual vowels and consonant sounds.

① 上海市浦东新区南码头小学朱黎授课。

☐ 4. To teach pronunciation means to ask learners to repeat after the teacher sound by sound or word by word.

☐ 5. If children can pronounce individual sounds correctly, they have good pronunciation.

☐ 6. Pronunciation should be tested in exams.

Discussion Point

This task aims to explore the following three issues: Is it necessary to learn pronunciation? What should be included in teaching pronunciation? Is it necessary to test pronunciation and how?

1. Is it necessary to learn pronunciation?

   Pronunciation is integrated in language learning and it plays an important role in listening, speaking and spelling. It is helpful for children to grasp good pronunciation. In communication, listeners need to be able to hear and understand English well and similarly, speakers need to be able to produce the language eligible enough for others to understand. Good pronunciation helps to make communication successful. What's more, phonetic knowledge can make word recognition and spelling much easier.**Reading 5.3.1A** analyzes the reasons why pronunciation should be integrated in teaching children English.

Reading 5.3.1A 《语音是小学英语教学的重中之重》（李兆增）

2. What should be included in teaching pronunciation?

   Pronunciation includes stress, rhythm and intonation as well as individual sounds. "Learning pronunciation should not be limited to finding primary stress and comparing individual vowel and consonant sounds in a given word, as has often been the case with pronunciation learning in the past". For children, it is more important to help them develop phonemic awareness(See **Reading 5.3.1B**) which means to be aware of the connection between letters and sounds, to be able to feel the rhythm of the language, and to understand and produce sounds.

3. Is it necessary to test pronunciation and how?

   Cambridge young learners' English test does consider pronunciation as one of the important criteria for the final score of the oral test. It is good for teachers to know how good their students' pronunciation is and it might also be a good idea for learners to know their problems. However, when testing pronunciation, teachers need to be more tolerant of children. The criteria of testing should not be "perfection" but "intelligibility" (Harmer, 2007).

5.3.2 Should we teach phonetic alphabet as a starting point for teaching English to children in order to help them get correct pronunciation?

TASK 5.3.2A

Work in pairs and reflect on your own experience of learning English.

Did you learn IPA (International Phonetic Alphabet) when you learned your English?

If yes, at what stage did you learn it, at the beginning or at a later stage?

How did you feel about learning IPA, interesting, boring, useful, or motivating?

What benefits or problems do you think there might be in learning IPA?

Do you agree that IPA should be taught to primary school children at the beginning? Why and why not?

TASK 5.3.2B

Read the following statements and tick the ones that you agree with. Then discuss them with another teacher.

- ☐ IPA helps with pronunciation.
- ☐ IPA helps with spelling.
- ☐ IPA helps with reading.
- ☐ IPA is not useful.
- ☐ IPA makes learning boring.
- ☐ IPA makes learning difficult.
- ☐ IPA works better with adults than with children.
- ☐ IPA is useful for self-directed learning.

Discussion Point

In many countries it has been popular in the past to use the phonetic symbols of the IPA as a starting point for learning to read and write in English. Research and experience have shown, however, that this approach is not successful with many learners except for those mature and academically oriented learners. According to Harmer (2007), learning phonetic symbols "places unnecessary burdens" on learners. It is certainly not recommended for use with children. The problem with it, especially in situations like China where the writing system is not alphabetical, is that it requires the learner to learn an extremely complex phonetic system with 44 distinctive sounds [phonemes] and a writing system with 26 letters in the alphabet. What is more, there is an extreme mismatch between the sound system and the symbols available for representing it. For young children, whose focus is not on the forms of language at the best of times, this could be a most confusing and distracting experience.

The best solution, in the view of the writers of this book, is to work with the "normal" alphabet, but to take extreme care when introducing them and to make sure that the children are already familiar with the oral form of the words that they are going to meet in the written form. Teachers should also not expect very quick success with their children learning to pronounce English words from the printed form, given the fact that success does not come quickly even for most English native speaking children. It should be recognized that learning to decode in English is a long hard job, whatever your language background.

5.3.3 Can pronunciation help with reading and writing?

TASK 5.3.3

Discuss in groups the relationship between pronunciation and reading and writing. Do you think learning pronunciation is helpful in improving reading and writing? If so, can you give some examples?

Discussion Point

It is important to remember that it takes a long time for children to learn to read Chinese. We should not have too high an expectation of them when they learn to read English, as they are dealing with a completely different system of writing.

Children already know a lot of their own language aurally and orally when learning to read in their own language. In foreign language learning, it is better to follow the same process, establishing a good aural/oral command of a wide vocabulary before the teacher asks children to start reading and writing. Of course, learning to read means more than simply being able to say the words on the page. However, this is an essential first stage.

The English writing system is very different from that of Chinese. In English, letter symbols represent sounds in words. This helps the reader work out the pronunciation of a word that he or she may see for the first time. However, the writing system of English is not completely consistent or logical. The symbols may help to some extent, but they are not a guarantee. Look at the common examples below. At the same time, you can add as many such examples as possible.

Words with different spellings but exactly the same pronunciation

sea	see	
hear	here	
I	eye	
two	too	to
by	buy	bye
meat	meet	

Words with the same spellings but different pronunciation

present tense:read [ ]	past tense:read [ ]
noun: tear [ ]	verb: tear [ ]

This means that learning to read words aloud in English is not just a matter of learning the symbols and pronouncing the corresponding sounds. Readers need to use other strategies, too. One is to recognize the general shape of a whole word. This is called "Look and Say". Our children are probably very good at this, since it is similar to the way in which reading is done in Chinese. Many very common words in English have very irregular spellings, so a "Look and Say" recognition approach is recommended.

Even for native children, reading English words is not an easy task and the beginning stage needs to be carefully planned. Therefore, our expectations of children in China, learning English as a foreign language, should not be too high. We need to take a realistic attitude and try to create a relaxed, friendly, enjoyable learning environment for children to experience reading in another language.

In learning to read, "Look and Say" alone is not enough since it will not help readers work out words that they have never seen before. For this, they need to learn the 26 English letters and use the clues that the letter symbols can offer.

5.3.4 How to help children improve their pronunciation

TASK 5.3.4

Look at the descriptive standards for phonetic knowledge in the 2022 Curriculum and tell your partner what you can or will do to help your students meet these standards.

Level 1 Descriptive standards phonetic knowledge

1. Identify and read the 26 letters in upper and lower cases;

2. Perceive the sounds of letters in words;
3. Perceive simple spelling rules , and use them to help spell words;
4. Perceive and imitate speaking English, and recognize word stress and the rising and falling tones of sentences.

Discussion Point

In this part, we will focus on the teaching of phonics based on the second requirement in the above list. First of all, what is phonics? Phonics is a method of teaching students to read, spell, and pronounce words by understanding letter-sound relations. With the knowledge of letter-sound relations, students will be able to pronounce a word by blending the letters following certain sound and spelling rules. A lot of research has suggested that phonics skills are both effective and fundamental for developing English reading and writing skills.

While we agree that phonics skills are important for all learners of English, we should be aware that children learning English as their native language and those learning English as a foreign language have obvious differences. For native children of English, by the time they learn phonics, roughly around the age of 4-5, they have already accumulated a large amount of vocabulary and rich listening and speaking experiences. All they need is to establish a connection between the sound of language and the words in their written forms so that they will develop reading and writing skills to lay a good foundation for formal education. However, children in China are different in many ways when they first start learning English. For Chinese children, they do not know any English vocabulary, neither do they have listening and speaking experiences with English when they start learning English. Let's look at an example. When a child in China hears the word "tree", he or she will not be able to recognize its sound, neither will he or she know its meaning or spelling. Therefore, he or she has to learn to recognize it by sound, also learn how to pronounce the word, and at the same time, learn how to spell the word on paper. For a native child, things are quite different. When he or she hears the word "tree", he or she will immediately recognize the sound and the meaning of it at the same time. However, he or she may not be able to recognize the words in its written forms or spell out the word on paper. Therefore, the first and foremost task for native children is to learn phonics so that they can use the sound-spelling rules to recognize words in reading and spell words out in writing.

Well, it is generally agreed that developing phonics skills are beneficial for all children to learn to speak, read and write English, the question is: should we teach the letter-sound relations to Chinese children in the first place as native children in school? The answer is: NO. We should be aware that children in China lack listening and speaking experiences with the language and they do not have a vocabulary base. If we teach the rules of spelling as a knowledge system, it can demotivate children for learning the language. Therefore, the first and foremost task to help Chinese children learn English is to help them accumulate some English vocabulary and develop preliminary experiences in speaking and listening in meaningful contexts. With more experiences with the language and a collection of English words, the teaching of phonics will facilitate their learning in reading and writing.

As we discussed in Unit 1, children learn better when they are engaged in meaning exploration, when they are involved in both mind and actions with the language.Therefore, when teaching children new English words, the first thing to do is to let children hear the word, understand its meaning with the support of pictures or gestures, and then help them say the word or words out loud. After that, ask them to read and write the word or words down. Remember that it is important to help students accumulate some spoken vocabulary first and develop their listening and speaking skills before helping them with phonics skills to enable them to read and write more effectively through a variety of interesting activities.

5.3.5 What activities are helpful in teaching phonics skills?

TASK 5.3.5

Look at the following suggested activities. What do you think are the purposes? How would you organize them? Can you improve them to better teach phonics? Write your ideas down after each activity.

Activity 1

Listen to the words the teacher says and tick the correct pictures.

Purpose: ______________________________.

Teaching suggestion: ______________________________.

Activity 2

Teach this to your students:

A	says /a/	/a/	/a/	in apple.
(CLAP)	(CLAP)	(CLAP)	(CLAP)	(CLAP)
B	says /b/	/b/	/b/	in book.
(CLAP)	(CLAP)	(CLAP)	(CLAP)	(CLAP)
C	says /k/	/k/	/k/	in cookie.
(CLAP)	(CLAP)	(CLAP)	(CLAP)	(CLAP)

Purpose: ____.

Teaching suggestion: ____________________________________.

Activity 3

Select an object in the room. Think of its initial sound. Tell students: "I spy something that begins with the sound __________."

The first student guess the correct object selects the next object.

Purpose: ____.

Teaching suggestion: ____________________________________.

Activity 4

Give each student a word card and ask them to find friends. For example, ask your students to find friends who have the same vowel in the word they have.

Purpose: ____.

Teaching suggestion: ____________________________________.

Activity 5

Ask students to write simple rhymes using their imaginations and creativity.

Example:

A fat cat has a black hat.

The black hat is in the backpack.

Purpose: ____.

Teaching suggestion: ____________________________________.

Discussion Point

As you have probably noticed, these activities all aim at raising students' phonemic awareness.

Activity 1

This one is designed to help children distinguish the sounds they hear. They are trained to identify meaning of the sounds they hear by matching the sound and the picture. This could be carried out as a whole class activity or group activity. When carried out in groups, it is also a good opportunity to see whether children can pronounce the sounds correctly.

Activity 2

This is called "alphabet chant", a commonly used activity for helping children learn the sound of each letter. When children can say this correctly, they should be able to remember the sounds. What's more, each sound is produced in a word, it is much more meaningful. Teachers can then stimulate children's creativity by asking them to change the words in each line. This could be fun. This activity can be carried out in different ways and for different purposes. Teachers can ask children to say it with action, say it loudly or softly, fast or slowly. It can be used to teach a new sound or to review old sounds.

Activity 3

This is called "I spy". "I spy" is a good activity for teaching pronunciation and vocabulary. In this activity, children need to think of the English name of an object and identify the initial sound in it and see if it is the same as what the teacher requests. It is helpful for establishing connection between sound and letters. This can be done in the whole class or in a small group. It can also be changed to asking children to find something that contains a particular sound or ends with a particular sound.

Activity 4

Children like to play games and this is a fun game for them. Once the instruction is given by the teacher, children should be allowed to walk in the classroom to find their "friends". After small groups have been formed, a report should be given from each group and feedback should be provided. If this is too chaotic, teachers can also organize children to stand in a circle or simply sit in their seats. Each one is given 2-3 flashcards with words on them. The teacher pronounces a sound and those who have the sound in their words should come to the center or stand up and say the words.

Activity 5

Writing Simple rhymes is more challenging to pupils and therefore should be used at a later stage. The teacher can help by eliciting words that contain the rhyme and children can work in groups to put the words together to form meaningful sentences.

There are many more activities teachers can use in teaching phonics and get the students engaged in learning English. For example:

(1) Using songs.

Singing songs together is a good way to raise children's awareness of sound-spelling relations. Choose a song that has rhyming words and repetitive lyrics. Many children's songs have such features. For example, "Ten Little Monkeys" and "Old MacDonald Had A Farm" are easy for children to learn with fairly simple vocabulary and sounds that all children will find interesting to learn. Hold up pictures of animals with words in them as you sing these songs together, so that the students can associate the images with the sounds and the written forms of the words. After singing the same song a few times, pause so your child can sing the lyrics without your help. Then, you can encourage your children to look for words that have similar sounds and spelling. You can also encourage them to make up their own rhyming words in sentences and sing them together to learn and remember more new words.

(2) Using pictures.

Expand your students' English vocabulary with pictures and objects. Use a large picture of a person or maybe a photo of one of your students. Point to parts of the body and say the name aloud. Have your students repeat the words after you a few times. Then point to each part and ask your students to tell you what it is. Gently prompt him if he forgets. Use other pictures and objects such as fruits and vegetables to teach your students new English vocabulary. Then, immediately follow this with the English words to help your child build the association among the sound, meaning, and form of a word.

(3) Using stories to enhance phonics skills.

Using stories to teach your students is an ideal way to build their phonics skills and expand their vocabulary. When you read to your students, they hear new words in the context of the story. This will help them hear the word while understanding its meaning in context. By reading aloud or answering questions based on what they read, they can see the shape of the word. In this way, they are using more of their senses to learn the words. They can also try to act the story out. Incorporating more senses in teaching children to read can improve your students' ability to comprehend and remember the words with ease. As many lower level English stories are written with phonics built in, by asking children to identify as many words that have sound and spelling relations as possible, their phonics skills can be enhanced.

Reading

Reading 5.3.1B

Phonemic Awareness for Young Learners (selected)

By Tsvetelina Harakchiyska

Phonemic awareness

Language learners should possess not only knowledge of the phonological system of the target language, but also the ability to segment and manipulate the sounds of speech skills that are included in **phonemic awareness instruction** which "is more complex than auditory discrimination [i.e. hearing a difference]... [and which] entails a level of analysis of the constituent sounds of a word". Or in other words, students are expected to be able to auditorily discriminate the phonemes within syllables and words in English and recognize and identify single phonemes and their allophones in a word or sentence. Therefore, it can be said that phonemic awareness builds links between auditory sounds and the letters by which they are represented and is related to the structure of words rather than to their meaning. In fact, phonemic awareness provides learners with the abilities to compare and contrast phonemes, to "play" with the sounds of English, to correctly articulate them and increases their "ability of decoding and spelling words and... [of] comprehend[ing] text". That is why, phonemic awareness training accounts for the development of the four skills: reading, writing, listening and speaking.

How to develop phonemic awareness

The basic question that this paper aims to answer is "How can teachers develop phonemic awareness skills in young learners of English?" Teachers of English should take into consideration the following guidelines for planning phonemic awareness activities:

(1) Identify the phoneme awareness task you want to use and select appropriate activities for engaging students in the task. Choose activities that are fun and involve playing rather than drilling.

(2) Focus the attention of learners on the sounds not on the letters. Explain to students that in English one sound may be represented by two or more letters. You may first want to target on the auditory perception of a specific sound and then on its production.

(3) Bear in mind that continuant sounds like /i:/ or /a:/ are easier to manipulate and hear than stop consonants like /p/ or /b/. For example, "When you introduce continuant, exaggerate by holding on them: /r/-/r/-/r/-/r/-/r/-ing; for stop consonants, use iteration (rapid repetition):/k/-/k/-/k/-/k/-/k/-atie".

(4) "When identifying or combining sound sequences, a CV pattern should be used before a VC pattern, followed by a CVC pattern (e.g. pie, egg, red)".

Some of the tasks that I would like to offer correspond to the above mentioned principles and involve more direct instruction in the building of skills in students for phoneme identity and phoneme manipulation.

Task 1 Rhymes

Repetition of the same word endings. This could be used in songs or in poems or silly rhymes. You may also encourage children to create their own new rhymes.

Task 2 Alliteration

Repetition of an initial consonant sound in several words.
E.g. *Six snails sell sodas and snails.*

Task 3 Assonance

Repetition of vowel sounds within words, often combined with rhyme.
E.g. *The leaf, the bean and the peach are all on the beach.*

Task 4 Sound blending/synthesis

- Blending an initial sound onto a remainder of a word—*/l/* + */ait/* = */lait/*.
- Blending syllables of a word together—e.g. Listen to the sounds.What is the word they make?
- Blending isolated phonemes to a word (phoneme counting)—e.g. Listen to this word—*sat*. How many sounds do you hear?

Task 5 Segmentation

Isolation of the sounds in a spoken word by separately pronouncing each one in order. This is one of the most difficult tasks for young learners.

- Syllable—e.g. Listen to this word: *table*. Say it syllable by syllable. (*/tei/...ble*)
- Onset/rime—e.g. Listen to this word: *pan*. Say the first sound in the word and then the rest of the word. (*/p/...an*)
- Phoneme by phoneme—e.g. Listen to this word: *sat*. Say the word sound by sound. How many sounds do you hear?

Task 6 Phonemic manipulation

- *Initial sound substitution*—***mat*** *->* ***sat***
- *Final sound substitution*—***mat*** *->* ***map***
- *Vowel substitution*—***top*** *->* ***tap***
- *Syllable deletion*—Say "*baker*" without "*ba*"
- *Initial sound deletion*—Say "*sun*" without"*s*"

- *Final sound deletion* — Say "*best*" without"*t*"

Some of these tasks may be incorporated into the following activities:

Activity 1 Minimal pairs

Listen to the pairs of words. If they sound the same, write [+]. If they are different, write [–]. (*For example: bag—beg cat—cut too+two fill—feel ice—eyes*)

Note: *The teacher gives out to each learner the "Answer handout". Learners only listen to the pairs of words pronounced by the teacher. They do not see the pairs written. Students only write* [+] *or* [–] *depending on whether they hear the same or different pairs of words.*

Activity 2 Three word combinations

Listen to the words and say which of them are the same:

(1) *year*	*hear*	*hair*
(2) *thin*	*tin*	*thin*
(3) *that*	*that*	*that*
(4) *send*	*sand*	*sand*
(5) *three*	*tree*	*tree*

Note: *Learners only listen to the groups of words pronounced by the teacher. They do not see the groups written. The teacher can either give students the Answer handout presented in activity 1 or ask learners to clap their hands if the words are the same or stump their feet if they are different.*

Activity 3 Count the sounds

Listen to the sentence. How many times do you hear the sound /θ/ in the sentence?

E.g. *My father and mother live together with my brother.*

Martha Smith is an author and an athlete.

There are three trees in the tram.

Note: *This activity focuses the attention of learners on one particular sound that they should identify in the words within the sentence (in the example sentences it is the phoneme /θ/). You can allow students to have the sentences written when they hear them pronounced.*

Activity 4 Rhymes

Write as many words that rhyme with the word as possible:

- grow -> *blow, snow, show, throw*

- pan -> *man, van, ran, plan, can*
- cry -> *fly, try, die, buy*
- beat -> *meat, meet, sweet*
- come -> *some, drum, plum,*

***Note:** Give students only the initial word to which they should write rhymes. You can also add a competitive element and ask students to work in groups. Think of an "award" to the winners!*

Activity 5 Different vowel sound

Read the words and circle the one with the different vowel sound.

(1) *what*	*hot*	*lost*	*salt*
(2) *snow*	*low*	*cow*	*show*
(3) *tea*	*see*	*bee*	*be*
(4) *shoe*	*love*	*true*	*book*
(5) *cheap*	*sheep*	*jeep*	*chips*

***Note:** Students are given a handout with the words written. Each student in class receives the same handout. Students work alone. They are given time to read the groups of words and decide which is the "odd-one-out". If the task is not clear to students, you may give an example to illustrate what you expect them to do.*

Activity 6 Story writing

Write a story with your class using the sound you are learning. (Ask pupils to fill in the gaps with words that have the sound you are learning.)

Our Story

My best friend is an apple. Her name is Ann. She lives in a black hat. She is a happy girl. She has a cat. The cat likes to eat ham. It is a very bad cat.

***Note:** You can also use pictures to help students visualize the story they are writing.*

Activity 7 Word-picture matching

Listen to the word the teacher tells. Tick the picture representing the word you hear.

***Note:** If you are good at drawing you can draw pictures of pairs of words that differ in only sound, e.g.* cat-bat, sun-son, bag-back. *Glue them together on a piece of paper. Each student in the class has the same handout with the pairs of pictures. Say the word representing only one of the objects in each picture pair. Ask students to tick the picture that represents the word they hear.*

Unit 6

Teaching Language Skills

Aims of the unit

In this unit, we are going to focus on the following:

6.1 How to teach listening to children

6.1.1 What do children listen to in their daily life?

6.1.2 What are the principles and models of teaching listening to children?

6.1.3 What do you think of the practice of teaching listening to children?

6.2 How to teach speaking to children

6.2.1 What are the aims and objectives of teaching speaking to children?

6.2.2 What are the principles of teaching speaking to children?

6.2.3 What are information gap activities?

6.2.4 What activities are suitable for listening and speaking?

6.2.5 How effective is the following speaking activity?

6.3 How to teach reading to children

6.3.1 What are the aims and objectives of teaching reading to children?

6.3.2 What are the principles of teaching reading to children?

6.3.3 What can we do to help beginner readers?

6.3.4 An example of teaching reading

6.4 How to use stories for teaching English to children

6.4.1 What are some of the advantages of using stories in language teaching?

6.4.2 How can we use stories in teaching?

6.4.3 What activities can be used for using stories with young learners?

6.4.4 What are some of the features of a good lesson using stories?

6.5 How to teach writing to children

6.5.1 What are the aims and objectives of teaching writing to children?

6.5.2 What can we do to teach writing to children?

6.5.3 What are the principles and models of teaching writing to children?

6.5.4 How can we make the teaching of writing more effective?

6.6 How to integrate the four skills

6.6.1 What are receptive and productive skills?

6.6.2 How can we design an integrated activity?

Language skills include listening, speaking, reading and writing. In primary schools, teachers need to realize that learners are at a young age and are just beginning to learn English. Developing their interest and love for the language is the first step to help them learn the language. Therefore, the activities for developing language skills should be fun and motivating and children need to be encouraged to take part in all sorts of activities and tasks to experience the skills. Moreover, language skills should not be dealt with separately as they are rarely used separately in real life communication. Teachers should think of ways to integrate them in their teaching.

6.1 How to teach listening to children

课例示范：听力教学①

Children listen to different things compared to adults and they also listen for different purposes. In teaching, we need to take these into consideration when designing listening tasks. In general, children should be trained to understand what they hear and show it by acting, drawing or providing simple responses.

6.1.1 What do children listen to in their daily life?

TASK 6.1.1

Brainstorm what children listen to in their daily life.

For example:

- Instructions
  —Come here.
  —Brush your teeth.
  —Pass me the apple, please.
  —
-
-

① 上海市古美学校王敏静授课。

Discussion Point

Long before children are able to produce any language, they have already been very experienced and efficient listeners in their first language. Parents talk to them everyday no matter whether they understand or not. Gradually they can follow instructions like "Smile! Give this to Daddy. Don't touch it, etc." Taking this into consideration, we would find it easy to understand that in English classes, we can offer similar opportunities for our pupils. This means that before we ask children to speak or repeat after the teacher or the recorder, they should be allowed to listen and respond with gestures and actions as a way to show their understanding. This would prepare them for speaking. Furthermore, children like participating in actions and they seldom get bored when they are involved in the activity. Slattery & Willis (2001) point out that if a teacher asks children in English to do something, he/she is using language for a purpose, e.g. the teacher is giving pupils an opportunity to show that they understand; or she/he is giving them an opportunity to acquire the language; or she/he is giving them an opportunity to absorb the sounds and patterns of the language naturally. Therefore, we can conclude that "Listen and do" is a natural and effective way of teaching listening to children.

6.1.2 What are the principles and models of teaching listening to children?

TASK 6.1.2

Please study the following listening activities (Figure 6.1.1) and decide whether they are suitable for teaching listening to children. Discuss with your partner the basic principles for designing listening activities for teaching children.

(a)[①]

(b)[②]

① 选自北京师范大学出版社的义务教育教科书《英语》（三年级起点）三年级下册 Unit 10。
② 选自北京师范大学出版社的义务教育教科书《英语》（三年级起点）四年级上册 Unit 1。

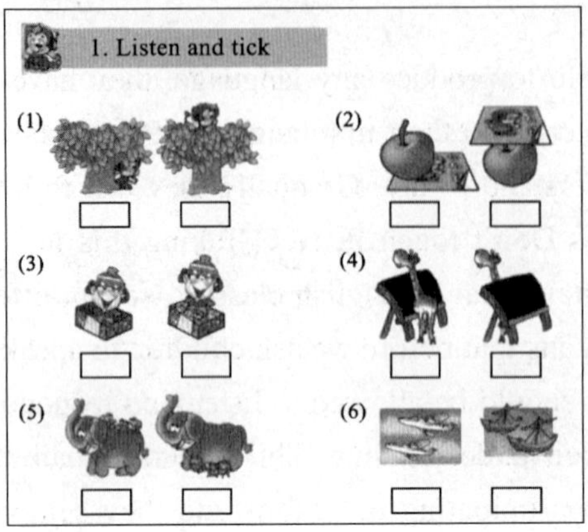

(c)

(d)

(e)[①]

(f)

Figure 6.1.1 Listening activities

① 选自外语教育与研究出版社的义务教育教科书《英语》（三年级起点，主编陈琳）三年级下册 Unit 2。

Discussion Point

Traditionally, the teaching of listening is mainly done in the form of "listen and repeat". Children are asked to listen and repeat after the teacher or the recorder word for word and sentence for sentence. The problem with this kind of listening is that children get bored easily as they can repeat without understanding or thinking.

The listening activities you have seen in Task 6.1.2 are very different from the traditional kind of listening exercises. They all involve children in understanding and in doing things based on listening. For example, they listen and do coloring, numbering, ticking, pointing, or matching. Without understanding and thinking, it will be difficult to complete the tasks required. Moreover, these activities help develop children's real-life listening skills. They practice listening with a clear purpose and they listen to get things done.

The following is a list of other possible listening activities.

A. True or False?

B. Listen and draw.

C. Listen and choose.

D. Listen and discriminate, e.g. "sheep or ship".

E. Listen and follow directions.

F. Listen and order.

G. Listen and compare.

H. Listen and solve the problem.

I. Listen and fill in the table.

J. Listen and finish the dialog.

K. Listen and write.

L. Listen and complete the flow chart.

M. Note-taking.

Some of these activities are easy and simple while some are more challenging. Therefore, some are more suitable for beginners or lower primary pupils and some are better for higher level learners. When pupils reach grades 4, 5 and 6, listening can be made more challenging. E.g. pupils can be asked to do note-taking and problem-solving activities. Also, more attention should be paid to training listening skills.

There are several things to be considered when teaching listening:

- Give children confidence. We should not expect them to always understand every word and they should know this.
- Explain why children have to listen. Make sure they are clear about why they are

listening. This is a good way of preparing children to listen for meaning and for information. E.g. what the main point or purpose of the activity is.

- Help children develop specific strategies for listening. An important strategy that the teacher should teach is "intelligent guesswork". Pupils are used to drawing on their background knowledge to work out something they are not sure of.
- Set specific listening tasks. Try to think of listening in three stages, pre-listening, while-listening, post listening and have activities for each stage.

Two more things to keep in mind include:

- Let children listen to authentic English (such as songs, rhymes, dialogs or short passages with natural English pronunciation and intonation) as much as possible.
- Let children be active in listening. Always remember to involve them in doing something when asking them to listen. For example, children must listen and act out what they hear. In doing such activities, usually it is the teacher who gives instructions. The teacher should remember to give the chance to children when they are ready. Let them take the lead and try to be a little teacher. This will motivate learners more in participating in listening activities.

6.1.3 What do you think of the practice of teaching listening to children?

TASK 6.1.3

Look at the following two extracts taken from real lessons, discuss the effectiveness of each with your partner before looking at the comments provided below.

Extract 1

The teacher is trying to teach prepositions.

T: Victor, put the pencil on the desk. Put the pencil on the desk.

S: (*Does not know what to do.*)

T: Where's the pencil?

S: Pencil.

T: Yes, pencil. Put the pencil on the desk.

S: (*Does not know what to do.*)

T (*to the whole class*): Ok, help him. Here's the pencil. Put the pencil......look at Nick (*a puppet*). 看尼克怎么做。 Put the pencil on the desk. (*The teacher holds Nick's hand and puts the pencil on the desk.*) Understand? 明白吗？

S: (*Nods his head.*)

T: OK, again. 我们再让他试试好不好？

Ss (*the whole class*): 好!

T: Hold the pencil. (Have *the pupil hold the pencil.*) Listen, Victor, put the pencil on the desk.

S: (*Still does not know what to do.*)

T: Put the pencil on the desk. (*Slows down and pronounces every word clearly.*)

S: (*Still does not move.*)

T: Ah, put the pencil on the desk. (*The teacher holds Victor's hand and helps him to complete the action together.*) On the desk, on, on, on.

Extract 2

This teacher has just taught prepositions and in this lesson she is going to play a card game, but she notices that there are a lot of things on pupils' desks so she makes an on-the-spot decision.

T: ...Let's play a card game. Now take out your cards. You all have 5 cards, right?

Ss: Right, yes.

T: OK, listen. Please look at me. ...OK, now show me your paper, this one (holds up the paper). Put your paper on your desk. OK, now next show me your books. Right. Put your books on your desk. OK, now last, show me your pencil box. Put it on your desk, too. OK, Good. ...Now put your cards on the desk, on the left side.

Discussion Point

In the first extract, the teacher tries to ask pupils to listen and do. Obviously this student Victor is a weak one and he finds it difficult to understand the teacher's instruction no matter how many times it has been repeated. The teacher tries to demonstrate the action through a puppet and say the instruction slowly and clearly, but Victor fails to do so. There might be several reasons for this. It could be that the teacher has not demonstrated it clearly before she asks pupils to do this. It could be that Victor is very nervous in front of the whole class. Another reason might be that the sentence is too difficult for him. For example, both *pencil* and *desk* are new words and the structure "put...on" is new and of course "on" is new too. Imagine if we are given a similar instruction in Spanish or any other language that we know very little of, we will find it difficult, too. The suggestion is that teachers should demonstrate more so that children get familiar with the sounds and meaning and gradually build up a link between the sounds they hear with the objects or actions they see. Then we can ask them to listen and do or listen and point.

In the second extract, the teacher creates a very natural and real situation for the pupils to practice the language structure just introduced. She asked them to put things away from their desks and this has not only given pupils a good opportunity to practice the structure and become aware of its functions but also for the teacher to find out whether children have actually understood the language. Please note that she breaks the actions into two steps. As the first step, she asks children to show her the objects, which helps her check whether they have picked up the right things. Then, she asks them to put it in the place that she wants them to. As we can see, the way how activities are organized is important for their purpose and effectiveness.

6.2 How to teach speaking to children

Speaking is fundamental for communication and is essential for developing interpersonal skills. Very often the first impression we give to others is whether we speak the language fluently and clearly. Listening and speaking usually go hand in hand in real communication. For children's language development, listening and speaking are often more important at the beginning as they are the first two language skills for anyone who starts learning the first language. Also, children are interested in communicating with others through listening and speaking. If they are good at listening and speaking, it will give them the confidence in learning the foreign language. Therefore, as teachers, we have the responsibility to prepare children as much as possible to be able to understand and speak English in the real world outside the classroom.

6.2.1 What are the aims and objectives of teaching speaking to children?

TASK 6.2.1

Which of the following do you think are the aims and objectives of teaching speaking to children?

- To know the difference between spoken and written language.
- To be able to communicate with others.
- To be able to repeat after the teacher.
- To be able to answer the teacher's questions.
- To be able to identify different sounds.

Discussion Point

—Is there any difference between teaching speaking to children and to adults?

—What should be the focus when teaching speaking to children?

Obviously, children and adults are quite different in their ways of learning and thinking. Thus, the objectives and methods for teaching children and adults should also be different. Adults are good at making sentences using grammar rules, but they are afraid of losing face in front of others when speaking, so they need a lot of encouragement to speak in public. Children, on the other hand, are not afraid of making mistakes and they love talking, showing off and acting. The problems children encounter are that their emotions and interests are not stable which can be easily influenced by outside factors. When teaching children speaking, teachers need to consider these special features of children and design motivating activities and games. Repetition and answering questions are necessary but should not be the only forms. Instead, teachers should try to make children repeat in different forms with a focus on meaning as repetition is a useful way for memorization. Besides, grammar rules though important, should not be taught explicitly and forced into children's head. It is better for teachers to let children experience the language with meaning first before discussing grammar rules. Identifying sounds is vital but again should not be done mechanically. What is important is to involve children actively in speaking activities and encourage them to use the language creatively. Helping children experience the target language and use it to communicate with their friends is the key to successful development of speaking skills.

6.2.2 What are the principles of teaching speaking to children?

课例示范：speaking①

There are some principles that teachers need to consider when designing speaking activities. Let us look at some sample speaking activities. What are their shared features? Do you think children will like them? Why? Do the following tasks and then summarize the principles for designing speaking activities with a partner.

TASK 6.2.2A

Imagine you are going to organize a party. You need to find out about your classmates' special abilities. Please interview your classmates and find at least one person for each item.

Find someone who is able to...	name
cook	
sing English songs	
dance	
decorate the classroom	
draw beautiful pictures	

① 上海师范大学附属外国语小学黄春霞授课。

continued

Find someone who is able to...	name
write beautifully	
host a party	
make good use of money and buy food for our class	
play instruments	

TASK 6.2.2B

Please reflect on the task you just did with a partner and discuss the benefits of using this type of activity for teaching speaking.

Discussion Point

In the above activity, children are using the language for getting information. And because they are involved in finding out what their classmates are able to do for the class party, they focus on meaning rather than form. During the process of completing the task, the pupils also integrate listening and speaking skills. Activities like this can easily help teachers successfully create a need for using English in the classroom.

The most important features of good communicative listening and speaking activities include:

— learner-centered — interactive — meaning-focused
— collaborative — purposeful — task-based

6.2.3 What are information gap activities?

TASK 6.2.3

Study the following two activities. What is the shared feature? Do you think children will like them? Why? Discuss with your partner.

(1) Spot the differences (Figure 6.2.1). Work in pairs and look at the two pictures very

carefully. Student A should not look at Student B's picture and vice versa. Each one of you should describe your own picture to the other so that you can find out the 5 differences between the two pictures. Please use "In my picture, there's/there're..."

(2) Work in pairs (Figure 6.2.2). Each of you will get a map of Green Tree Town. There are many buildings on the map, some have names, some don't. You need to ask your partner to tell you the missing names so that you can write them down on the buildings on your map. Your partner would also ask you about the missing names on his/her map. Write down all the names of the buildings. In the end, both of you will get a complete map. But before the end of the activity, do not show your map to your partner.

(a)

(b)

Figure 6.2.1 Spot the differences

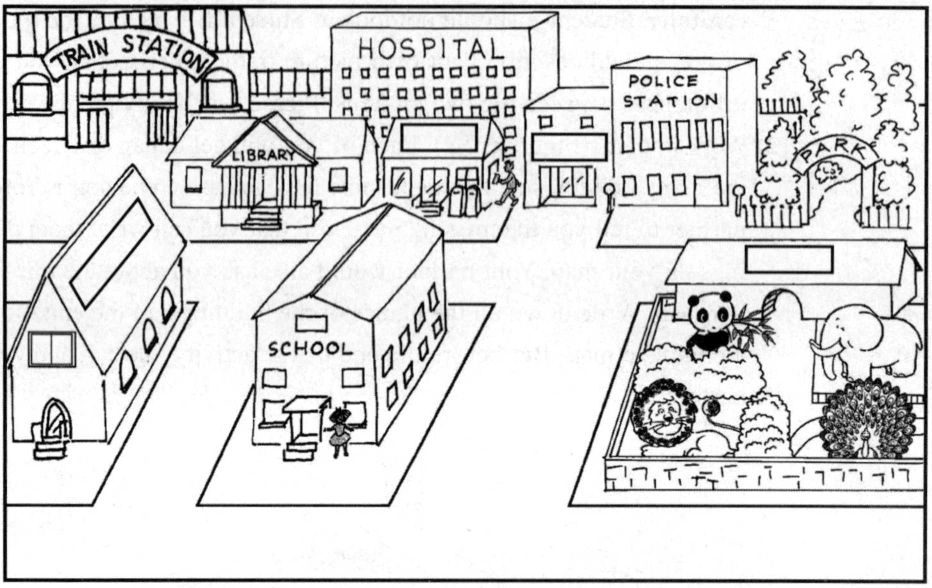

(a)

(b)

Figure 6.2.2 A map of Green Tree Town

Discussion Point

Please read **Reading 6.2.3** and try to answer the following questions:

—What kind of activities are information gap activities?

—How can teachers create an information gap?

—What are the benefits of using information gap activities?

—What are the characteristics of a successful speaking activity?

—How can teachers satisfy the criteria of successful speaking activities?

—What are the possible problems in organizing information gap activities?

6.2.4 What activities are suitable for listening and speaking?

TASK 6.2.4A

Work in pairs and think of as many listening and speaking activities as possible that you can use in the classroom. Make a list and then discuss with another pair.

TASK 6.2.4B

Imagine that you are going to teach one of the following three topics to your pupils along with their relevant structures and vocabulary in a textbook. Work individually to design a series of listening and speaking activities. Please use **Reading 6.2.4** as a reference. Work on your instructions very carefully. Then work in groups to try them out and discuss how they can be improved with other group members.

(1) weather

—What's the weather like today?

—It's sunny/cloudy/windy...

(2) clothes

A: Can I help you?

B: I want a skirt.

A: What about this one? It's beautiful.

B: I like it. It's my favorite color. How much is it?

A: It's 50 yuan.

B: I'll take it.

A: Here you are.

B: Thank you.

(3) animals

—What's your favorite animal?

—My favorite animal is dog.

Discussion Point

Listening and speaking are very important skills for beginners. Children learning their native language begin by understanding through listening. They comprehend the language long before they can speak it. With primary school pupils, it is better that we let them listen and understand the language first. Let them speak gradually when they feel ready and comfortable with it. In fact, listening and speaking are always used inseparably in real life situations. However, listening is an important basis for speaking. Reading 6.2.4. has provided you with some listening and speaking activities you can use in the classroom. As we all understand, to tell you how to fish is much more useful than just to give you fish. Therefore, we hope these activities are just something triggering more of your own brilliant ideas. In your future teaching, there are many other factors you need to consider before planning your lessons such as learner differences and learner needs. You need to plan your lessons according to your children's needs and your teaching contexts. Be creative, imaginative and practical.

6.2.5 How effective is the following speaking activity?

TASK 6.2.5

The following is an extract of a speaking activity. Read it and discuss its effectiveness in developing pupils' speaking skills.

T: OK. I put some toys here, then you touch it, then others to guess what's in it, OK?... Mary, come here. OK now, first you touch it. Tell me do you know what it is? (S1 whispers the answer to the T) OK. Who want to try to guess it? You must say "Is it a...?" "Is it...?" For example, if you guess, is it a ball? Is it a teddy bear? Is it a car? OK, now Lora you try.

S2: Teddy bear.

T : OK, say the sentence. Is it a teddy bear?

S2: Is it a teddy bear?

S1 : No.
T : No, it's not. OK. Another one. Cyndy.
S3 : It...(Teacher waits for 3 seconds.)
T : Is it a...?
S3 : Is it a doll?
S1 : No, it's not.
T : No, it's not. OK. Another one. OK, Diana.
S4 : Is it a truck?
S1 : Yes.
T : Yes, it is. OK, have a look. Oh, what a beautiful truck!

Discussion Point

This is an information gap activity but it is done in the form of a guessing game. The children who ask questions to guess what it is are eager to make a correct guess, so they try very hard to think of the words they know. The student who answers the questions has to listen carefully to judge whether his/her classmates' guess is right or wrong.

This activity seems to be easy but the way it is organized needs to be improved. Instead of giving long explanations to tell children how to guess or ask and answer, the teacher could demonstrate to the students by saying: "OK. Look, there are some animal toys in this bag. But what are they? Let me try to touch and make a guess (T tries to touch one animal inside the bag). OK, now I know what it is. Is it a teddy bear? No, it isn' t. Who can make a guess? Is it a...?" Then children will try to guess in the same way the teacher demonstrates it.

课例示范：
Let's talk①

The task can also be adapted for higher level pupils. The teacher can ask the one who touches the toy to describe it for other students to guess. For example, "it has four legs and a short tail". Also, other students can be encouraged to ask different kinds of questions to find clues about it, e.g. "Does it have wings? Can it jump?" etc.

6.3 How to teach reading to children

6.3.1 What are the aims and objectives of teaching reading to children?

We read to gain pleasure or get information. For children, reading for pleasure is the

① 广东省东莞市常平镇教育管理中心张春艳授课。

most important element. How to raise and keep their interest in reading is a big challenge for teachers. Meanwhile, reading involves a variety of content among which the following are particularly important for children:

— Recognizing the script of the language, e.g.title, cover page, concept of a sentence, punctuation, capital and small letters, etc.
— Building links between words, sounds and their meanings.
— Raising phonemic awareness by reading.
— Understanding main ideas.
— Understanding relations between parts of the text.
— Predicting the content or ending.

When children reach a higher level of English, they may also be helped to develop more complicated reading skills, such as understanding the implied meaning and recognizing cohesion devices, etc. The key issue teachers need to keep in mind is that we teach reading not to test children and make them afraid of it but to help them love it and know how to read.

TASK 6.3.1A

Look at Figure 6.3.1 and write down what you think it is. Write as many as possible. Then share them with your group members.

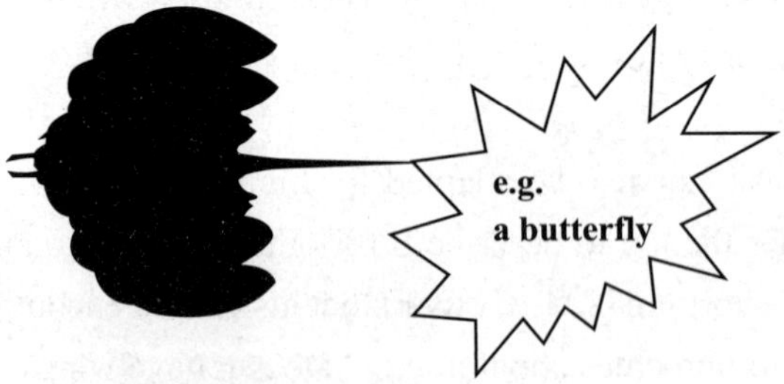

Figure 6.3.1 What is it?

TASK 6.3.1B

Look at Figure 6.3.2 and tell each other how many people you can see in this picture. Then try switching from one to another as quickly as possible.

Figure 6.3.2 How many people in the picture?

Discussion Point

From the above two tasks we understand that people see things differently. Even when we look at the same picture, we may get different images. In fact, the picture in Task 6.3.1A is only a drop of ink. This activity mirrors the reading process very well. When the author is writing a piece of text, he/she may have an idea of what it is about. But when the readers read it, they may interpret it very differently. Does it matter what the original idea is? The answer is no. As long as readers enjoy reading the piece of writing, it becomes a pleasant and successful reading experience.

People have great imaginations. If they are given time and chances, they can be very creative and enthusiastic. Reading is the same because it is also a mental activity. If teachers want to involve children in a reading activity, they should provide them with opportunities to guess and predict based on their experience or imagination. For example, if the story is about why turtles do not have smooth shells, teachers may ask pupils to provide as many reasons as possible. Then when they read the story, they will get interested because they are eager to find out whether their predictions are true or not. As teachers, we should try our best to cultivate children's imaginations and encourage them to show or express their own points of views on understanding about the things they read. For example, when they read "Three bears and Goldilocks", they should be encouraged to share their opinions on the bears and the little girl. Some of them might say the little girl is rude to go into someone's house without permission. Some of them might say she should not be afraid of going out again just because of this experience. She should be braver and well prepared for the adventure, etc. Different interpretations of the same story should be encouraged so that children develop their own reasoning abilities. And because of the different points of view, children will get motivated and excited about reading. The important thing for children is to be motivated to read, to enjoy reading and to learn how to read with understanding.

6.3.2 *What are the principles of teaching reading to children?*

Teaching children to read in English sounds quite ambitious. How can children who know very little vocabulary and very few structures be able to read in English? In the past, we often focused on the teaching of listening and speaking. In fact, children start to "read" in their native language long before they go to school. They read picture stories and all kinds of children's books with their parents. This type of reading becomes a very important experience for children's later reading in school or in life. As for learning another language in school, children have already had the experiences of reading in their native language. What's more, no one can avoid written language in their everyday life. So in English classrooms teachers do not need to avoid reading either. However, when we teach reading to children, there are certain things we need to bear in mind. For example, what kinds of texts are suitable for children, in other words, what do they read in their real life? Only when children are given appropriate reading materials can they enjoy reading and learn how to read successfully. The things children often read in their life can be modified for the purpose of teaching. We should not confine reading materials to texts only. Children can be offered different kinds of reading materials such as road signs, posters, labels, cards, and simple picture stories so that they can accumulate reading experience.

TASK 6.3.2A

What can be used to teach reading in English? Please check the things and explain why and how you're going to use them.

picture stories
cartoons books posters newspapers
postcards E-mails poems
novels greeting cards letters magazines
street signs instructions song lyrics
messages

TASK 6.3.2B

Figure 6.3.3 taken from primary English textbooks. Do they seem attractive to children? Study them carefully. What are some of the common features that you can find about them? Can you think of other kinds of reading activities besides these?

(a)①

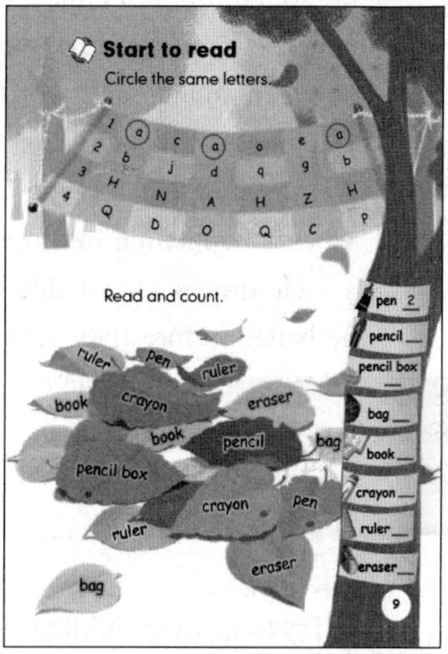

(b)②

(c)③

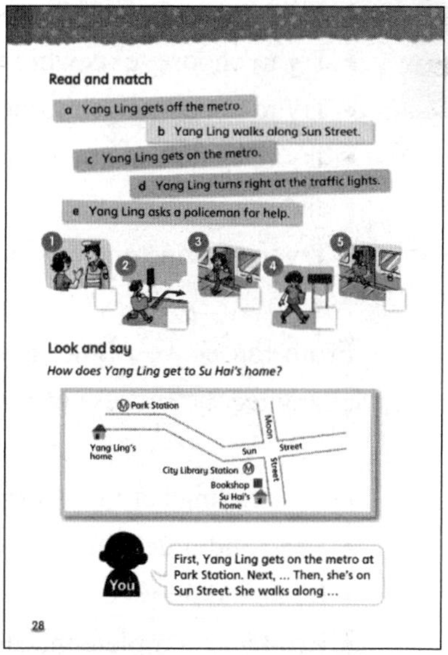

(d)④

Figure 6.3.3 Examples of textbooks

① 选自北京师范大学出版社的义务教育教科书《英语》三年级下册 Unit 10。

② 选自人民教育出版社的义务教育教科书《英语》（PEP）三年级上册 Unit 1。

③ 选自外语与教育研究出版社的义务教育教科书《英语》（三年级起点，主编陈琳）四年级上册 Unit 2。

④ 选自译林出版社的义务教育教科书《英语》（三年级起点）三年级下册 Unit 2。

Discussion Point

Both reading and listening are receptive skills. Teachers need to check whether children understand what they read. To do so, it is better for teachers to ask children to do something after they read a text. For example, children can be asked to color, count, mime, or match, etc. The main purpose is to help them build up a relationship between sounds and words as well as the print and meaning. At an early stage of teaching reading, children often need visual support when they read. So, we can start our teaching by drawing children's attention to some pictures and have them guess what is happening in those pictures or what they can see in those pictures. By doing so, children's knowledge about the topic and familiar words and structures can be activated before they actually start reading. When we teach very young children to learn to read, they can be encouraged to recognize the whole word first, and learn the letters and spelling later.

When trying to teach reading to children, we might want to pay attention to the following things.

- Try to involve children as much as possible by asking or eliciting answers from them.
- Try to use different types of texts with your pupils.
- Try to arouse their interest in reading.
- Try to choose texts which contain repeated structures or vocabulary.
- Try to encourage children to think and to learn more knowledge of other fields.
- Try to include some basic reading skills such as predicting and guessing, skimming and scanning, etc.
- Try to provide enough guidance and assistance.

From these, you must have noticed that involvement, interest and encouragement guarantee the success of reading.

Other reading activities include:

- Read and order (pictures or sentences).
- Read and draw.
- Read and complete the story.
- Read and retell.
- Read and correct mistakes.
- Read and complete a flowchart or a table.
- Read and act it out.

6.3.3 What can we do to help beginner readers?

TASK 6.3.3

What are these teachers trying to do? Why do they do this? Do you think it is necessary? Please share your opinions with your classmates.

Teacher Talk 1

- Jessie, that's a great T-shirt you're wearing today. It has words on it. What do you think those words say?
- Look at the sign above the door. It says, "Exit." What do you think that word means?

Teacher Talk 2

- We need to make a sign for the fish tank. Let's see, can you help me? "F-I-S-H", we need to start with "F."
- Wow, you made a castle. Do you want to make a sign for your castle? Do you want the sign to say "Tim and Harry's castle"? OK, T-I-M, (say slowly, sounding out the word) "T" (say the sound) we need to start with a "T" (say and write the letter).
- We use this door to come in and this one to go out. These signs I've made say, "In" and "Out" .

Teacher Talk 3

- I'm going grocery shopping later, so I wrote this list of the things I need to buy. Can you tell me how many things are on the list?
- I want your parents to know how well you're doing, so I'm sending them an e-mail.
- Here's today's newspaper. I like to read papers every morning so that I know what's happening in the world.
- Let's go over to the computer and see if we can find out some more information about butterflies.
- Look at this menu I brought from my favorite restaurant. Here are some pictures of their desserts. This one looks good. It is a cake. Let's read it. C-A-K-E (sound out slowly).

Discussion Point

As we mentioned previously, nobody can avoid written words in our life. We cannot just let children listen and speak. They have the desire to read when they see signs of written language around them. Therefore, teaching reading should be brought up as early as possible. As an English teacher, we want our children to:

- Recognize words in their surroundings.
- Understand that words carry meaning.
- Know that words are used for many purposes.
- Learn about words through experimental writing.

However, we cannot force children to read. And we do not want to make children lose their interest in reading. We can encourage children to try to read by showing them the following examples in the classroom:

- Books and other printed materials for children to look at and pretend to read.
- Photographs and pictures with captions and labels.
- Posters, calendars, and bulletin board displays.
- Labels and signs for special areas in the classroom.
- Menus, order pads, and play money.
- Recipes, empty food cartons, and marked plastic measuring spoons and cups.
- Old telephone books, memo pads, envelopes, and address labels.
- Price tags, stickers, and large paper bags (with printed words).
- Toy cars, trucks and construction equipment (with printed words).

In task 6.3.3, the teacher is doing exactly these. He/She makes use of objects in the classroom and every opportunity to introduce the idea of reading and show all sorts of reading materials. With the help of these real materials, children will get the impression that English is an existing language in their life. It is not difficult for them to see the written language and it is very useful if they understand the language. They will be motivated to learn to read more in English. Besides, they get excited when they are able to read English books. Meanwhile, they can develop the ability for life-long learning during the process of learning to read. Once they know how to read in English, they can get what they are interested in through reading.

6.3.4 An example of teaching reading

TASK 6.3.4

The following is an example showing how to teach reading to children. The teacher is teaching Clive Taylor's story book *Presents*. How did she handle this? Could you work with your partner and find out the beliefs underneath?

<table>
<tr><th>Book</th><th>Teacher and children</th></tr>
<tr><td>
</td><td>T: What can you give to a turtle?
C: A scarf!
T: Good. Why?
C: Because it has a long neck. It feels cold.
T: Very kind of you. What else?
C: A hat!
T: Right! Why?
C: It has no hair!

The teacher may go on asking the kind of gifts we can give to a turtle. Write them down.</td></tr>
<tr><td>
</td><td>T: Look! Some skates for the turtle! Why?
C: It can move fast. It will run faster than a rabbit!
T: Yes. How many skates do we need to buy?
C: One, two, three, four! Four skates!
T: Clever boy! What color are the skates?
C: Green.
T: Do you want to give the turtle green skates?</td></tr>
<tr><td>
</td><td>T: What's this?
C: A big fish.
T: No, it's a seal. It lives in the water. What can you give to a seal?
C: Goggles.
T: Good idea. Anything else?

The teacher keeps on eliciting more answers from them.</td></tr>
<tr><td>
</td><td>T: What is the present?
C: A straw?
T: Looks like a straw. It is a snorkel. Why does the seal need this?
C: It can breathe under the water.
T: Very good. Do you need a snorkel for swimming?</td></tr>
</table>

Discussion Point

Notice that in the above example the experience of reading is like a conversation between the teacher and the children. The teacher invites the children's comments and leaves space for their imaginations. She listens to what they say patiently and encourages them to make sense of what is happening in the story. She tells the children new information that will help them understand and enjoy the book more.

Reading to young children is important because it helps them acquire the information and skills they need to succeed in school and life. By reading to them, we are helping them:

- to become familiarized with the knowledge of printed letters and words and the relationship between sound and print.
- to learn the meaning of many words.
- to understand how books work and to experience a variety of writing styles.
- to understand better the world in which they live.
- to become aware of the difference between written language and everyday conversation.
- to get the pleasure of reading.

6.4 How to use stories for teaching English to children

6.4.1 What are some of the advantages of using stories in language teaching?

TASK 6.4.1

What is the role of stories in language learning for children? Write at least three reasons for using stories in the language classroom. Are there any problems then?

Reasons for using stories in the language classroom
• • • •
Problems or difficulties for using stories in the language classroom
• • • •

The benefit of using stories in the language classroom is quite obvious. By using stories as learning materials, children can learn the language in a more natural way. Stories usually provide comprehensible input based on meaningful context from which children can induce the language and its meaning from the input they receive. Children tend to identify with story characters and can become personally and emotionally involved in the story. They react to stories with laughers, sadness, disappointment, and anticipation (Brewster, Ellis, & Girard, 1992). The input is likely to lay the foundations for meaningful output as children will engage in post-listening or post-reading activities as well as language-related activities. As we can see, stories not only help promote children's linguistic development, but also cognitive, social and affective development.

Discussion Point

Your list of reasons for using stories may include the following:

- Learners love stories and feel at ease with them.
- Story language is often repetitive. With the help of pictures learners can easily understand the meaning.
- It helps learners learn the language with a focus on meaning instead of just form.
- Stories often go beyond language learning for social, emotional, and moral development.
- Stories make a nice change from the normal language learning activities.

Children enjoy listening to stories in their native language and this is a familiar experience for children to be introduced to a foreign language. The following are some further reasons identified by Brewster, Ellis, & Girard (1992) for teachers to use stories.

- Stories are motivating and fun and can help develop positive attitude towards the foreign language and language learning, and create a desire to continue learning.
- Stories exercise imagination. Children can become personally involved in a story as they identify with the characters and try to make their own interpretation of the narrative and illustrations. The imaginative experience helps them develop their own creative powers.
- Stories are a useful tool in linking fantasy and imagination with the child's real world. They provide a way of enabling children to make sense of their everyday life and forge links between home and school.
- Listening to stories in class is a shared social experience. Reading and writing are often individual activities; story telling provokes a shared response of laughter, sadness, excitement and anticipation which is not only enjoyable but can help build up the child's confidence and encourage social and emotional development.
- Children enjoy listening to stories over and over again. This frequent repetition allows certain language items to be acquired while others are being overtly reinforced. Many

stories also contain the natural repetition of key vocabulary and structures. Repetition also encourages participation in the narrative, thereby providing a type of "hidden" pattern practice in a meaningful context. Following meaning and predicting language are important skills in language learning.

- Having children listen to stories allows the teacher to revise or introduce new vocabulary and sentence structures by exposing them to language in varied, memorable, and familiar contexts, which will enrich their thinking and gradually enter their own language production.
- Listening to stories develops the child's listening and concentrating skills via:
  —Visual clues, for example, pictures and illustrations.
  —Their prior knowledge of how language works.
  —Their general knowledge.
- Stories create opportunities for developing continuity in children's learning since they can be chosen to consolidate learning in other school subjects across the curriculum.
- Learning English through stories can lay the foundations for secondary school learning in terms of basic language functions and structures, vocabulary, and language learning skills.

However, there might also be potential problems with using stories in the classroom. The most recognized one would be the discipline problem as children may get over-excited with stories and the teacher may find it hard to control the excitement. Besides, there are teachers who are not confident with their own English, and sometimes, appropriate visual aids might not be available for some stories. Therefore, it requires a good preparation beforehand to ensure the success of using stories in the classroom. For example, the teacher may need to practice telling the story to a mirror before telling it to the class, or to another teacher if possible, making gestures and adding sound effects whenever necessary. If the learners really enjoy the story, they would not notice that they are actually learning the language and there might not be any discipline problems.

6.4.2 How can we use stories in teaching?

TASK 6.4.2

If you were to use a story with your students, how would you do it? The following is a list of things that a teacher can do for using stories in the language classroom. Read and decide how you are going to interweave them into a story telling lesson. Tick the activities that you might choose to do from the list and order them into steps of teaching. Then, discuss your choices and procedures in a group of four.

Preparation

- Prepare a simplified outline of the story in English.
- Practice telling the story to the class, paying attention to voice, intonation, pace, and body language.
- Make large pictures of the story for the whole class to share by using multimedia technology.
- Think of a pre-story activity, for example, using pictures to teach the key vocabulary.

Delivery of the lesson

- Ask children if they know the story in Chinese.
- Ask children to look at the pictures and tell the class or tell each other what they know or see—the people, the setting, the objects, and the possible storyline.
- Tell the story while pointing at the relevant pictures.
- Tell the story, while asking children to observe pictures and to think and predict what will happen next.
- Tell the story the second time, but pause at places for children to join in.
- Point at the pictures and provide only the beginning words, let children say the rest of the lines.
- Find volunteers to take part in the story telling.
- Make masks for children to act out the story in groups.
- Ask children what they like about the story or what they have learned from it.

Others

- ____

Discussion Point

The phrase "tell a story" is somewhat misleading, that's why the phrase "use stories" is used instead as the title of this chapter. Since we have used stories for language learning purposes, there should be more than just telling a story from the beginning to the very end. We need to involve children both physically and mentally, to enjoy the story, to develop their cognitive ability and their overall language ability as well. In achieving these, different teachers may employ different methods and activities. However, good and successful use of a story should include the following procedures.

- Activate children's background knowledge and relate the story to their experience. The background knowledge helps readers understand better.
- Pre-teach some key vocabulary. A story may contain quite a number of new structures and vocabulary. Some teachers believe that we have to teach our students all the

new words before they can understand the story. This is not necessarily true. In fact, we do not need to pre-teach every new word or structure before reading. If we do so, we would deprive children's opportunities to take a risk and explore the meaning by themselves. Therefore, we only need to pre-teach those words which are central for comprehension. Other words can be left for students to guess and learn while reading the story by taking advantage of the clues that are available in a story.

- When telling a story, have children observe and understand the situation where language occurs. Try to give children opportunities to express their feelings, ideas and opinions, so that they can observe and think, and experiment with the language. In this way, you are actually making the story interactive, leading them into the story. All these make them active participants instead of passive receivers who seemingly listen to you but actually do not hear anything. At this stage, the focus should be placed on meaning.
- Children have their own ways to understand meaning. Pictures provide very good context for them and besides, the teacher's body language and the use of the voice or intonation can also help them understand. So when using stories, do not READ them but TELL them. Use your voice to "color" it (Tann, 1991) and give extra emphasis to key words or key points.
- After the first round of presentation where children feel the language either by listening, reading or watching video, it is time to go around the story again with more detailed information. You might need to clarify the meaning of some vocabulary or certain sentences, explain what happened and why certain things happened in the main plot. You may also ask questions to check their understanding, or their opinions and comments over certain things in the story. At this step the focus is still on meaning but the language forms are foreshadowed and children are drawn to NOTICE the language forms embedded in the discourse.
- So far, the children will have achieved comprehension and understanding of the story. They have also become aware of certain sentence structures and their meanings and this will lead them to reflect upon the language system. Then they need time to consume and internalize all these input. What you need to do is to give children a break, give them time to read the story by themselves, exchange their ideas, feelings or opinions to each other. Do not think this step is a waste of time. They need it.
- Finally, it comes to the extension stage where you could ask children to role-play, retell, or do follow-up activities based on the story. Then you can put the story telling to an end temporarily until the next lesson, where you are going to focus more on the language embedded in the story.

6.4.3 What activities can be used for using stories with young learners?

Using stories in the language classroom does not simply mean telling the story or having fun. We need to design different activities to help children practice using the language.

TASK 6.4.3

Choose a story that is appropriate for classroom teaching and then think about what kind of activities you can use with it. Write all the possible activities in the space provided and then compare your list with your partner's.

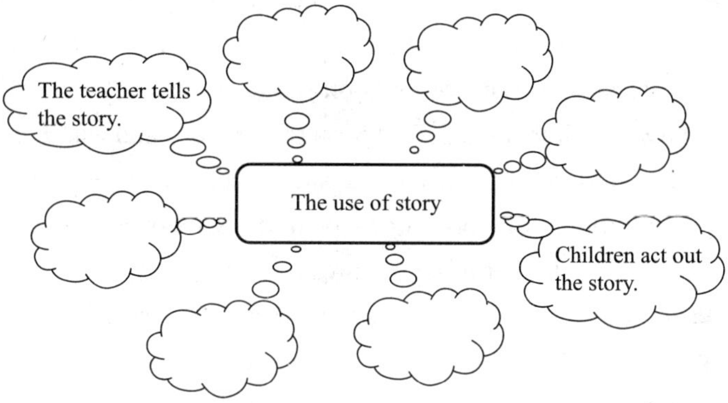

Discussion Point

There are many different activities which can be used with stories. Figure 6.4.1 Shows several possibilities when using stories in the classroom.

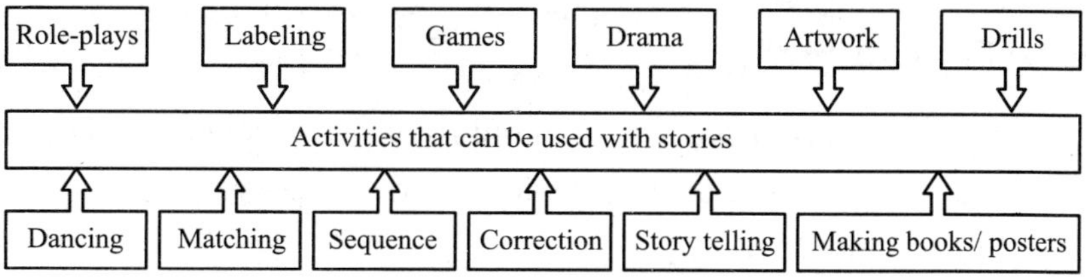

Figure 6.4.1 Activities that can be used with stories

The following suggestions are examples showing how we can design different activities for using stories (adapted from Phillips, 1993:18). Please note that some of the activities are simpler and some require more language. You can decide which activities are best for your students or try to adapt them to meet your needs. For more techniques for using stories in teaching children, please go to **Reading 6.4.3**.

- Show children a picture with all the key words around it. Ask children to find the right picture and match it with the right word.
- Teacher tells the story while children listen and mime out the actions based on understanding.
- Give children scrambled sentences from the story, ask them to rearrange them in the right order. You can do several sets of these and put them in different envelopes for group work if you are working with a fairly large class to see which group gets the story done first and then ask them to read out loud their stories to the whole class.
- For a beginning class, you can give picture stories in a different order, and ask children to put them in the right order according to the story they have heard and talk about the pictures.
- In groups, give each child a picture of a part of the story. Each child is to describe his/her own picture and the whole group can put the story together.
- Give children the story in split sentences and ask them to match the halves.
- Give children a gapped version of the story and ask them to fill in the gaps.
- Get children to dramatize the story, perhaps using puppets.
- Get children to work in groups to draw their own pictures of the story and then write simple captions for the pictures.
- Put a few vocabulary cards together, take one of them away, and then show the rest of the cards and ask children which card is missing.
- Write the story with some wrong information in it. Ask children to read it and correct the wrong information.

6.4.4 What are some of the features of a good lesson using stories?

TASK 6.4.4

The following are two examples of using stories in language teaching. Compare them and try to identify some features of a good lesson using stories in the classroom.

Example 1

Topic: *Tec and the Hole*（大猫英语分级阅读，2 级）

Level: students in grade 2

Length: 45 minutes

Teacher：Ren Yanzhu

一、教材分析

大猫英语分级阅读中的故事主题丰富，内容有趣。其中，科普类故事能帮助学生增长见识；许多有寓意的小故事能加强对学生的思想教育，教会学生做人、做事。

本课是第 2 级的第 1 个故事，故事的主人公是 Tec 侦探。故事由 Tec 发现的一个坑引出了一个非常有趣的小故事。最终 Tec 发现是他的小狗挖了这个坑，更为有趣的是小狗一直跟随着 Tec 寻找坑的主人。

本课作为故事学习的第 1 课，侧重培养学生对故事内容的预测能力和理解能力。本课教学借助图片，让学生预测故事的发展，培养学生用英语思维的能力；借助故事情节，培养学生的情感态度和价值观。

二、学情分析

本课的教学对象是我校二年级（一）班的学生，学生有一个学期的“X 计划”阅读经验，他们对故事非常感兴趣，大部分学生能够关注封面、题目、作者和绘者信息、正文图片，并通过图片提取信息，预测故事情节发展。

三、教学内容

核心词汇：who、dig、hole、rabbit、squirrel、girl、man。

阅读策略：（1）关注封面上的图片、作者和绘者等信息。

（2）借助图片信息，预测故事情节发展。

四、教学目标与教学重难点

（一）教学目标

在本课学习结束时，学生能够：

- 通过观察图片，分析故事中不同坑洞的特征，合理猜测挖洞人。
- 借助图片描述故事。
- 尝试评价故事中的主人公并表达个人观点。

（二）教学重点

在图片的帮助下预测故事情节，读懂整个故事。

（三）教学难点

在预测故事情节时，通过观察、对比图片，合理推测故事结局。

五、教学用具

自制课件，准备配套音频、板书、示意图、卡片、侦探帽、放大镜、“Who dug the holes?”活动纸。

六、教学过程

（一）导入

1. 教师与学生问候，如：

Hi, boys and girls. Glad to see you again.

How are you today?

What’s the weather like today?

It’s a nice day. We can play outside.（呈现户外场景）

2. 师生分享场景图片。

教师引导学生观察图片，提问：Look, what can you see in the picture?

学生观察图片，说出看到的景物：I can see... (trees, flowers, a boy, a park...)

教师根据学生说出的景物提一些相关问题，与学生进行简短交流。

交流举例：

当学生说出 tree 时，教师回答：Maybe there are some animals in the tree. But we can't see them.

当学生说出 flowers 时，教师提问：What color are they?

当学生说出 a boy 时，教师提问：Where is the boy? What is he doing? Do you like to play on the swing ?

教师指着场景回答：It's a colorful and beautiful place, right? The story happens here.

【设计意图】与学生进行有关生活实际的交流，拉近与学生的距离，并引出故事发生的场景。

3. 呈现关于 hole 的图片，帮助学生理解 hole 的意思。

教师引导学生发现地上的一个坑，说："Wow, there is a hole."。然后教师简单谈论一下坑，引导学生进行初步猜测："What do you want to know about the hole? Do you have any questions? Wow! Yes! Who dug this hole?"。之后，教师引出故事主人公 "Look! A man is coming to help people. Who is that man?（His name is Tec.）"。教师拿出侦探帽戴在自己头上，说："Now，I'm Tec. I can help you."。教师引导学生迅速进入角色，说："Who wants to be Tec?"。学生戴着帽子，手拿放大镜，体验当大侦探的感觉。

【设计意图】让学生真正体验当大侦探的感觉，戴上帽子，拿着放大镜到坑边去观察，激发学生参与、探究、体验的兴趣。

（二）阅读准备

1. 教师呈现动画帮助学生理解 dig—dug。

T: Tec went to find out who dug this hole. 教师贴图片（hole），呈现动画（dig）。教师在黑板上贴图：Who dug this hole? 提问：Now, you are Tec. Who wants to try?

2. 了解文本信息。

教师出示读物，带领学生了解封面、书名、作者和绘者。

提问：

Do you want to read the story?

What is the title? The story is called *Tec and the Hole*.（在黑板上贴图）

Who wrote the story? Who drew the pictures?

【设计意图】学生学会认识封面、标题、作者以及绘者等，能够观察主题图，为预测故事奠定基础。

（三）图片环游

1. 猜测故事情节。

教师引导学生猜测故事情节："Who dug this hole?" "Can you guess?" "Why do you say so?"。教师呈现句型："Was it the… " "Now, let's search with Tec."。

【设计意图】激发学生已有生活经验及认知，让学生思考可以挖洞的人或动物，大胆猜测是谁挖的洞。鼓励学生说出理由，引导学生进行逻辑推理（可以用中文）。

2. 根据图片信息进行合理推测。

学生在教师的引导下进一步推测是谁挖了这个洞（课件呈现放大镜在寻找的图片，放大镜停留在兔子身上）。

提问：

What do you think? Can the rabbit dig the hole?

What's the rabbit's hole like? Let's have a look.

教师呈现兔子洞的图片，引导学生观察兔子洞："The rabbit's hole is very deep." "They can go into the hole to protect themselves."。

教师用兔子洞的图片做对比，提问："Is it deep enough?"（明显比较浅）。

教师提问："What's your idea?"。学生得出结论，好像不是兔子挖的。

教师故作疑惑状："Who dug this hole?"。学生推测是谁挖的。

教师再次呈现放大镜搜索的图片，放大镜停在松鼠处，让学生学习 squirrel（松鼠）的读音。

教师提问：" What do you think about the squirrel?"，课件呈现松鼠在树上的图片。

教师提问：" There is a squirrel in the tree. It lives in the tree. But it can dig the hole near the tree. Why?"。

课件呈现松鼠和洞的放大照片，教师说："Because it can put the food into the hole."。

对比之前发现的洞，教师提问："Was it the squirrel?"（学生推测）。

教师："But Tec is not sure. So he searches again."，继续播放课件，放大镜停在小姑娘那里。

提问：

What's your idea?

学生观察图片并发表自己的想法："The girl is digging. She is digging the sand for fun."。

3. 教师引导学生认真观察图片。

学生和教师一起发现线索："Wow, there is a man. He is carrying a spade."。

教师呈现男子挖坑的图片，提问："What's your idea? Was it the man?"。学生大多认为是他挖了这个坑。

【设计意图】教师通过人人都是大侦探的猜测活动，激发学生积极探究、积极思考并主动参与语言实践的欲望，引导学生养成观察图片获取信息的习惯，鼓励学生积极思考，发展学生的预测能力。

4. 教师与学生共同讨论男子挖坑的原因。

教师提问："Why does the man dig the hole?"，学生对比两个洞的不同。"Look at this hole, there aren't any flowers near the hole. And it is small." 学生推测，教师故作无能为力状，引导学生跟随 Tec 回到土坑处去观察和发现。教师说："I have no idea. Who dug this hole? Let's return and have a look! Oh, there isn't anything. So let's dig the hole again."，请大家帮助 Tec 继续挖一挖这个坑，看看有没有什么新发现。"Can you dig this hole? Let's dig. Dig, dig, dig..." 学生做挖的动作，边挖边读 dig。课件慢慢呈现坑中的物品，教师提问："What's it?" 的同时，课件逐渐呈现骨头，"Wow, it's a bone."。教师提问："Who dug this hole? Why?"，线索逐渐清晰。学生齐声说："It was the dog."。教师引导学生说出原因："Because there is a bone in the hole."。

【设计意图】通过带动学生一起做挖坑的动作，吸引学生继续探究到底是谁挖的这个坑；培养学生积极的参与意识，并再次激发学生的兴趣，将故事情节推向高潮。

（四）读后活动

1. 内化语言：教师播放录音，学生打开书，认真跟读小故事。

2. 学生通过观察图片，理解故事，试着评价故事中的主人公。

教师提问：What do you think about Tec and the dog?

Tec is a ________ detective.

What a ________ dog!

3. 学生两人一组朗读对话，一人朗读，一人指图，进行图文匹配活动。

【设计意图】故事表演的方式，有助于学生融入故事中的角色，学习语言并体会不同角色的情感，培养学生描述图片和复述故事的能力，培养合作学习的意识。

（五）迁移创新活动

1. 教师呈现活动纸："Now, we know that the dog dug this hole. But there is another hole. Do you know who dug this hole? Why?"。学生看图片中的坑，说一说是谁挖的那个坑以及原因。

2. 教师呈现更多的坑，让学生两人一组逐图充分练习表达，说一说是谁挖的那个坑以及原因。

3. 请学生自己画一个坑，让他人猜猜是谁挖的以及原因。

【设计意图】学生自己设计挖坑的人或动物，并让其他人来猜的方式有助于学生将所学语言自然地运用其中。

七、家庭作业

- 熟读故事。
- 让父母猜猜你画的坑是什么。

Example 2

Topic: Rooms in a house

Level: students in grade 3

Length: 45 minutes

Procedure	Teacher/Student activity	Purpose or Language involved
A game: Simon Says	Ss follow T's instructions and perform the actions.	Vocabulary: eating, sleeping, playing Structure: You are washing.
A chant	Ss say the chant from the previous unit with audiotape.	Reviewing.
Story Learning I	Ss watch the multimedia of the story.	
Story Learning II	T sets a question and Ss watch the story again and find out the answer.	How many rooms are there? What are they?
Vocabulary Presentation	T presents vocabulary with pictures. Ss repeat after T.	bedroom, living room, kitchen, bathroom This is the (bedroom).
A Vocabulary Game	T Shows pictures and children say the name.	bedroom, living room, kitchen, bathroom.
Present the written form of the vocabulary	T puts pictures on the blackboard and writes out the name, demonstrates pronunciation and children repeat.	bedroom, living room, kitchen, bathroom.
A Game:Pass the secret message	Ss pass on a secret message in groups. The fastest one to get it right wins the game.	The Message: This is the bathroom /living room.
A Game: Find the appropriate place for the activities	Ss find the right room for their activities written on the card.	Four rooms—playing, sleeping, reading, cooking. What are you doing in the kitchen? We are cooking.
Story Learning III	Ss watch the video again and then describe the characters' activities in different rooms.	This is Bobby's house and this is the living room. Bobby's sister is sleeping.
Listen and say	Ss watch and repeat the story with the multimedia support.	

continued

Procedure	Teacher/Student activity	Purpose or Language involved
Role-play	Teacher-student demonstration of the role-play. Ss prepare in groups. Ss' presentation in groups.	
My house and my activities	Ss draw and describe their own houses and activities.	This is my house. This is my living room. This is my bathroom. I'm washing.
A song		Ending

Ss=students, T=teacher.

Class assignment

Choose a story and think about how to use it with your class. Prepare an instructional design.

Discussion Point

There are several distinctive differences between the two lessons which make Example 1 a better one. In Example 1, the teacher provides a full instructional design which includes all the important elements of a lesson, e.g. text analysis, student analysis, teaching content analysis, lesson objectives with main focuses and potential difficulties for teaching the lesson, teaching aids, teaching procedures, assignments, and blackboard design. Other specific features include:

- The lesson objectives are designed using action verbs aiming to help children not only process the meaning of the story while acquiring the new words and expressions, but also develop their thinking skills by asking children to evaluate the story.
- The teacher asks children to examine the cover of the book and elicit what students know about the topic and the language.
- The teacher tries to help children establish the book concept by guiding the children to find out about the book title, the writer, and the illustrator, etc.
- The teacher motivates children to read the story by asking them to find solutions to the problem "Who dug the hole?".
- The teacher involves children to co-construct the story.
- The children observe, predict, think, and guess when reading the story with the teacher.
- The children have a say in the story and their opinions are respected.

The second lesson also has points that are worth noticing, for example, the teacher tries to relate the content to children's life and experience. However, the lesson is more like story-based vocabulary teaching. The lesson would take a better look if the teacher can:

- allocate more time on story learning and involve children's active thinking in the process;
- direct children's attention to the comprehension and meaning of the story;
- put vocabulary learning in a separate class that comes after.

In the current design, children's attention is divided between the story and vocabulary, the result of which is that not all of them achieved understanding of the story, nor have they learned the vocabulary as expected.

6.5 How to teach writing to children

6.5.1 What are the aims and objectives of teaching writing to children?

Reading and writing in the first language take place much later than listening and speaking. Children can communicate with their mother tongue long before they can read and write. Writing often comes last. Therefore, a lot of people think that children learning English as a foreign language need to develop skills in listening and speaking first and teaching writing at an early stage might demotivate them. In fact, if writing is taught tactfully it can produce a sense of achievement and therefore motivate children.

TASK 6.5.1

Please discuss with your group members the following questions:

(1) In learning another language in school, when do you think we should start teaching writing? Give your reasons.

(2) What do you think written communication skills involve?

(3) How should we develop writing skills with children when they are beginners?

Discussion Point

When children start learning English at the age of 7 or 8, the focus of teaching will mainly be on oral communication skills with a minimum requirement for reading and writing, especially at the beginning stage. However, we need to be aware that children need to be introduced to reading and writing gradually with support at the beginning. Also, we know that children have in general developed their skills of reading and writing in their native language. Therefore, they can bring into the learning of English some experiences of reading and writing in Chinese. Do not forget that these are important resources for developing reading and writing in English. Of course the reading and writing skills at this stage will be very basic with the main purpose of developing their interest in reading and writing in another language. Gradually, we can move to more strategy training which leads to better reading and writing.

Obviously, writing comes last in our first language learning. Most children formally learn to read and write when they start school at the age of six. In fact, many children learn to write their names and some simple words before they actually start school. Most of the time, they are very actively involved and interested in this kind of writing because they get a sense of achievement. Similarly, in English teaching we can start teaching writing with very simple tasks at an early stage. All we need to remember is that we should be very cautious not to discourage them at the beginning with writing.

6.5.2 What can we do to teach writing to children?

TASK 6.5.2

Suppose you are going to teach writing to a group of young primary school children, what possible writing tasks would you give to your learners? Make a list and then compare it with your partner.

For example:

Copy words and sentences

Discussion Point

How many writing activities have you listed? Some of them may be more suitable for younger children and some for older children. The following suggests some writing tasks for both younger and older children.

Writing tasks for younger children

- Copying
- Making a shopping list
- Completing sentences
- Writing an invitation/a greeting/ a note, etc
- Card writing
- Labels of products
- Making a class timetable
- Making a poster
- Spelling games
- Making a cartoon story

Writing tasks for older children

- Writing a letter/ postcard/E-mail
- Writing poems/songs/ rhymes
- Keeping a diary
- Writing a summary
- Writing a story
- Writing a notice
- Writing instructions
- Writing an advertisement
- Writing an essay

The lists are by no means complete. From the two lists, we can see that writing has a very important function in social communication and we can create something for others to read through writing.

The purpose of teaching writing then is to help children experience the charm of the written language, to stimulate their creativity in using the language, and to guide them through the writing process. How to spell correctly, how to produce grammatically correct sentences, how to find the best words, how to make writing interesting, how to organize thoughts, etc. all need to be included in the teaching of writing.

6.5.3 What are the principles and models of teaching writing to children?

TASK 6.5.3

Look at the following activities. Discuss the types of activities and the purposes and benefits of each type. Then summarize the principles behind the design of each writing task.

- **Handwriting.** The first experience of children with the writing of English will be the handwriting practice. They need a lot of practice to develop familiarity with the English writing with big letters and small letters and to be in good control and keep tidy. In fact, it takes native children many years to develop good handwriting. Beginning writing activities will involve tracing letters and copying words and sentences.

- **Spelling activities**

(1) Have children use their fingers to practice writing letters in the air. For example, the

teacher says a letter or a word, then checks if the children can write the letter or word by asking them all holding their finger high to write in the air.

(2) Teacher writes a word on the board in a vertical way then pupils are to work in pairs to write out different words in a horizontal direction. For example:

- Labeling pictures or objects, e.g. body parts, colors, things in the classroom, etc.

- Write captions for pictures.

Jack is a teacher.

They are singing.

This is Jack. He is a handsome snowman.

- Write birthday/holiday cards.

Dear Ding Lin,
Happy Birthday!
Mark

Dear Miss Wang,
Happy Teacher's Day!
Class 3

- Write out one's own time table in English.

Time	Monday	Tuesday	Wednesday	Thursday	Friday
8:00–8:40					
8:50–9:30					
10:00–10:40					
10:50–11:30					
13:30–14:10					
14:20–15:00					

- Read the chart and write sentences about Jack and Mary.

Who	Football	Volleyball	Tennis	Swimming	Jogging	Skating
Jack	×	×	√√	√	√√	√√
Mary	√	√√	√√	√	×	×

√√ = like a lot √ = like × = don't like

Write sentences:

Jack likes ____.

Mary likes volleyball and tennis a lot. She likes football and swimming, too. But she doesn't like ____________________________________.

- Fill in simple forms

Name:	Age:	Telephone:
School:	Class:	Hobbies:
Father's name:		
Mother's name:		

- Write to key-pals or e-pals (a friend you keep in touch only through the internet) with older children under teacher's guidance: Please note that a website is provided for making a key-pal connection around the world at the end of the next section on the use of resources.

- Writing simple poems, e.g. Noun + Noun, Noun + verbs, Adjectives + Noun, etc. For example:

Spring birds	Elephant walks	Blowing wind
Summer roses	Rabbit runs	Sunny sky
Winter snow	Frog jumps	Green trees
Autumn leaves	Duck swims	Red flowers

Discussion Point

As in listening, speaking and reading, writing activities also need to have a purpose. Problems with many of the current writing tasks are (Wang, 2006):

(1) mainly accuracy-based

(2) no sense of audience

(3) imitating rather than creating

(4) test-oriented

(5) insufficient preparation

As language is used for communication, this communicative element should be integrated into teaching writing. When designing writing activities, teachers need to consider the following questions:

— Why do I ask my children to write this?

— Who are they writing for?

— How can I create a writing task that is similar to real life situations?
— How can I arouse my pupils' interest in writing?
— How can I help them write better? What kind of strategies are involved in this piece of writing?

If these questions can be tackled, pupils will have a clear purpose and a sense of readers in their mind when writing and be ready to make their writing personal and interesting.

6.5.4 How can we make the teaching of writing more effective?

Brookes & Grundy (2000) have produced many good examples of writing activities at different levels. Let us look at one example for lower level and one for higher level learners.

TASK 6.5.4

Look at the two examples and work in pairs to discuss how effective they are.

For lower level learners—Making word lists (Brookes & Grundy, 2000).
Specify a text (a unit in the textebook, for example) and ask the students to copy down words in a certain category. The category will depend on the level of your students. Good categories include two-letter words, three-letter words, words ending in *-ing*, *-ed*, or in *-er*, *-ness*, *-ly* and *-wise*. Or words with prefixes, words with initial capital letters, time words, activity words, personal and place names, colloquial expressions, words relating to people, to occupations, to home, to travel, words you don't understand. The list is endless.

For higher level learners—Writing instructions to accompany a picture sequence (Brookes & Grundy, 2000).
(1) Distribute the picture sequence and ask the students to write a set of instructions to accompany the pictures. As they finish writing, encourage them to compare what they have written with their neighbours.
(2) Ask for a volunteer to write their suggested text on the board and invite comments on it. It usually works best to keep the volunteer at the front of the class so that they can amend their instructions if they are persuaded by what their classmates suggest. If necessary, guide the discussion to the most important issues, which include:

— whether to use more formal or less formal vocabulary (e.g. *extract* versus *pull out* for the second picture in the sequence supplied);

— whether to use definite articles or not (e.g. *pull out bag* versus *pull out the bag*), and how consistent to be about this;

— how much work to leave to the pictures and how much to let the words do. You can also discuss how the instructions would be different if there were no accompanying picture sequence.

Discussion Point

Although the first writing task is the simplest kind of copying activity, "it enables the students to teach themselves quite a lot about English as they do it. If you teach intermediate-level pupils, from time to time you can ask them to write about what they have learnt from their word lists" (Brookes & Grundy, 2000). With lower level pupils, teachers often find it difficult to design writing activities other than copying. In this example, the authors open a new window for us. They show us that even the simple activity such as copying can be used creatively. We can imagine that children's feeling of the language can be stimulated by completing this activity and their awareness of word formation can be developed.

The second writing activity appears quite easy to do, "but the discussion stage reveals how much can be learnt about this sort of writing and that the choices facing the writer are much more extensive than they might at first appear to be" (ibid). If you want to challenge your children, you can ask them to place the pictures in the correct order before writing the instruction. This seems to be irrelevant to language learning, but it helps to develop children's logical thinking ability. What is more, if they place the pictures in a different but acceptable order, they should be encouraged because of their effort and creativity. The discussion after the writing is very important because it widens children's view about writing and improves their writing ability.

6.6 How to integrate the four skills

课例示范：综合技能①

In real life, we often use more than a single language skill. After all, listening, speaking, reading and writing are parts of a whole if we consider language as a whole. In teaching, we sometimes might need to train them separately but most of the time we need to integrate them.

① 上海市长宁区江苏路第五小学冯宇亮授课。

6.6.1 What are receptive and productive skills?

TASK 6.6.1

Can you put the four skills into the table?

Medium	Receptive skills	Productive skills
Oral medium		
Written medium		

Discussion Point

Listening and reading are receptive skills, speaking and writing are productive skills. How do we integrate them? As you have probably noticed, course book writers often integrate listening and speaking together and reading and writing together. Listening and reading materials often serve as models for speaking and writing. Acting out dialogs, retelling stories, writing summaries, composing similar texts, etc are commonly used activities for integration. Sometimes the four skills can be combined differently. For example, listening can be integrated with writing where children create a piece of class news after listening to a school news report. Reading can serve as a trigger for oral discussion where children voice their opinions about what they read or it can be changed into a dialog for performing.

6.6.2 How can we design an integrated activity?

TASK 6.6.2

Work in pairs and discuss how to integrate the skills in teaching. Come up with an activity and design a procedure for using it in the classroom.

Discussion Point

There are various ways of integrating the four skills. Here are three examples.

Example 1

(1) Prepare a piece of paper on which a number of questions are listed. Stick copies of them on the wall.

(2) Divide the class into groups of four.

(3) Ask group members to take turns to go to the wall and remember one question, then go back to their group and recite the question.

(4) The whole group read the text and find the answer to that question. Meanwhile, they need to write down the question and the answer in their own words.

(5) In the end, the whole group needs to produce a summary of that reading text.

In this activity, speaking, reading and writing are successfully integrated. If you want it to be more challenging, you may ask group members to come to you in turn to get the question by listening and memorizing it. They go back to their group and repeat the question. In this way, listening is also practiced. This activity is fun but it might take a long time and requires good organization.

Example 2

This lesson is designed for students of Grade 5. The class is organized around the topic of "My Favorite Person". In this lesson, the students will learn how to talk and then write about a favorite person. For example, from what aspects can they describe a person they like? Based on what they have learned, each student will decide on his/her own favorite person and introduce him or her to the class both orally and in writing.

Example 3

(1) Tell the children that they're going to hear a passage/a story about... (tell them the topic). Ask them to raise a question about it and try to guess what they'll hear.

(2) Read the passage/story to children twice. Children listen to it carefully and try to remember the main idea (allow them to take notes if they want to).

(3) Ask them to work in pairs to reconstruct the passage/story as closely to the original one as possible.

(4) Give the children a copy of the passage/story for them to check.

(5) Ask them to retell the passage/story to a different partner. (Or ask them to change it into a short play and act it out if suitable.)

In this activity, all of the four skills have been tackled. Children need to listen to it first and write it down, next they need to read it and check, finally they need to change it into a play and act it out. During the process, the pupils have not only been trained the strategy of predicting in listening, but also the skills of writing by reconstruction.

Reading

Reading 6.2.3

Using Information Gap Activities in the Second Language Classroom

By Violet Raptou

One of the challenges many second language teachers face is motivating their students to speak in the target language. Confident students always participate and students who are less confident are reluctant to speak. Even when students speak in the target language, they are usually answering a question and this approach greatly limits student output. Oral presentations provide opportunities for students to speak in the target language for an extended period of time and these activities are useful, but they should not be the only opportunities students have to speak at length. Because students prepare for these presentations by writing a script and then rehearsing it, they have difficulty speaking in the target language spontaneously because they are given little opportunity to do so. When students choose to learn a language, they are interested in learning to speak that language as fluently as possible. I teach Core French at the secondary level and students complain that when they go to a French-speaking part of the world, they cannot say what they wish to say in French, even though they have had years of French education. We, therefore,need to actively engage students in speaking activities that are enjoyable and that are based on a more communicative approach. One solution is using information gap activities.

In an information gap activity, one person has certain information that must be shared with others in order to solve a problem, gather information or make decisions. These types of activities are extremely effective in the L2 classroom. They give every student the opportunity to speak in the target language for an extended period of time and students naturally produce more speech than they would otherwise. In addition, speaking with peers is less intimidating than presenting in front of the entire class and being evaluated. Another advantage of information gap activities is that students are forced to negotiate meaning because they must make what they are saying comprehensible to others in order to accomplish the task.

Ur (1996) lists the characteristics of a successful speaking activity:

— **Learners talk a lot.** Most time is occupied by the learner talking.

— **Participation is even.** Classroom discussion is not dominated by a minority of talkative participants: all get a chance to speak, and contributions are fairly evenly distributed.

— **Motivation is high.** Learners are eager to speak,because they are interested in the topic and have something new to say.

— **Language is of an acceptable level.** Learners express themselves in words that are relevant, easily comprehensible to each other, and of an acceptable level of language accuracy.

Information gap activities satisfy all of the above criteria. The teacher simply explains the activity and reviews the vocabulary needed for the activity. Students are then on their own to complete the task. Each participant plays an important role and the task cannot be accomplished without everyone's participation. Many information gap activities are highly motivational because of the nature of the tasks. Activities that require the solving of a problem or a mystery are especially effective. As teachers, we know whether an activity is of an acceptable level of difficulty for our students. If students are sufficiently prepared for the activity, the level of language accuracy will be acceptable.

Information gap activities can also reinforce vocabulary and a variety of grammatical structures taught in class. They allow students to use linguistic forms and functions in a communicative way. These activities bring the language to life for students. Grammar is no longer a concept they have difficulty applying to their speaking. Students have the opportunity to use the building blocks of language we teach them to speak in the target language.

Creating a variety of information gap activities that will satisfy Ur's criteria listed above is not an easy task. If our goal as second language educators is to have our learners speak with confidence in the target language, then we must make an effort to provide our students with a greater variety of opportunities to speak in the target language. Information gap activities are an effective means for accomplishing this goal.

Reading 6.2.4

Listening and Speaking Activities

Listening activities

• Listen and repeat.

Listen and repeat can be done with words or sentences, with individual pupils, or groups of pupils, or the whole class. The purpose of listen and repeat is to get pronunciation and intonation right and for enjoyment and encouraging participation and confidence.

- Listen and guess.

  The teacher describes something and the pupils are to guess what it is. For example: "It is very tall. It has four legs but it can not jump high and it can not run very fast. It has a long neck. What is it?" "It's a giraffe."

- Listen and join in.

  This is often done with rhymes, songs and stories. Let children first listen for a few times, when they feel they are ready let them join in by saying part of it and with practice they can finally say them by themselves with little teacher support.

Speaking activities

Speaking activities do not need to be always reading aloud, reciting dialogs or repeating what is said by the teacher. When we speak, we speak with a purpose and we speak with interest as well. Therefore, we need to create interesting topics and genuine purposes for children to speak the language. Of course some imitations and repetitions are necessary to prepare children to speak, but even with imitations and repetitions, we can make them more interesting and meaningful. The following are some speaking activities. Some of them are basic speaking practice activities and some of them are more advanced speaking activities. They can only be applied with different levels of learners and in different contexts.

- Draw and ask questions to find out.

  Ask each child to draw a character, an imagined character in whatever ways they want to. Then write down his/her name and age. Let children work in pairs and ask each other questions without showing the picture to each other to find out about the characters. For example, *what's his name? How old is he? How many legs has he got? What color are his eyes? What does he like?* etc. While asking the questions, the child can also try to draw the character out. Then they can show each other the pictures and compare their own drawings with the originals.

- Whisper a sentence.

  Tell the class you are going to pass on a message by whispering it in someone's ear. The first child who hears the message will whisper it to the next until the last child hears it. He is to say it out loud to the whole class.

- Pairs finding.

  Give the class a set of cards. If you are teaching a big class then give the cards to a group of ten to twelve children. Every pupil should be able to find another (only one) classmate who has the same card as his/hers. Each pupil will have to ask questions to find out about his/her pair. The questions asked can be "Have you got a ...?" "Do you like...?" "Do you have...?" "What do you have on your card?" etc.

- A class quiz.

  Divide the class into two teams. Ask a question or give a task to one team at one time. If one team fails to do the task, it moves to the other team. Each time a question is answered or a task is done, certain points will be added to the team. The team that has the highest points will win the quiz. For example:

  You have 30 seconds to give me the following answers. The time starts now.

  (1) The twelfth month of the year.
  Six forms of transport.
  The seven days of the week.
  Six kinds of fruits.
  Ten different kinds of animals.
  Names of four vegetables.
  Five subjects of your study.

  (2) Eight parts of your body.
  Seven different colors.
  Eight different types of clothing.
  Say a rhyme with numbers in it.
  Say a rhyme with colors.
  Tell me six things you can do.
  Tell me six things you like to eat.

- Speaking chains.

  Based on what pupils have learned, you can start a sentence using the main structure that has been taught to ask children to do chain practice both for the familiarity of the structure and for the practice of vocabulary. Look at the following examples:

  (1) I have a banana. I have a banana and a pear. I have a banana, a pear, and an apple. I have a banana, a pear, an apple and an orange.

  (2) I'd like to have a cup of tea. I'd like to have a cup of tea and a hamburger. I'd like to have a cup of tea, a hamburger, and some milk. I'd like to have a cup of tea, a hamburger, some milk and an orange.

- Find someone who...

  You can organize this activity in groups or in one class. Ask each child to move around and find out some information about each other. For example, find out someone who...
  likes to get up early.
  doesn't like music.
  likes cooking.
  doesn't like watching TV.
  doesn't like shopping.
  likes swimming, etc.
  Children move around and record their findings and then each report to the group or the class their findings.

- Telling or retelling stories.

  The teacher can find or draw a series of four pictures. Put them in the wrong order. Pupils work in groups to put the pictures in an order that they think they can make a logical story. Then the group will tell the story in the order that they have arranged the pictures. With this activity, the stories from different groups may be different so that different groups will remain interested in finding out about what the story is from other groups. Retelling is an activity related to stories that have been told. After hearing a story for a few times, children can be asked to retell the story with support of some pictures.

- Guessing games.

  Guessing games can create very good opportunities for pupils to practice speaking as they give a good reason for speaking or guessing.

- Questionnaires and surveys.

  Questionnaires and surveys will be very good activities for developing a variety of skills in learners. First of all, they help develop integrated skills in listening, speaking, reading and writing as pupils will have to ask questions to get information and listen carefully to record information, and read the information to summarize the result and to report back the information in a presentation. They will have the opportunity to practice collation skills and oral presentation skills. They also give the pupils a genuine purpose for using the language. For example, a survey on the favorite food, favorite sports, favorite movie stars, favorite pets, and food, etc. will give pupils the opportunity to use the language for some genuine purposes as the answer is unknown until it is found out through the activity. Such activities can be used to practice different kinds of language structures and communication strategies.

Reading 6.4.3

Useful Strategies for Teaching Stories
By Wang Qiang, Chen Zehang, Qi Xianglin

Picture Tour

The term "picture tour" is used here to describe a teaching strategy similar to shared reading. In the classroom, teachers engage students in reading graded readers page by page while helping students learn unknown or unfamiliar words from the context with both lower-and higher-order thinking questions to encourage observation, prediction, comprehension, analysis and evaluation, and share their feelings or personal interpretations about the book. During this process, students learn vocabulary and grammar to aid the construction of new knowledge and to achieve better understanding of the book. The kind of picture tour adopted for this study includes the following six basic steps:

(1) Warm-up

Songs, pictures or videos are used to activate students' vocabulary knowledge and interest in reading.

(2) Developing book concepts

Students look at the cover page of the book and try to identify the title, author, illustrator, publisher, etc. and use the cover page to predict a possible story line or content for establishing the concept of books.

(3) Picture Tour

Teachers and students go over the book page by page. Students predict what is going to happen based on the pictures or words. They may raise questions and try to offer solutions to any problems in the book. Then, teachers and students together construct a story map using a mind map or flow chart to illustrate the main plots or concepts.

(4) Internalizing, summarizing and evaluating

Students use the flowchart or mind map to talk about the main plots or concepts, summarize the main idea and make comments.

(5) Individual reading

Students read the book silently and aloud individually to review the details, consolidate the language knowledge learned and form their own understanding.

(6) Discussion and sharing

Students discuss the underlying meaning of the book and then work together to act it out. Finally, they may add new plots or create their own stories with drawings to be shared in class.

Jigsaw Reading

Jigsaw reading is a teaching strategy used widely with the purpose of promoting cooperative learning and autonomous learning. In jigsaw reading, we first divide a book into 4 to 6 parts and divide the class into several corresponding groups. Each part of the book is given to a different group. Each student in the group reads the same part individually first and then together to make sure that everyone gets the same information. Such a group is called "base group" . Then each student takes their part of the book to go and form a new group and share what he/she has read to construct a logically connected complete story. Then everybody learns about the whole story. The new group is called the "experts' group" . Such a reading activity is claimed to promote cooperative and autonomous learning, which also create motivation or purpose for interaction and communication.

Reading Circles

In this study, Reading Circles proposed by Bookworms Club Bronze is adopted. Normally, students work in a group of six with each taking a role and completing one type of reading task. The six roles are Discussion Leader, Summarizer, Culture Collector, Connector, Word Master, and Passage Person. In Reading Circles, students read individually to complete the task following the specifications required in the role card. Then, the six roles meet to share what each has accomplished. The group work is normally organized by the Discussion Leader. Finally, a class presentation is organized to encourage students to present their work as a group to the class. Reading Circles require each student to read carefully, think deeply, take responsibility for his/her learning, and help and support each other when sharing.

Sustained Silent Reading (SSR)

SSR is a practical way to help students develop their reading habit at school. It encourages each student and the teacher to read quietly for 5 to 15 minutes every day without any forms of testing or evaluation after reading. SSR has been proved to have a positive effect on students' performance in reading comprehension as the students' reading assessment scores from the experimental group was found significantly higher than the control group in both L1 and L2 learning. Moreover, it is demonstrated that SSR has a strong impact on students' reading habit and attitude towards reading. Also, another very important finding is that the longer students practice SSR the better results it will bring.

Unit 7

Practical Techniques for Teaching Young Learners

Aims of the unit

In this unit, we are going to focus on the following:

7.1 How to use songs and rhymes

7.1.1 What are the purposes for using songs and rhymes for teaching English to children?

7.1.2 How to use a song or a rhyme

7.2 How to use games in the classroom

7.2.1 What are the benefits and problems of using games in the language classroom?

7.2.2 How to select appropriate games for your students

7.3 How to use mind maps

7.4 How to use projects in teaching

7.4.1 How do you understand projects?

7.4.2 How does doing a project feel like?

7.4.3 What are the criteria for choosing project topics?

7.4.4 What kind of projects are suitable for children?

7.5 How to use board writing in teaching

7.5.1 What kinds of writing styles are best for teaching purposes?

7.5.2 How can we better organize the blackboard to support learning?

7.5.3 Why and how to use stick figures?

7.6 How to use resources in teaching

7.6.1 What resources can teachers use in the classroom?

7.6.2 What other resources can teachers use?

7.1 How to use songs and rhymes

The value of using songs and rhymes to teach English to children has been widely recognized internationally. More and more teachers in China are now using songs and rhymes in their classrooms. As we all know, songs and rhymes can be used for different purposes, at different stages of a lesson and using different methods.

7.1.1 What are the purposes for using songs and rhymes for teaching English to children?

TASK 7.1.1

Think about all the reasons or purposes for using songs and rhymes in language classes, write down as many as you can. Then compare your list with your partner's.

课例示范：
Monkey Fun①

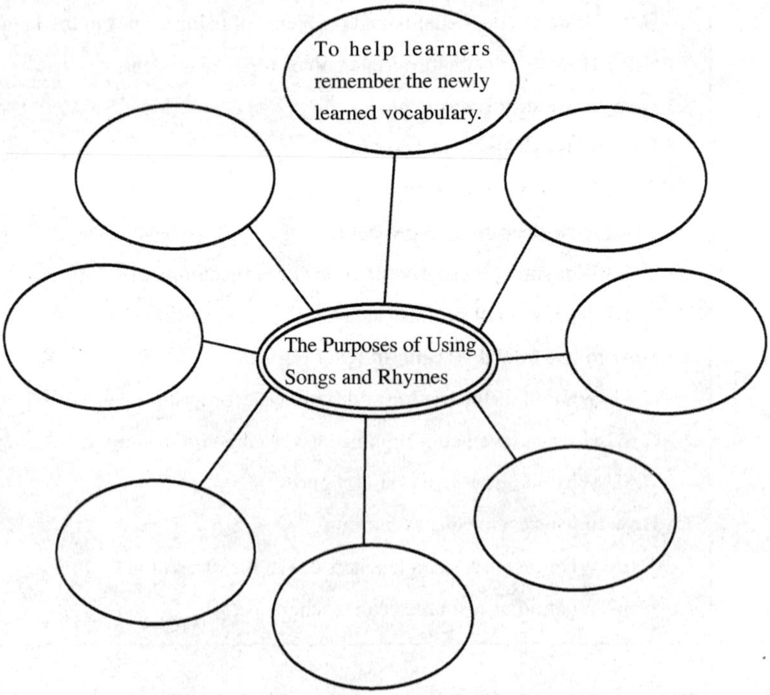

Discussion Point

Both teachers and learners find songs and rhymes interesting and relaxing. Using songs and rhymes in class can often bring a change to the routine procedures of language presentation and practice. They are magic teaching tools to develop learners' language

① 广东省东莞市南城阳光第二小学杨沛珊、许宇华提供。

abilities. They can be used to teach language items like pronunciation, vocabulary, or a particular structure. They also can help children better understand and remember the newly learned language, because singing songs and saying rhymes with actions can help internalize the structures which may be difficult for young beginners to understand through explanation. On the other hand, songs and rhymes can help teachers to create a relaxed classroom atmosphere where learners feel safe and non-threatened. Some teachers also use songs or rhymes to call attention, keep discipline, as a warm-up or an end-of-class activity for a lesson.

Why are young learners so interested in songs and rhymes? Basically all children enjoy singing songs and saying rhymes in their native language. Therefore, they will naturally enjoy doing the same in another language. Songs and rhymes sometimes are good attractors that can draw back learners' attention to ensure the smooth running of a lesson.

Songs and rhymes demonstrate very clearly the rhythmic nature of the English language. The interchange of stressed and unstressed syllables is emphasized. When learners sing a song or say a rhyme they will certainly practice the timing of stressed syllables. Once they learned the songs and rhymes, those songs and rhymes will stick in their mind for the rest of their lives.

At the beginning stage of language learning, it is important to expose learners with language chunks (set phrases, like "I don't know." "See you later.", etc.). Moon (2000: 6) states that in learning a foreign language, teaching children chunks may be very helpful in the early stages of language learning. "They can take over and use for themselves these ready made bits of language" so that they can join in communication gradually. Songs and rhymes are usually rich in these language chunks. Therefore, teachers should use songs and rhymes in the classroom as an important way of language input to learners and encourage learners to say them not only in the classroom but also to their family and friends.

7.1.2 How to use a song or a rhyme

TASK 7.1.2

Here is a rhyme from a primary English textbook(Figure 7.1.1). Work in groups and discuss how you can use it with your future students. Prepare a mini-presentation for the class and think about how you can make it interesting and attractive to all your classmates. Compare your plan with the Lesson Notes in **Reading 7.1.2A.**

Figure 7.1.1 A rhyme[①]

Description of the class: Grade 3 with 40 students in one class.

Teaching procedures:

Step 1

Step 2

Step 3

Discussion Point

The methods or techniques for using songs and rhymes may vary, depending on when and for what purpose we are using them. However, a formal presentation of songs or rhymes is often the first step which generally starts from the comprehension of meaning. We may start by drawing our students' attention to the illustrations accompanying the song or rhyme. Asking them a few questions to familiarize them with some words

① 选自北京师范大学出版社义务教育教科书《英语》（三年级起点）三年级下册Unit 11。

that may appear in the song or rhyme. Then play the audio tape for pupils to listen to figure out what it is about. This first step is important because it gives students the opportunity to experience and feel the song or the rhyme as a whole and think actively in order to understand its meaning. There might be some new words or structures, but if they do not affect the overall understanding, there is no need to teach them all to children at this stage.

If the first step is to give students a feel of the song or rhyme as a whole, the next step will shift to draw children's attention to more specific meaning and the language used and this is where teachers' help becomes obvious. The teacher can have children listen to the song or rhyme again and clarify its meaning by asking questions or explaining some new words. The teacher may also demonstrate the pronunciations but wouldn't go that far to formally present and practice them, since the overall purpose at this stage is to make sure children really understand the song or rhyme.

It is a good idea to relate the song or rhyme to actions. Young learners will certainly be interested in what you have them do, if it is physically involving them. This is because, at this stage, children learn about the outside world mainly through what they do, what they see and what they hear and say (Bruner, in Williams & Burden, 1997). If a song or rhyme can involve them physically, it will increase learning effectiveness since they will willingly sing and chant. In most cases, finding or giving each key word an action would help learners understand what the song or rhyme is about. The rhyme below would be a perfect demonstration.

Do not expect children to be able to say the rhyme immediately after the first lesson, because it takes time for them to understand and internalize the song or rhyme. Children need repeated practice and revision before they can actually sing the song or say the rhyme. You have every reason to be happy if they show great interest in your teaching and be able to produce one or two lines after the very first lesson.

Compared with songs, not all rhymes are easy to say. Some rhymes will give you a harder time with their rhythmic patterns. Generally, the content word or the word that carries important meaning would be stressed, while the functional words such as *a, the, this, etc.* would be unstressed in a rhyme. A stressed word and an unstressed word normally appear in pairs, but this is not always the case. Some teachers may worry that they are not able to say the rhymes correctly themselves. The good thing is that almost all primary English textbooks provide audiotapes to teachers, so that the audiotapes will help a lot in this issue. If you do not have audio resources, clapping hands might be a simple but effective solution. You can try to say a rhyme and at the same time clap your hands. Stress the words on which you clap you hands. In this way there would be obviously stressed and unstressed syllables. Here is an example:

An elephant* can walk*.
Walk*, walk, walk*.
A frog* can jump*.
Jump*, jump, jump*.
A fish* can swim*.
Swim*, swim, swim*.
An egg* can roll*.
Roll*, roll, roll*.

For more ideas on using songs in the classroom, please refer to **Reading 7.1.2B.**

The teacher in the Reading 7.1.2 A started teaching the rhyme with vocabulary and led children to "co-construct" the rhyme. In the lesson, children had plenty of opportunities to mime animals, do role-plays and finally they were able to produce parts of the rhyme.

As we can see from the lesson notes, the teacher tried to relate the meaning to actions. She encouraged children to observe, to think, to guess, to act, and to role-play. The process of learning also provided a good opportunity for real communication in the classroom. The teacher did not force the children to produce any lines of the rhyme in the class, instead she repeated a lot. Gradually some children were able to follow the teacher in saying the rhyme while miming the actions.

As you may have noticed, in this lesson, the teacher talked a lot. It is worthwhile to discuss why the teacher's talk dominated the class from the very beginning. Go over the lesson again, you will find that the class relies heavily on the cooperation between the teacher and the children who are invited "to discover" the rhyme with the teacher. The requirement seemed a little bit too much for most pupils, therefore the teacher has to take the responsibility of discovering the rhyme by herself. On the other hand, the lesson takes an indirect way to introduce the rhyme. It gives the children a hard time predicting where the lesson is going even after it had started for five minutes. It probably would be clearer and easier to start directly with the whole rhyme using illustrations and audio tapes. And this will save up to half of the class time for other activities.

7.2 How to use games in the classroom

7.2.1 What are the benefits and problems of using games in the language classroom?

TASK 7.2.1

Do you have any experience of playing games in your learning of English? Discuss in pairs the benefits or potential problems of using games in the classroom. Do you have any suggestions for how to overcome the problems so that the learners can benefit most from playing games while learning?

Advantages	
Possible problems	
Possible solutions	

Discussion Point

What are the benefits of using games in the classroom? The first and foremost reason is that "games are fun and fun elements can create a desire for children to communicate and games can also create unpredictability" (Halliwell, 1992). For example, it will be more interesting and effective to have children find out and hang up clothing items on a "washing line" according to your instructions than have them just learn a list of clothing vocabulary and structures. Besides, games can create helpful frameworks for further learning. Games like bingo, dominoes, noughts and crosses, etc. can provide a framework for teachers to give children practice on almost any linguistic content at the primary level. Used properly, games can engage the whole attention of the learner and help facilitate necessary repetition of the language in a more meaningful way. In addition, games can help develop children's interactive competence, confidence and fluency (Sharpe, 2001). Cant and Superfine (1997) also point out that games can provide a meaningful context for learning and help develop both a positive classroom atmosphere and a more effective learning environment.

You may say that there are both benefits and problems in using games in language teaching. We quite agree with you at this point. The main problem perhaps is the discipline problem or the lack of space and resources. However, we can try to overcome these problems. In fact there are many games which are quite simple and easy to manage with large classes and they do not require a lot of resources. If we can organize games well, discipline should not be a problem.

As you may have all noticed, children are not very good at **direct learning.** That is to say, when you ask them to sit down and learn something, they will feel that you are taking away their playing time and they can not concentrate for very long. However, children have a strong capacity for **indirect learning**, when they are enjoying themselves and focusing on meaning without noticing that they are learning the language. As far as teaching is concerned, we need to create fun activities to engage them with meaning. Games will have a role to play here. For example, guessing games often provide such opportunities for learning to take place in fun. When involved in a guessing game, children are not trying to learn the phrases or structures; they are concentrating on trying to guess right. By the time they finish repeated guessing, they will have used the words and structures they only half knew at the beginning. They will have got the phrases or structures firmly into their minds. Guessing is actually a very powerful way of learning phrases and structures (Halliwell, 1992). It is through indirect learning that children grasp the language. This is the way we learn our mother tongue.

7.2.2 How to select appropriate games for your students

TASK 7.2.2

What language activities and games do you know? For what levels of proficiency and class size are they appropriate? Look at the following games and discuss: What skills do they focus on? What adaptation can you make for large classes? Write your analysis on the lines provided.

Running dictation

Print a story on a piece of paper and cut it up into four parts with each having several sentences.Put them in four different places in the classroom. Students work in pairs with one acting as a runner who runs to look at the sentences and then dictates to the other who acts as the listener and writer. The first pair to complete the whole story correctly wins the game.

This game involves all the four skills. The "runner" needs to read and recite, while the other needs to listen and write. It is not a real communicative activity, but there is information gap in the game and the students learn to cooperate with each other. However, with a large class, the class could be easily out of control.

Bingo game

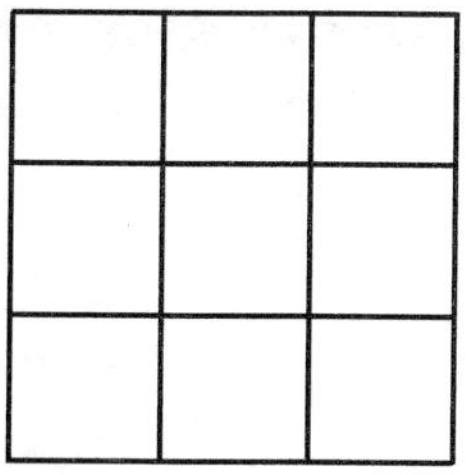

Each learner draws a diagram like the one on the right. Prepare 10 to 15 word cards. Have the learners choose 9 cards and put them in the chart randomly. When they finish, pick cards randomly from the word cards and call out the words. The learners cross out the word they hear. The one whose crossed words forms a line either horizontally, vertically or diagonally says, "Bingo". The game can be continued until all the words are crossed out, in which learners say, "Full house!"

Listen and point

Prepare four pictures and pin them up on the blackboard. Say the name of a picture and have the children point in the direction of the picture. To make it easier for students to point, better arrange the pictures in the form of a cross.

"I spy with my little eyes something ... "

This is an activity that involves children in guessing words from context. The teacher writes down a word on a piece of paper and says "I spy with my little eyes something beginning with 'p'". Invite learners to guess and find out what the word is, which could be "pen" or "pencil". The game can go on with other children.

Pic-a-boo

In this game the teacher covers a picture, for example a flash card of an apple, with a piece of paper and then shows it bit by bit. Students try to guess what the picture is with the visual clue they get.

Back to the board

Have a student come to the front of the classroom and stand with the back towards the board. Put up a picture on the board. The rest of the class help the student find out what the picture is by answering the student's questions. But they can not mention the name of the picture in their answers.

Describe and draw

This game is played in pairs. Each child in a pair has a simple map. One child has the route and tries to describe it to the other child who is to draw the route out on his/her map. Alternatively, you can give every child an unfinished picture. Ask one child from each pair to close their eyes and you show the whole picture to the other half who are to describe the picture to their partners. Their partners try to finish the drawing according to what they hear.

Discussion Point

At the end of this long list of activities, we'd like to draw your attention to three points:

First of all, always be aware that classroom games are not simply for playing, there should be language practice elements and purposes within them and make sure this is considered in your design of the games.

Secondly, as communicative games/activities are designed for promoting fluency, linguistic games are often needed before communicative games can successfully be carried out. The more careful and adequate the code-controlled games/activities are done, the better prepared the learners will be for the communicative games/activities.

Thirdly, error correction may take place during the linguistic games/activities. While doing the communicative games/activities, learners should be encouraged to take risks to meet the challenge of using the language learned to get a message across using as many different strategies as possible. Make sure that you do not interrupt the activity for the sake of error correction. You may take a note of the errors and work on them afterwards or take the chance to get information for the focus of your next class of teaching.

In addition to the three points raised above, there are a few other issues that worth our attention. First, it is important to bear in mind that simply putting games together does not automatically make a lesson interesting, attractive or effective. Games are elements that help you to achieve your teaching goal and they should be arranged in relation to the teaching objective. You need to consider if a specific game is relevant or helpful to develop certain knowledge or ability, and then decide when and where to use it and how to use it. In this way a game can be helpful both for teaching and for learning.

There are also management issues to consider before using games. For example, you need to consider if any preparation is needed before the lesson. For example, do you need to use special facilities, like a dice, a ball, or other equipment, such as a chair, a board or a recorder? Make sure you get these resources ready before class; otherwise, you will surely encounter problems.

Since we use games for language teaching and learning, it is important to get children linguistically prepared for the games you are going to use. Children need to know what language structures are used and what vocabulary is needed. This step is crucial for the successful implementation of a game, but unfortunately is often overlooked by many teachers which results in a frequently observed phenomenon in the classroom that children turn to Chinese or their mother tongue in the game while the teacher keeps asking, "English only, please. English only." To avoid such embarrassment, do remember to review the language that is necessary before the game.

The successful conduct of a game relies also on clear instruction and demonstration. Remember that the reason some children could not finish the task is not because they lack the ability required but because they do not know what they are supposed to do. To avoid this, the instruction of a game must be verbally simple but clear. You need to provide demonstrations so that children can understand the instruction not only through listening but also by observing. A demonstration from the teacher is often enough in most cases, but for some games where there are interactions between two or more children, you can do a demonstration with a student. In this way, children can understand what they are expected to do and what to do, and whether they should do it in pairs or in groups.

During the implementation of a game, the teacher should be fully aware of language problems occurring in the game. These problems are often indicators where children need help. Then after the game, you need to consider if a follow up activity that focuses more on the problem areas is needed or if special practice on certain aspects is necessary for the classes that come after.

Class assignment

Choose a unit in your book and prepare a review lesson using as many games as possible. Write out the lesson plan and if possible make a presentation in your class.

7.3 How to use mind maps

Task 7.3.1A

Look at the two mind maps below for teaching a fiction ***Tricky Aliens*** (Figure 7.3.1) and a non-fiction ***In a Nutshell*** (Figure 7.3.2). Can you tell what each text is about? Why do you think you can do so? In what ways do you think they may be used to help students in reading, writing, or speaking? Discuss in groups and give your reasons.

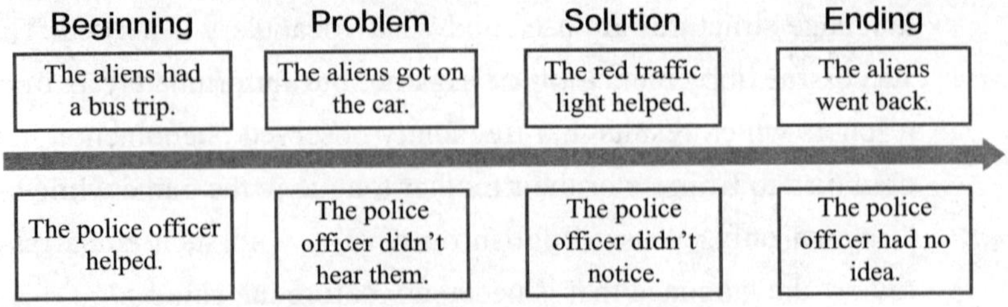

Figure 7.3.1 A mind map of *Tricky Aliens*

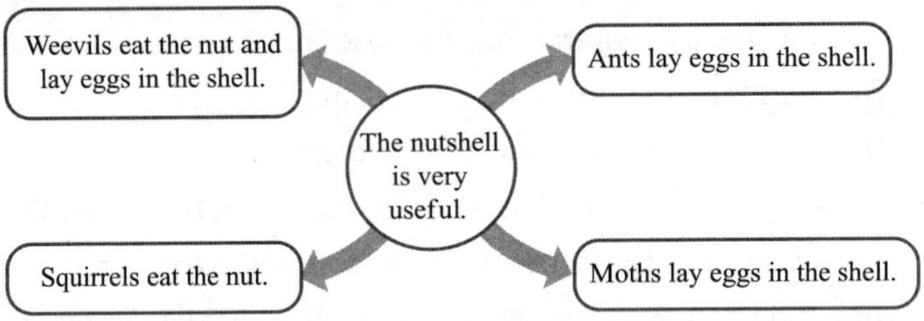

Figure 7.3.2 A mind map of *In a Nutshell*

Discussion Point

In recent years, mind maps have become a very popular instructional or learning tool for both teachers and students in language classrooms. This is because mind maps can help organize information, concepts, ideas, facts, or events into a logically connected structure for better understanding and retention of information. The key is that mind maps can represent the relationship of ideas or items around a central key word or concept (Deshatty & Mokashi, 2013) by a visual organizer to facilitate logical thinking and avoid scattered learning.

In language classrooms, mind maps, or more accurately, visual organizers, are useful activities to involve students in active learning. For example, by inviting students to use a mind map to illustrate what they read, they are immediately engaged in meaning exploration. By doing so, they will make full use of their time processing information and transforming information into memorable structures with vivid images and attractive colors, connecting the new information with those stored in their memory, communicating the information they obtained, noticing the interrelation between points of communication. More specifically, visual organizers can be used for a variety of learning purposes, both comprehension-based and production-based activities. They can help not only improve the memorization of vocabulary but also serve as a basis for improving fluency in speaking and writing tasks.

As far as multiple intelligences are concerned, mind maps or visual organizers are also useful for promoting different learning styles. According to Sarasin (1999), categorization of learning styles includes auditory learners, visual learners, and tactile/kinesthetic learners. Lectures may be OK for auditory learners, but not enough for visual learners who need greater visual support, or tactile learners who need to be engaged in hands-on activities for more effective learning. However, mind maps capture a specific topic in a nonlinear fashion and incorporate graphics and colors, and thus, the construction of mind maps provides a learning experience for visual and tactile learners who are not as well served by traditional lectures. As we can see, mind maps facilitate classroom teaching in being responsive to diverse learning styles (Sarasin, 1999).

TASK 7.3.1B

Below are four mind maps (Figure 7.3.3 to Figure 7.3.5) created by Grade 5 students.[①] What topic and learning content has each mind map captured? What do you think students have learned by creating these mind maps? What activities can be designed based on the mind maps for language practice? Share your opinions.

Figure 7.3.3 Water-Splashing *Festival*

① Thanks to Ms. Liu Haiying for the mind maps created by her students from Changping District, Beijing.

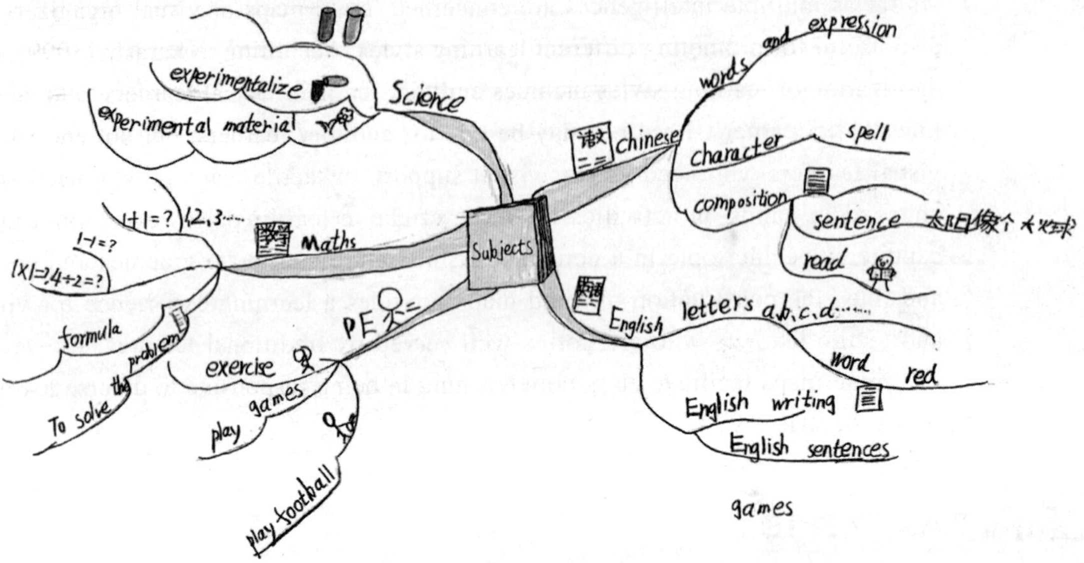

Figure 7.3.4 *Subjects*

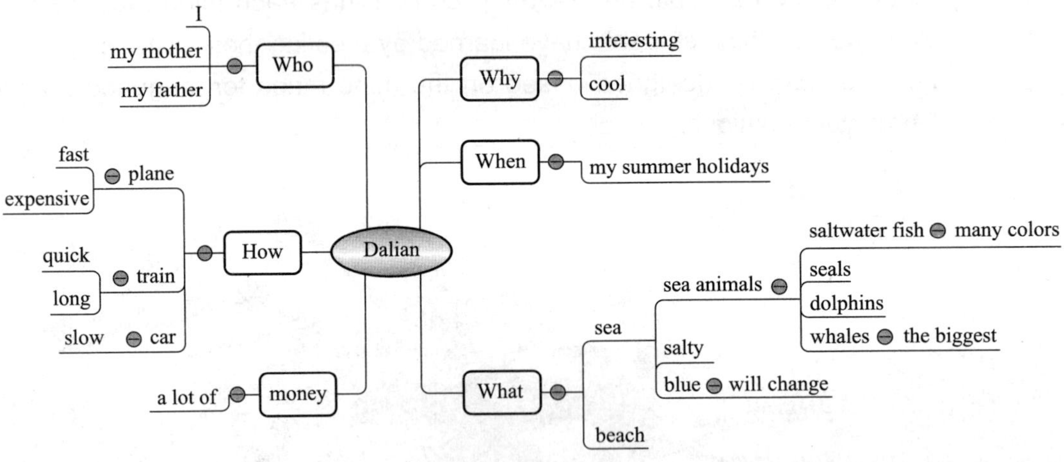

Figure 7.3.5 *Dalian*

Discussion Point

As we can see, the three mind maps, two by hand and one drawn digitally, are organized around three topics: Water-Splashing Festival, Subjects, and Dalian. Each topic is presented with a few related ideas or items, each of which is further connected correspondingly to more specific related words, ideas, or activities. For example, *Water-Splashing Festival* is represented with Date, Celebrations, Dress, and Symbols, each of which is further connected again to their respective words or phrases. Although each of these mind maps contains more or less some incorrect choice of word forms or inaccurate spelling, they clearly reflect the active learning processes of these students in terms of information processing and information presentation. The mind maps will prepare them for further activities of memorizing information and expressing meaning. We can see that by using mind maps, students no longer learn words or grammatical knowledge in a scattered or mechanical way, but in a holistic and meaningful way organized around the main topic of what is being presented.

7.4 How to use projects in teaching

Using projects is not new for teachers now, but how to use them successfully with children is an important issue that needs further exploration.

7.4.1 How do you understand projects?

TASK 7.4.1

Brainstorm your understanding of project-based language teaching. What is a project? What is the purpose of using projects in the primary school English classroom? Are children able to do projects?

Step one: My understanding of project-based language teaching.

A project should include:

-
-
-

Step two: The following statements try to describe the main characteristics of a project. Read them carefully and decide whether they are true or not. Discuss with each other and share your opinions:

T / F A project is just like a classroom exercise.
T / F A project is often easy to carry out.
T / F A project is simple to do.
T / F A project is not structured.
T / F A project can be of any topics.
T / F The things that can be studied in a project should be in the real world.
T / F Projects can only be done by older children or adults.
T / F A project mainly involves making things with your hands.
T / F A project can be a piece of research.
T / F A project engages children with interest and effort.

T / F A project often requires cooperation.

T / F Project work can involve more than just language skills.

T / F Children in the primary school do not have the ability to carry out projects.

Step three: Please summarize the main features of a project.

Discussion Point

A project is a kind of in-depth investigation of a real-world topic worthy of children's attention and effort. A project may be carried out by a class or by small groups of children and it can be undertaken by children of any age. Children can be highly motivated if the projects involve them, interest them, and engage them in activities that bring them experiences to work together, to get to know each other, and to use language to create their own world of life. Older learners can be highly motivated if the projects bring them the opportunity to use their knowledge learned in other school subjects for developing language, communication, and other abilities.

In other words, projects can enrich children's dramatic play, construction, painting and drawing by relating these activities to life outside school. Projects can offer older learners opportunities to do firsthand research in science and social studies and to represent their findings in a variety of ways. In doing project work, children will have many occasions to apply basic math, language skills and knowledge in solving problems and in developing overall abilities. What is more, children will not feel the pressure of learning a language. Instead, they see the language as a tool to fulfill a task.

7.4.2 How does doing a project feel like?

TASK 7.4.2

Work in groups of 4 or 5. Complete the following project. Reflect on your experience of doing this project. Refer to **Reading 7.4.2** and pick out any useful information you can find.

Reading 7.4.2

A project for you

Step 1 Choosing a topic

Choose a question from the following list to do a small research project. Or you may choose your own topic. Follow the guidelines given below.

(1) When should children start to learn a foreign language? Is it the earlier, the better?
(2) What are the qualities of a good primary school English teacher?
(3) What are the possible projects for primary school students? How to carry out projects successfully in primary school English teaching?
(4) How to integrate other school subjects in English teaching?
(5) What are the criteria for evaluating a successful primary English lesson?

A: Write down the possible ways of getting information for your research topic.

e.g.

1. interview
2. Internet
3.

B: How are you going to present your result?

1. oral presentation
2. present a demonstration lesson
3. pictures
4. written report
5. other ways

Step 2 Conduct your research

Work in groups and write down the questions you may ask for finding out information about your chosen topic. Each group member should interview at least four people.

Types of questions

(1) Open questions: e.g. What do you think of ...?
(2) Yes/No questions: e.g. Do you like ...?
(3) Multiple-choice questions: e.g. I think ... is _____.
A. too low B. just right C. too high

Research Topic:

Questions	Person (1)	Person (2)	Person (3)	Person (4)
1.				
2.				
3.				

continued

Questions	Person (1)	Person (2)	Person (3)	Person (4)
4.				
5.				
6.				

When all of you are ready, you may start interviewing your classmates. The following are some useful phrases for you to conduct your interview.

- Introducing yourself

Excuse me, my name is ... I am from group ... Hello, I'm ... from group ...

- Explaining

I'm carrying out a survey on ... (topic) I'm doing a survey on ...(topic)

- Asking for permission

Have you been interviewed by my group?

May I ask you a few questions? Would you mind answering a few questions?

After you have collected all the answers, you may come together again and decide how to make use of these answers. Please work on your statistics and your report.

Step 3 Finalizing your report

Please take some notes from the books and materials you have read through. Write out a report for your group. Each of you should contribute some ideas for the final report.

7.4.3 What are the criteria for choosing project topics?

TASK 7.4.3

Not all topics are equally appropriate for children in terms of their educational values. Consider the Figure 7.4.1 (deliberately a very mixed bag!). Which of these are better topics for projects? Why do you think so? What are your criteria to help you decide?

food trees
Valentine's Day animals
making an advertisement
going shopping weather
water roads/traffic
the six senses dinosaurs
children's favorite books
cartoon character

Figure 7.4.1 Topics

Discussion Point

The following are some criteria for choosing a good topic.

Criteria Checklist

(1) How interesting is the topic for the children?
(2) Is it a real world topic?
(3) Is there a certain amount of personal experience they already have with the topic?
(4) How easy will it be for them to have hands on (first hand) experience (field work)?
(5) How dependent will they be on adults or books for information?
(6) Will there be many different questions that children will want to ask about the topic?
(7) Will there be opportunities for the children to investigate their own questions actively?
(8) Will there be many different ways that children can be helped to represent their findings?
(9) Will there be opportunities for children to take roles in dramatic play?
(10) Will there be any large constructions for children to build and play with or in?
(11) What will there be to count, measure, and compare?

(12) How can shapes, colors, texture, or size be explored in the study of this topic?
(13) What expertise can I draw on from among the parents of the children?
(14) If the topic is of short-lived interest, is there a natural follow up for a new project?

Are your criteria similar to these?

Some basic steps found in most projects include: selecting a topic, making plans, researching, developing products, and sharing results with others. For doing a successful project, group effort and cooperation are very important. Activities that engage learners in communication and in peer- and self-evaluation can help create a proper learning environment. Information gap activities, interviews, role-plays,and writing tasks can support learning and help prepare learners for project work.

Project-based teaching provides children opportunities to use English in real communication. You might want to have a try when you are ready.

7.4.4 What kind of projects are suitable for children?

TASK 7.4.4A

Study the following examples taken from some primary textbooks (Figure 7.4.2 and Figure 7.4.3). Decide whether they are good projects or not. If not, can you make them better ones?

Figure 7.4.2 Project 1:make a salad[①]

① 选自人民教育出版社的义务教育教科书《英语》（PEP）四年级上册Unit 5。

Figure 7.4.3 Project 2: do a survey①

Discussion Point

For young learners, projects should be easy and motivating. They need to be guided by their teachers. For older learners, project work can be very effective in helping children integrate all the disciplines and knowledge and skills as well. It is useful to help them develop greater autonomy in language learning.

These two examples are suitable for practicing newly introduced structures. However, after students have carried out the survey, there should be a stage when they can share the result, which is a crucial step in a project.

The two examples represent the current form of projects in our textbooks. There is nothing wrong with them, but for older learners they can be extended to include cross-curriculum study so that learners can exercise and develop a wider range of knowledge and skills.

Take the second project as an example, "calendar" is a very good topic for carrying out a more challenging and motivating project. The following are some of the things a teacher can do if he/she wants to use "calendar" as a topic for a project.

(1) Invite students to bring photos of their pets at home and make a class display.
(2) Ask students to do a survey and make a bar graph titled "Our Favorite Pets".
(3) Make a simple pet dictionary with names and pictures.
(4) Design a poster for their own pet with photos/pictures, name, age, favorite things to do, favorite food, habits, things that make them different from others, etc.

① 选自人民教育出版社的义务教育教科书《英语》（PEP）四年级上册Unit 5。

(5) Design an advertisement for a pet shop.

(6) Visit pet shops and discover goods for pets and their prices.

(7) Introduce an imagined student and his/her situation and then ask students to help him/her choose a suitable pet.

(8) If it is possible, teachers can buy or ask students to donate pets for classes and ask them to observe these animals and keep a class log.

(9) Students work in groups and study one kind of animal carefully. Prepare pictures showing parts of the animal or other information they want to share with their classmates. Language should be helped and guided by the teacher.

For each of these things, students need to have time to share the results with each other such as making a wall display, doing a presentation, and making a school display.

The teacher needs to notice the change of roles in the classroom. In project work, the teacher is more of a guide and facilitator. He/She should try hard to make the best of students' ability and creativity.

TASK 7.4.4B

Choose a topic from any textbook that you have and work out a detailed plan for a project with your group members. Please point out the specific age group. Write out your plan in the space provided below.

Discussion Point

Use the following questions as a checklist to see if the project you designed satisfies the features of a good project for language learning.

- Is the topic chosen relevant to the learners' experiences of life?

- Is the language required to complete the project within the ability of the learner?
- Is the knowledge required to complete the project within the learners' current cognitive ability?
- Does the project help develop the learners' ability in dealing with real-life problems?
- Does the project foster integration of a whole range of knowledge and skills?
- Does the project give learners the first-hand experience in learning to do things?
- Does it allow children with different talents or intelligences to give individual contributions to the project and cooperate together?
- Will learners be able to get the information they need? Or do they have access to the resources they need?
- Are learners given enough time to complete the project?
- Have you set up clear criteria for assessing the projects?
- Have learners been informed of the criteria?
- Are learners invited to participate in the activity of setting up the criteria?
- Does the project allow a lot of interaction among project members?
- Does the project encourage the use of English in all the four skills?
- Will the project help develop learners' learning strategies?
- Will the project help develop learners' cultural or other knowledge?
- Will the project give learners the opportunity to present themselves and their learning achievements?

Self-evaluation

How would you rate the design of your project?

☐ Excellent ☐ Good

☐ Needs improvement ☐ Needs to be redesigned

7.5 How to use board writing in teaching

Despite rapid development in educational technology, the blackboard will continue to be one of the most commonly used teaching aids for most teachers in the classroom. How to use it well to serve the purpose of teaching and to support the students' learning is not as easy and simple as one might think. It seems easy as all you need is a piece of white chalk, or sometimes colored chalk, with an eraser or a piece of cloth. However, a good teacher should not only have the ability to write clearly and gracefully on the blackboard but also have a clear mind for planning board writing so that what you write, how you write, and where you write will help and support your students' understanding and remembering of the content learned. There are cases when some teachers who failed to organize their board well, failed to achieve the teaching effectiveness intended.

7.5.1 What kinds of writing styles are best for teaching purposes?

TASK 7.5.1

Look at the following board writings. Are there any advantages and advantages of each of the writing styles? What kind of learners are they appropriate for? Discuss with a partner.

1. *Do you like cats?*
2. **Do you like cats?**
3. *Do you like cats?*

Discussion Point

Board writing refers to the written words that a teacher puts on the black/white board in class. Different teachers might write differently since the style of handwriting is a very personal matter. However, certain points should be considered when writing on the board in order to better serve the purpose of teaching. They are clarity, size of words, style of writing, proper use of board space, and speed of writing.

Generally speaking, all the three kinds of writing styles are commonly used by teachers in most classes: they are italic, block letter and cursive style or print style of handwriting. We would like to recommend the italic style which most teachers use, as it can present words very clearly and also ensure a quick writing speed. The block letter style or print style makes words easy to recognize, as they are unconnected and upright. But it takes time to write. Young learners are often taught to write block words when they begin to learn to write. Cursive style enables writing a word in one stroke, so one can write quickly to save time. But as you can see that such a style of handwriting is much harder to recognize, particularly when students are trying to learn some new words. For advanced learners, cursive writing should be fine but it is obviously not suitable for young or beginning learners.

Good board writing is more than writing clearly on the board. It also includes how to use the board effectively. In other words, good board writing helps learners realize what is more important than others. It is in no sense simply writing the things that come to the teacher's mind. Therefore, it needs careful planning. The teacher needs to plan beforehand how the board can be divided for different functions, what needs to be written on which part of the board, and how writing should be presented, e.g. whether in colored chalks,and how important contents can be highlighted to help achieve effective learning.

7.5.2 How can we better organize the black board to support learning?

TASK 7.5.2

Evaluate the following layout of board writing and find out what problems do each example have. Discuss how it can be improved.

Unit 2 Lesson 2

I	like	apples.
He	likes	oranges.
She	likes	pears.
We	like	bananas.
They	like	strawberries.
It	likes	watermelons.

Unit 2 Lesson 2

I		apples.	◇
We	} like	bananas.	◇
They		strawberries.	◇
He		oranges.	◇
She	} likes	pears.	◇
It		watermelons.	◇

Adapted from *Cross*, 1992.

Discussion Point

You may agree that the first one is not a good example with the key structure unclear and un-emphasized. An improvement could be made to separate **He/She/It** from others with -**s** marker stressed. In this way the key structure intended would be more obvious. The second is a good example which classifies the sentences into two groups.

Board writing needs to be carefully planned before starting to write, or it will fail to reach the intended purpose. Board writing can be divided into two parts: the main board writing and minor board writing. The main board writing is carefully prepared by teacher and generally written in the middle part of the board. While the minor board writing provides notes or supplementary material for the main one.

There are certain rules and principles to follow when writing on the board. Cross (1992) suggested:

(1) Write clearly.

Board writing should look more like print than cursive scripts. Avoid using fashionable loops and circles that can be misread. Beginners would be confused by these writings. Write large so that the learners sitting at the back can read easily. Do not put too much writing on the board and make it look crowded.

(2) Write straight.

It is not easy to write straight if the line is too long. Therefore, keep your lines short and do not write a sentence all the way across the whole board. Divide the board into two or three sections, and this will help keep your writing short and straight.

(3) Stand sideways.

Do not stand with your back to the class as you write. Stand half way turn around and write with your arm extended. In this way you could write on the board and at the same time keep contact with your students over shoulders. This will also help you write straight.

(4) The talk and chalk principle.

Try to involve the students all the time, even when you are writing. Do not work in silence on your own. You can ask students to read out or comment on what you are writing.

(5) Economize on board time.

Do not spend long periods of time writing on board. Think and plan before class about what and how writings or pictures need to be presented or illustrated.

7.5.3 Why and how to use stick figures?

Teachers often find themselves in the position of drawing something in the classroom and nobody would deny the fact that not all English teachers are good artists. Some teachers use stick figures because they are easy to draw and require lower drawing ability. Generally speaking, stick figures do not have facial details, nor clothes unless you want them look more attractive and beautiful. A skirt is often needed to indicate a girl or woman. Follow the instructions below and try your hands with some stick figures.

TASK 7.5.3 A

Now work in pairs or groups. Each person gets a piece of paper and practice drawing your own stick figures following the instructions below.

(1) Draw a boy.

Step 1 Draw a circle for the head and don't forget to leave space for the body.

Step 2 Draw a line for the body.

Step 3 Add arms and legs. It should look like what is shown in the final picture.

Step 4 Practice drawing your own "boy".

(2) Draw a girl.

Step 1 Draw a circle for the head.

Step 2 Draw a triangle for the dress.

Step 3 Add arms and legs.

Step 4 Draw a girl yourself.

(3) Draw a boy with facial expressions

Step 1 Draw a circle for the head.

Step 2 Add the facial expression.

Step 3 Draw a line for the body.

Step 4 Add arms and legs.

Step 5 Now, draw your "boy" here.

(4) Draw a girl with hair and facial expressions.

Step 1 Draw a circle for the head.

Step 2 Add facial expression and hair. You can choose to draw different hair styles.

Step 3 Draw a triangle for the dress.

Step 4 Add arms and legs.

TASK 7.5.3B

Stick figures can walk, run, sing a song, sleep and do almost everything that you do. To draw stick figures of movement, you need just to pay attention to elbows, knees and position of the head. You can also dress your stick figures up by adding a simple bow tie, a T-shirt, pants, a dress or a hat and make them do different professions. Then, try to draw out the following professions, actions, and expressions. What else can you draw?

A girl	A businessman	A doctor
Painting	Dancing	Riding a horse
Happy	Sad	A cat

Discussion Point

As you see below (Figure 7.5.1), by "dressing up" with different clothes a stick figure could be a doctor, a business man, etc. Usually certain symbols are also attached to the figure to create context and surroundings.

Figure 7.5.1 Stick figures

TASK 7.5.3C

Stick figures can be very good visual aids for stories, songs and rhymes. Choose a song, or a rhyme, or a story in the book available to you and demonstrate it with the stick figures. Present your drawing to your class.

Your song with illustrations using stick drawing.

Your story with illustrations using stick drawing.

Discussion Point

It does not matter much if your stick figures do not look like the examples given. It is highly reasonable for you to develop your own stick figures and use them with your students. With only a little training, you will find that stick figures could almost give all the specific actions and expressions you need.

Even though you may not be able to draw as well as you expect, you do not need to worry too much. The purpose of drawing is to support teaching and learning and therefore, it is the effectiveness for using them that is more critical. The following short introduction on how to do simple sketching on the board may be useful for you to do further practice.

Drawing in the classroom expressions

Sketching on the board in class is something that most teachers do. As the saying goes, "a picture paints a thousand words". This is especially true in a language learning situation—ESL or EFL in this case—where a quick sketch can help students focus and generate language related to the sketches.

The key to drawing quickly is the fact that humans usually fill in the missing information. The difference between "happy" and "sad" is one simple stroke—a smile or frown. There are basically seven expressions which can be quick-

ly expressed in a few strokes of the marker or a piece of chalk and cover quite a wide range of situations.

Here are the other five:

Laughing—e.g. *Why is he laughing? What joke has he heard?*

Anger—e.g. *What happened to Tom? Why is he so angry?*

Pain—e.g. *Have you ever bitten into a lemon? Can you describe the taste*

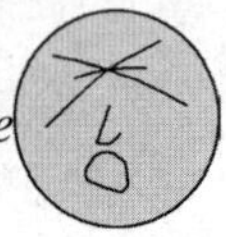

Embarrassment or insecurity — e.g. *Do you think Jenny has studied for the exam? What should she have done?*

Sleep well — e.g. *Do you remember any dreams from last night?*

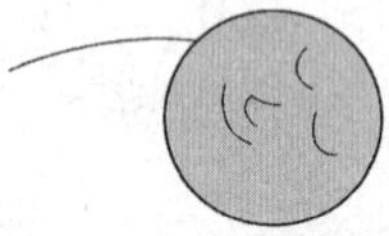

As you can see, these figures convey a wealth of information with very little effort. You can liven up class discussions—or get them going—by quickly sketching a few of these on the board and asking how the person feels and why. Students fill in the information taking the sketches as cues.

7.6 How to use resources in teaching

7.6.1 What resources can teachers use in the classroom?

TASK 7.61

First think about all the possible resources you may need for your teaching. Then complete the list below. Discuss with a partner, where can you find these resources? Can you make some?

• pictures	•	•
• real objects	•	•
• dictionaries	•	•
• the Internet	•	•
•		

Discussion Point

Obviously, in teaching English, we need a lot of resources to help us teach effectively.

Most textbook publishers provide a teaching package which may include flashcards, pictures, storybooks, tapes and videos or CD-ROMS. But you may not always find the things you need from it. As teachers are all very busy, it is difficult for them to find all the resources they need before every class. So what we suggest is that you need to start from the very beginning to establish the following:

- Your own file of pictures and cards. What do we mean by your own file of pictures and cards? You simply need to start by establishing an empty folder or file with different labels of categories you may need for your teaching. Then start collecting pictures and cards by taking notice in the magazines you read and the big calendar pictures you have seen and cut them out and collect those that may be useful for your teaching. The labels of categories will help you organize the pictures or cards, so that when you need them you can easily find them. For example, the categories may include Jobs, Hospitals, Transportation, Food and Drinks, Clothes, Weather, Sports, Famous People, Furniture, Animals, Colors, etc. Of course, if you can draw pictures or your friends can draw pictures, that will make things a little easier.
- Your own box of toys and objects. You should also put aside an empty box for collecting toys or useful objects that may be used for your teaching.
- Your own creativity and imagination for providing a better learning environment for the children. Think of ways that can help create a better learning environment for your learners, things that can be motivating and building up learners' interest and ability in learning. Write them down in a notebook and try them out to see how they work. Be active in attending workshops and seminars for teachers and learn from other teachers.
- Make children an important resource. You can invite children to help collect things for use in teaching, such as pictures, postcards, drawings, etc. Get children to help each other and act as resources for each other. Children can talk about their own clothes and the school things they have. Children act out in a role-play or action songs. Get children to perform for their parents what they have learned in class, etc. These are all important resources for learning.

You will have your resource bank and it will save lots of your time. The most important thing is that proper resources will make teaching and learning more effective. In fact, there are more resources we can explore in the classroom. They are not easily observable and we can say that they are hidden somewhere.

7.6.2 What other resources can teachers use?

TASK 7.6.2

Besides the resources mentioned above, what other things teachers can use in teaching?

1.
2.
3.
4.
5.

Discussion Point

The hidden resources we are talking about are things like our own imaginations, creativity, our own emotions, our environment, and our knowledge and skills. In the following session, we are going to provide some ideas for your reference to show how you can create your own resources for teaching and learning.

Use your imaginations

When we talk about imaginations, we mean the ability to see or hear things that are not there. You can create such a context for children to visualize things and talk about action sequences, and create situations in which a dialog takes place, etc. For example, you can use a piece of paper to make a telescope and you look into it to demonstrate to the pupils that you can see different things through it (Moon, 2000).

Use children's imaginations

For creativity, we may ask children to draw their own pictures with imaginations and then they can ask each other about their pictures. For example, children can be asked to draw their own monsters or friends living on Mars or their imagined pets. They then can ask each other about their drawings, such as their monster's names, hobbies, food they like and how they look like, etc.

Creating your own actions, songs and rhymes

For creativity, we can also make up our own songs and do actions with songs for children to sing and act with understanding as discussed in Section IV. You can use the same melody for different lyrics. We can do miming activities for guessing games and organize drama or role-plays.

Making use of children's drawings

For practicing sensitive adjectives such as thin, tall, short, solid, fat, etc., you can change the activity into a less personal one. Ask children to draw a woman or a man or an animal. They can decide whether she/he/it is thin, or solid, tall or short. After the drawing, they can ask each other questions about their own pictures or you can collect a few pictures and stick them on the board, then ask the pupils to describe their pictures to other pupils, and other pupils can guess which picture it is. With stories, drawing can be a follow-up activity. You can ask children to produce the pictures to illustrate the story in groups and then each group will try to talk about the story based on their own drawings.

Making use of the surroundings

The real context will be another important hidden resource. The classroom, the school, and the surrounding area can all be used as resources. For example, we can draw a map of the school area and have children practice asking about the way.

Making use of wall displays

In addition, we can always try to display things on our walls for creating resources. For example, we can put up the survey results we have done in class by drawing something based on survey questions: What's your favorite color? What's you favorite animal?

Exploring emotions

To explore emotions, we can do something to personalize children's learning. For example, after learning the twelve months of the year, we can create a wall chart to put all the months in it and write down the names of the pupils into the space according to the months of their birthdays. Then, each week you can ask children to find out about their classmates' birthdays and let the class sing "Happy Birthday" to the pupil(s) or you can have the class or pairs of pupils to make a birthday card for her/him to show care to each other. They can use the language they have learned and write it on the card with some drawings.

Telling stories and doing miming and TPR activities

We make use of our own knowledge and skills in doing story telling, creating quizzes, saying riddles, and miming actions, etc.

Letting children make their own dictionaries

Another idea is to direct pupils to make their own dictionaries. You may set up a dictionary making time once or twice a week. Such an activity will also help settle the class down after playing a game. You need to decide how you would want your pupils to organize the dictionary, whether in lexical sets according to topics such as family, school things, animals, food, clothes, colours, vegetables, etc. or alphabetically from A to Z. Our suggestion is that you start by lexical sets. After some time you may want your pupils to change it to an alphabetical one.

Encouraging children to build a WORDWALL

Creating a good environment is very important for language learning.Teachers can make use of limited resources to create a better climate for learning. The following are some ideas you may want to have a try or you may develop your own on the basis of these ideas.

(1) Use word bricks to build a wordwall such as the following (Figure 7.6.1):

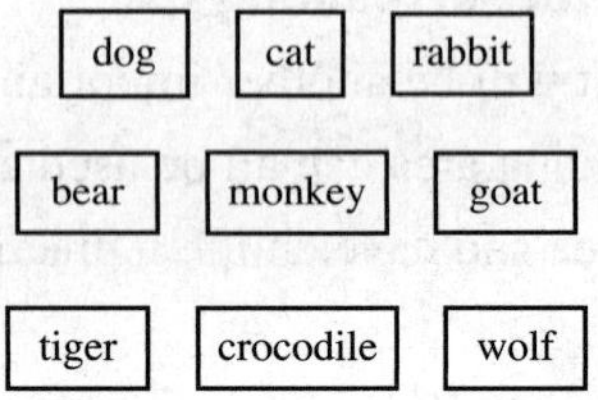

Figure 7.6.1 A word wall

(2) Instead of building a wall, you can let children do something different, maybe a building, a bridge, or a tree.

(3) Use footprints to show a path of learning on the wall. All you need to do is to cut out the paper into a bear's footprint and make a start from one corner of the room and let them go around the classroom to show progress in learning. It can be a lot of fun for children to decide where to put them. For example:

- Creating a word quiz on the wall. Each week, one group of pupils will be responsible for creating some word games on the wall for the class.
- For a newly learned structure, you can get pupils to think about their own sentences by creating a wall pocket with example sentences provided for the pupils to review the structures and then they can write their own sentences to put them inside the pockets.

Letting children make up their own quizzes

Finally, you can encourage children to make their own quizzes. Show them some ideas and then you can ask them to work in groups to make up their own quizzes for the other groups. For example (Figure 7.6.2):

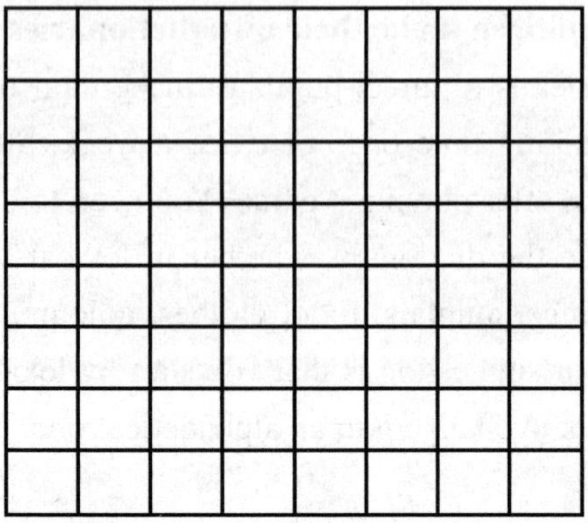

Figure 7.6.2 An example of the diagram

Developing your own drawing skills

A very simple way to make our teaching more efficient and easy is to be able to draw pictures ourselves. The pictures we need do not have to be very complicated and fancy. We can simply draw sticks or sketches to make teaching effective and dramatic. You can use them any time as you do not need to buy them or ask others to help you.

Internet as an important resource

With the rapid development of information technology, we can actually find a lot of resources for English language teaching. We can find teaching ideas, stories, songs and rhymes, even worksheets and test papers ready made. We can also use the opportunity to contribute our own ideas or ask questions about teaching. Believe it or not, you may get answers from teachers all over the world and sometimes from a very well known expert. The following are some of the websites you can start with. Once you start exploring them, you will be able to find more exciting places of resources and you can share them with other teachers.

Reading

***Reading* 7.1.2A**

Lesson Notes

Class description: 40 students in Grade 3.

Length: 45 minutes

Teacher's words	Teacher's actions	Children's actions	Children's words
Look at the picture.	*Shows a picture of a forest with animals in it.*		
There is a big tree. There are ...	*Pointing at the birds in the picture.*		Two birds.
Birds can ... This is an ... The elephant can ...	*Imitates a bird flying.* *Pointing to an elephant.* *Imitates an elephant walking.*	*Walk like elephants.*	Fly. Elephant. Walk.
Yes, the elephant can walk, walk, walk, walk.	*Imitates elephant walk.* *The teacher elicits more animals from the picture and reviews a chant from an earlier unit.* *"An elephant can walk, walk, walk, walk.* *A bird can fly. fly, fly, fly. ..."*	*Fly like birds.*	
There comes another animal. Guess, what it is? It's small. It has a long tail ...			(Shout) Crocodile.
A crocodile is very big. But this animal is small.			A small crocodile, A rat.
Yes, it's a little rat. Where do rats live? Do they live in my pocket?			No.
Do they live in a house?			No.
Where do rats live? Rats live in ...the field. FIELD.	*Demonstrates and indicates children to repeat.*		Field. (*Twice*)

continued

Teacher's words	Teacher's actions	Children's actions	Children's words
What can rats do? Rats can...	*Imitates the action of swimming.*		Swim.
The rats can...			Run.
How do they run? Do they run this way?	*Imitates walking of an elephant.*		No.
Show me how they run? Ok, rats run like this. Can you run like this?	*Imitates the action of running.* *To all children.*	*Imitate rats running.* *Imitate running like rats.*	
I have some rats. Guess how many do I have?			One /Two / Three.
Yes, I have three little rats.	*Show 3 paper masks of rats, and put the masks on three children's face.*		
Can you run? See how they run? Do they run fast or slowly?	*To the three children.* *To all children.*	*The three children run like rats.*	Fast.
Oh, yes. They run fast because a cat is chasing them.	*Put a mask of a cat on a child. "The cat" stands behind "the rats".*	*The cat starts to chase and "the rats" run away.* *Children laugh.*	A cat.
Next, the teacher organizes two more role-plays on this scene and all the children seem to enjoy it a lot. Then the teacher put pictures of rats on the board while saying the chant. The children say along with the teacher. *For the rest of the class, the teacher adopts more or less the same way to introduce the other two parts of the chant.*			

Reading 7.1.2B

How Can We Use Songs in the Classroom?

Listening activities

Using pop songs in the classroom is a common activity. They are an enjoyable alternative to traditional listening comprehension. Choose songs that are clear, make sense and do not contain a lot of unknown vocabulary. You may decide to pre-teach some key vocabulary.

Gap fills

Write out the song lyrics but leave gaps instead of some words. E.g. gap all the verbs or adjectives. Students listen and fill in the missing words. They may need to listen two or three times.

If you feel students will find this difficult, write the missing words randomly around the text and so the students have an idea what they are listening out for.

Jumbled lines

An easier activity—Write out the song lyrics, but this time jumble whole lines and students have to put them into the correct order while listening to the song. You may wish to cut up the lines, to make the task easier for the students—or get them to cut up the sheet before the activity. They can work in pairs.

Spot the mistakes

Write out the lyrics of the song, but make about 20 mistakes e.g. change the tense, write an opposite or synonym instead of the correct word. The students listen. The first time ask them to underline the words that are different and the second (or third) time actually write what they hear above the word or phrase that is wrong. After each hearing they can check with each other—in a mixed ability classroom this ensures no one is left behind and gets demotivated.

After they have checked that they got the right words, ask them to go through and see if the mistakes were words or phrases that were the same, similar or opposite in meaning. This is a good focus on vocabulary and/or grammar.

Songs—presentations

- Students can work individually, in pairs or small groups.
- They choose a favorite singer, group, musician, or composer.
- They research (Internet, magazines etc) the above.
- They produce a presentation—which can cover the biography of their chosen musician(s), and their career. It can be a talk, a role-play, an interview, or a sketch.
- They can use cassettes or CDs, posters, handouts to support their presentation.
- This could also take a written form—be produced as a poster, a booklet, or a magazine article.

Unit 8

Assessing Learning with Children

Aims of the unit

In this unit we are going to focus on the following:

8.1 What are assessment, tests and evaluation?

8.1.1 What is assessment? How do you understand assessment?

8.1.2 What is the relationship among these three terms?

8.1.3 What are formative assessment and summative assessment?

8.2 How can we set up targets and design assessment tasks?

8.2.1 How can we link assessment with teaching?

8.2.2 How can we design assessment tasks?

8.2.3 How can we design an assessment record for use in class?

8.3 What can we use to assess learning?

8.3.1 What are some of the useful ways to assess learning?

8.3.2 What is a portfolio and how can it be used to assess learning?

8.4 How can we give feedback to learners about their learning?

8.4.1 What are some of the ways for teachers to give feedback to pupils?

8.4.2 What is the role of self-assessment and how can we design self-assessment tasks?

8.4.3 How do you feel about doing a self-assessment task yourself?

8.5 How can we use tests to assess learning?

8.5.1 What are some common types of tests?

8.5.2 How can we test listening?

8.5.3 How can we test speaking?

8.5.4 How can we test reading?

8.5.5 How can we test writing?

In the previous units, we have been building up a picture of foreign language teaching that focuses on satisfying both the learners' affective needs (interest and motivation for learning) and their linguistic and communicative competence. If learners and learning are our central concerns, then assessment should contribute to the development of both the learners' interests and their learning process (Cameron, 2001). However, the ways that methods are used to assess learning have aroused a lot of debate.

8.1 What are assessment, tests and evaluation?

8.1.1 What is assessment? How do you understand assessment?

TASK 8.1.1

What is assessment? The following is a list of comments by different teachers about assessment. Tick the ones that are closest to your understanding. Then compare and discuss them with your partner.

- ☐ "Assessment means to give an evaluation to children by testing them."
- ☐ "Assessment is to help children find out how well they learn."
- ☐ "Assessment is a way to tell learners what they have not learned or mastered and I use it to keep a check on my children, by using spelling tests, small quizzes and things like that."
- ☐ "Assessment is an on-going process which focuses on the whole life of our school. Finding out if we are being effective."
- ☐ "I feel as though it is a big stick hanging over our heads. We are compelled to give constant tests and the results are compared by the school authority to evaluate our teaching."
- ☐ "It is to find out the strengths and weaknesses of our students and ourselves."
- ☐ "I use tests in my classroom. I also use quizzes—as a way of keeping a check on the children's learning. I also use it to find out what needs to be improved in my teaching and I make changes accordingly."
- ☐ "Assessment means to give a mark or grade to the learners. I sometimes give them comments or information about how well they have done their work."
- ☐ "I think it has something to do with evaluation."

Discussion Point

From the above statements, we can see that there is confusion about the terms of tests, assessment and evaluation. To understand assessment, we should first understand the differences among these three terms. Hence, we first provide the following definitions, hoping that they will help you find the differences among them.

(1) Tests often take the "pencil and paper" form and usually done at the end of a learning period, for example, at the end of a two months' learning, half a term's learning, a whole semester's learning or at the end of a whole program. The result is often expressed by a mark (60, 75, 90, etc.), a grade (A, B, C, D) or a ratio (7/10, 85/100, 95/120, etc.). Pupils' test scores are compared with each other and sometimes ranked for selection purposes.

(2) Assessment involves the collecting of information or evidence of a child's learning progress and achievement over a period of time for the purposes of improving teaching and learning. It is not based on one test or one task, nor is it expressed by a mark or grade, but rather in a report form with scales or levels as well as description and comment from the teacher. The report is written based on samples of the child's work, the child's self-assessment sheets, teacher's observation notes on the achievement of the child's linguistic ability, attitude, participation, cooperation and general cognitive development. Test scores may also be one source of the information. The child's achievement is often measured against his/her own starting point rather than compared against the skills or abilities of other children.

(3) Evaluation, according to Cameron (2001), can be concerned with "a whole range of issues in and beyond language education: lessons, courses, programs, and skills can all be evaluated" . It involves making an overall judgment about one's work or a whole school's work. It produces a global view of achievement usually based on many different types of information, such as observation of lessons, students' test scores, teachers' assessment reports, course documents, or interviews with pupils and teachers, etc.

8.1.2 What is the relationship among these three terms?

TASK 8.1.2A

Look at the diagram below and discuss your understanding of the relations among the three terms and discuss with a partner the following two questions:

- *Does this diagram, to a certain degree, help you understand the relations among the three terms?*

- *Explain to each other how tests are related to assessment and assessment to evaluation.*

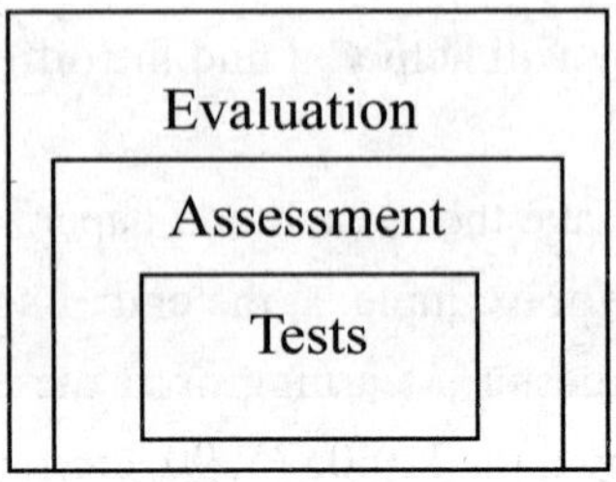

TASK 8.1.2B

According to what you have understood from the above discussion, complete the following table and share what you have written with your partner.

Issues	Tests	Assessment	Evaluation
Purposes			
Sources of information			
Report forms			
For whom?			

Discussion Point

Tests are perhaps the most familiar term to teachers. We often give tests or quizzes to our learners to find out about how well they learn and how effective we teach. In fact, testing provides only one source of information for us to find out about students' learning and it is limited in giving an overall picture. It often takes the "pencil and paper" form and is given at the end of a learning period. Questions such as "How much effort have learners put in learning during the process?" "What are their attitudes and degree of participation in classroom activities?" "What difficulties have they encountered and how have they dealt with them?" are often not answerable by tests.

Assessment, compared with testing, is more inclusive. It uses both tests and other forms of information to make judgments about students' learning. For example, teachers can collect information about students' overall learning from their oral performances in the classroom such as role-plays or interviews, from their written assignments, their project work and their cooperative attitude towards learning and the strategies they use in tackling learning difficulties, etc. Obviously, assessment can provide a much fuller picture about a student's learning progress and learning achievement than just a single score obtained from a test.

Evaluation involves making the final or overall judgment about the effectiveness of teaching and learning. Therefore, both information collected from assessment and scores recorded from testing can be used as evidence for evaluation. Evaluation is also done based on information through interviews, questionnaires, observations, and through examining documents of teaching materials and all kinds of necessary records. Evaluation can be used by a teacher to make judgments about his/her effectiveness in teaching and about his/her students' effectiveness in learning. It can also be used by a school authority or an educational authority to find out about the effectiveness of a whole school or the implementation of a new curriculum.

What are testing, assessment and evaluation for? Testing is for schools' or parents' benefits—for them to know exactly where each child stands among all the children tested and how well they do in such tests. Assessment is for both teachers and learners—for them not only to know how well they have done their learning or teaching but also for them to know where they have done well and where they need to make more effort. Evaluation is often for authorities who would want to know whether the money they spent or policy changed have had good results. As we can see, for educational purposes and for improving teaching and learning, assessment is far more important than testing. Therefore, in the following, we will focus more on understanding assessment and ways in conducting assessment.

8.1.3 What are formative assessment and summative assessment?

Assessment often includes two main kinds: formative assessment and summative assessment. The English curriculum issued by the Ministry of Education in 2022 Curriculum requires that assessment of students' learning should take both forms. Therefore, we need to, first of all, understand these two terms.

TASK 8.1.3

The following table provided by Hedge (2000) summarizes some major features of summative and formative assessment. Look at the table and discuss among yourselves whether you understand them and exchange your ideas with each other.

Summative assessment	Formative assessment
— does not necessarily relate immediately to what has been taught. — the judgment about a learner's performance is likely to feed into record-keeping and be used for administrative purposes, e.g. checking standards and targets. — is frequently externally imposed, e.g. by an institution or a ministry of education.	— is prepared and carried out by the teacher as a routine part of teaching and learning. — is especially related to what has been taught, i.e. its content is in harmony with what has been taught. — the information obtained from the assessment is used for improving teaching and learning; it is focused on each individual learner's specific strengths and weaknesses, as well as their needs, etc. — is not necessarily prepared and carried out by the subject teacher.

Discussion Point

Summative assessment is mainly based on formal testing. It is done mostly at the end of a learning period or a school year. Formative assessment is based on information collected in the classroom during the teaching process for the purposes of improving teaching and learning, therefore, it is sometimes termed as classroom assessment as well. Putting summative and formative assessment together, we will be able to form a sound basis for checking students' learning and teachers' teaching.

As teachers, we may be very familiar with testing or summative assessment, but quite unfamiliar with classroom or formative assessment. We often use tests to test students' knowledge and skills they have learned from the textbooks, which focus very much on memory work. They are often done at the end of the term and in the form of a pencil and paper test. The results of such tests, which are often presented in marks or grades, are then reported to the pupils, to the parents and to the school authorities. Can test scores be used to inform us of our overall teaching and learning effectiveness? The answer is: not exactly. Why? It is simply because children's ability and achievement in learning are not measurable in terms of one single test. Even if they can reveal some aspects of our teaching or our pupils' learning, it is often too late for us to do anything about them as it is already the end of a learning period.

Different from summative assessment, formative assessment focuses on the process of learning, that is, on assessing how well children understand concepts, perform tasks and make progress during the process of learning rather than on the final product or result of learning. This type of assessment will provide more information on children's learning during the learning process and will be more useful for teachers to adjust their teaching according to children's needs and base teaching on the easiness or difficulties of children's learning. Formative assessment should be an integral part of teaching and learning and it should not be threatening to children as a form of assessment. They should be similar to activities that are carried out normally in classrooms. You may develop your assessment tasks based on certain classroom activities and work out criteria to be followed when assessing children's performance and do record keeping.

8.2 How can we set up targets and design assessment tasks?

As teachers, we need to be aware that our assessment should be based on what is required from the curriculum and what the main objectives are for teaching English, so that we teach with clear goals in our mind and we know what we should try to achieve and how we can assess whether we have achieved what we are aiming for.

8.2.1 How can we link assessment with teaching?

Task 8.2.1A

List all the activities that you think you can do with children in the classroom. For example, reading aloud, children reciting a dialog, etc.

Activities that can be done in my classroom	
•	•
•	•
•	•
•	•
•	•

Task 8.2.1B

After you have listed all the activities you can do in the classroom, try to put them into the following columns with different headings given below.

Listen and Do	Speak and Sing	Play and Act	Read and Write	Audio and Visual

Discussion Point

In the past, many teachers are used to teaching according to the textbooks they use without knowing what the objectives and specific requirements are. The main problem is that teachers teach according to what is tested instead of what is required from the curriculum. A good teacher, however, teaches with clear objectives. He/She has a good understanding of the curriculum requirements and knows how to use the textbook and how to design classroom activities, in order to fulfill the teaching requirements and to achieve the stated objectives. Such teachers are more active users of textbooks rather than passively follow whatever they find from the textbooks. Understanding the requirements and the general objectives stated from the curriculum are very important for effective teaching and effective assessment. We will discuss in the next part how we can relate the general goals and objectives as well as the specific requirement to the assessment targets and how we can design assessment tasks.

8.2.2 How can we design assessment tasks?

TASK 8.2.2

Get into groups and find a unit from a primary textbook. Study the unit carefully and discuss together what the teaching objectives should be? Make a possible list of objectives for that unit and design a few assessment activities to assess whether your learners have achieved the stated objectives. Share your ideas with your group members.

Discussion Point

In order to assess our pupils' learning, we need to be aware of the requirements from the curriculum and also have to be very clear about the teaching and learning objectives of each unit in the textbook.For example, we need to assess pupils' learning from six fairly broad areas, as shown in the Figure 8.2.1.

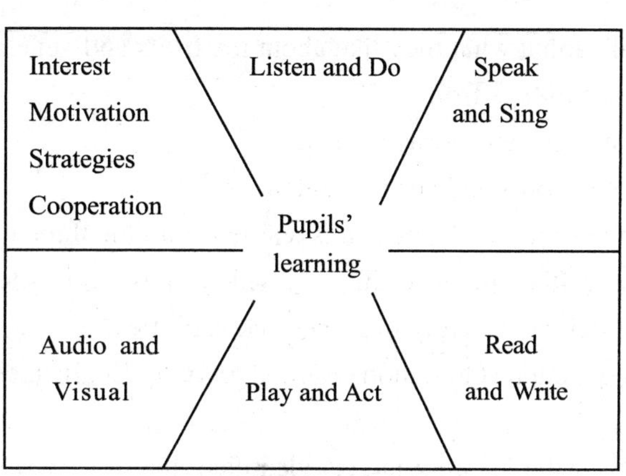

Figure 8.2.1 Pupils' learning

We can find specific performance descriptions for most areas from the curriculum. However, they are still quite general descriptions of learning goals and objectives. Regarding assessment, we need first of all to break the goals and objectives into observable behaviors or performances that are related to textbook contents, then we need to think about in what kind of tasks we can find out about our pupils' capabilities. Next, we can start designing tasks that can be carried out by our pupils in the classroom. In the meantime, we need to observe and record carefully children's performances. Of course, we need to follow certain kinds of criteria, too.

Now, we need to look at our course book and find out how we can relate the course book materials to the general learning goals stated from the syllabus. The following is an example we made up just to show you what steps are needed for designing assessment tasks.

First of all, we decide that we are going to assess the pupils after they have learned the first three units in the textbook. Let's say in these three units, they have learned the days of the week, the weather, numbers 11–20, names of some animals, and some fruits and vegetables. Therefore, we decide that our pupils should be able to do the following things by the end of the three units:

- Listen and understand the days of the week;
- Listen and understand the animal names;
- Listen and understand the fruits and vegetables;
- Name the seven days of the week;
- Name the animals;
- Name the fruits and vegetables;
- Talk about the weather;

- Talk about what they like about the fruits and vegetables;
- Say numbers from 1–20;
- Spell the new words learned;
- Copy words and simple sentences;
- Say rhymes and sing songs learned from the three units;
- Understand the recording and video shown at this level;
- Participate actively in games and activities;
- Show interest and motivation in learning English, etc.

With all the learning targets identified, the next step would be to decide on assessment tasks, e.g. when and how we are going to assess whether our pupils are able or not able to reach the above targets. Perhaps we decide to use TPR to assess their understanding of the days of the week, names of animals and names of fruits and vegetables. We also decide to use guessing games for checking whether they can name the animals or fruits. We may also design a survey activity for the pupils to ask each other questions about what they like about the fruits and vegetables. For assessing their use of the numbers, we may want to use a Bingo game to check whether they have learned the numbers or not. Before we assess them, we tell them that they are going to be assessed about their understanding and abilities in using English to name things. During these activities, we take notes while observing not only in terms of their linguistic abilities but also whether they show interests in learning or they are active or not in participating in the activities. We need to take a note on who are doing well and why, and who are not doing so well and what the problems might be. The criteria you use and the areas you are observing should be open to the pupils. For example, you should tell the pupils that you are not just observing their use of the language, but also their confidence in learning, their cooperative attitude and their use of strategy, etc.

8.2.3 How can we design an assessment record for use in class?

There are three examples of record sheets provided below. They are not intended to be models for you to follow without questions, but rather as a starting point for you to think about what may be appropriate for your pupils or for your school. With a record sheet, you need to decide how frequently you are going to record, whether you will assess at the end of each week with only one group at a time, or if you are going to assess after a particular skill is practiced, or you may assess at the end of every two units, or half a term.

TASK 8.2.3

Work in groups and discuss the purposes and functions of the following three samples. Are they useful? If yes, in what ways? If not, how can you adapt them?

Example 1

Areas of skills	Self-assessment ☺😐☹	Teacher assessment ★ ▲ ○
1. I can say numbers 1–10.		
2. I can write letters A–G.		
3. I know big and small.		
4. I can say my age.		
5. I can say father and mother.		
6. I can ask and tell my name.		
Parents' comments: ______ Signed	Teacher's comments: ______ Signed	Classmates' comments: ______ Signed

★ Very well ▲ About average ○ Needs more practice

Example 2

Student names	Speaking and listening Confident? Independent? Guided? Supported?	Problems Whose problem? Teacher's or pupil's?	Possible actions

Example 3

Class________ Teacher________ Date________

Items	Pupil A	Pupil B	Pupil C	Pupil D	...	...
Answer and ask about each other's names.						
Understand simple instructions, such as point at red...						
Answer and ask about fruits.						
Name and answer about vegetables.						
Ask about the color of animals.						
Introduce family members.						
Use plural nouns and singular nouns in simple questions and answers, e.g. What is this? What are these? Is it a pear?						
Ask and answer about how many (within 10).						
Say names of animals with pictures.						
Guess objects and answer questions, e.g. Is it a pear? No, it isn't.						
Say things you can do.						
Match pictures with words.						
Recite a rhyme in front of the class.						
Play the Bingo game.						

Adapted from Cameron, 2001.

Discussion Point

In order to find out how well learners do in learning, teachers need to observe carefully and record systematically how students have been learning. Therefore, it is advisable for teachers to develop an assessment record book for each class. With a record book, each student can be given a separate page so that the teacher can record information about every student on his/her learning in terms of his/her strengths or weaknesses during activities and performances. You may also record the children's use of strategies, their attitudes, and participation as well as cooperation with others. With large classes, teachers will not be able to assess every child in one class. She/He can choose to assess a group of students at one time, so in a week or two she/he will be able to make a record of every student observed in class. The information the teacher gets from such observations will give feedback to his/her planning for teaching immediately.

In order to keep a record of your observation, you need to develop a way, for example, use a three-level scale to record pupils' performance: 3 for "can do well"; 2 for "basically can do it"; 1 for "need more practice". With your records and notes, you will know each individual student very clearly in terms of their strengths and weaknesses. Whereas without a record book or notes, a teacher can only get a very general impression of his/her teaching and the pupils' learning. As a result, the teacher is often unable to offer necessary help needed by the learners.

8.3 What can we use to assess learning?

How can we get the most accurate information about a child's progress and achievement? When we are meeting the parents, is it very useful for us to just give the test scores to them? A test result is only an end product; it will not carry much information about how the child has tried to get such a result or what problems he/she may have for getting a low score. A specific test is only one indication of learning (Vale and Feunteun, 1995; Dean, 2001) and often does not reflect a whole picture or provide a fair measure of overall achievement. Young children usually can show remarkable progress within a short period of time, but may not be very skillful in taking tests. They sometimes become confused by the way the question is asked rather than by the task. Alternatively, a sample of a child's performance which the teacher sees or records is more likely to be a more valid way to assess the child's achievement and learning potential.

8.3.1 What are some of the useful ways to assess learning?

TASK 8.3.1

Discuss the following questions in groups:

- According to your experience, what would be some useful ways to assess children's learning as far as English is concerned? Why?
- What information do we need to inform our learners, their parents, ourselves as teachers, as well as the school authorities of the learning results?

Discussion Point

As teachers, how can we ensure that learning takes place and how can we be certain that learning has taken place? Obviously, we need to be able to show evidence of our pupils' learning. Therefore, the purpose of assessment should focus on what children can do rather than what they cannot do. And the information we get about things that children still cannot do well should immediately inform us about our teaching and our planning for the next stage. The way we assess children should be positive and non-threatening and allow children the opportunity to work co-operatively with others in the class. Also, we need to remember that generally speaking, success leads to success and the teacher's task is to design and organize assessment activities so that every child is able to succeed at some level (Dean, 2001). In general, we can use the following ways to collect information about children's learning.

- Observing children in activities: this requires pupils to proceed through a series of tasks individually or in teams. The teacher or a group of teachers may work together to develop some kinds of rubrics or standards to assess pupil's performance during an activity.
- Project work: requires pupils to complete a set of tasks designed to explore certain ideas of a concept. For example, to find out the difference between one zoo in China and one zoo in Africa and make a poster to illustrate the differences.
- Portfolios: consist of pieces of work done by the pupil over the term, which will be further discussed in the following section.

8.3.2 What is a portfolio and how can it be used to assess learning?

TASK 8.3.2

Work in groups and discuss the following questions:
- How can we help learners create their own portfolios?
- What may be included in a portfolio?
- What kind of criteria can we use to assess pupils' learning?

Discussion Point

A portfolio is a file which is created by pupils themselves for collecting and presenting their progress of learning which may include their designs, photos, writings, drawings, reflections, such as selected samples of writing with first draft, second draft, third draft, etc. self-evaluation records, feedback from peers and the teacher, plan for the next stage, etc. Things that can be included in a portfolio may include the following:
- Oral performance records (self-, peer-, and teacher evaluation), such as story-telling, interviewing, dialog performance, etc.
- Collection of pictures and art works reflecting the child's learning.
- Drawings, picture stories, diagram descriptions by the child.
- Acting performance records for role-plays, action performance, reciting, and music performance.
- Collection of the child's writings, such as self introduction, summaries, letters, poems, and stories.
- Multimedia project work and displays done by the child or a group of children, such as picture texts/ displays.

With a portfolio, we need to make clear to the pupils the criteria for assessment. These criteria should not only be made known to the pupils but also can be developed jointly with the pupils. For example, both the teacher and the pupils will agree on the inclusion of a certain required number of entries, the quality of the final products, seriousness of revisions, layout and design and keeping up to the time schedule (Smith, 2002). Children, therefore, need to select and put the samples of their work done by themselves in a folder, discuss with the teacher about what they have done. The teacher can also help the pupils set targets for their future performance through their self-assessment, e.g. to be able to say 10 words this week, learn to ask one question, write five words for five picture cards, etc.

Setting up clear criteria for assessment is very important when introducing the use of portfolios. The criteria for assessing portfolios can be discussed with the children and, of course, it can be done in the children's native language, so that they know in what aspects they will be assessed and what will be the expectations. Smith (2002) has suggested the following be included as the criteria for assessing pupil's portfolios:

- Inclusion of all the required entries.
- Quality of final products.
- Seriousness of revisions.
- Depth of reflections.
- Layout and design.
- Keeping to the time schedule.

On the last page of the portfolio, there can be a summary report by the child and by the teacher. We can gain a lot of insights and information about what the children can do and how they have done it by looking through the portfolios with children's self-assessments and teacher's comments. The use of portfolios can also provide teachers with valuable information for planning parent-teacher conferences.

You may ask whether portfolios will increase the workload of teachers and pupils. Our answer is: if used properly, it will not. With the use of portfolios, we need to change our way of giving regular homework assignments. In fact, some of the regular homework will be replaced by working with a portfolio and the usual homework will take on another form. Some portfolio work can also be done in class. However, with portfolios, the learners will definitely need to spend more time working with self-planning, use of imagination, meaningful language use, creative thinking and reflections. They are required to revise their assignments at least once. So when an assignment is handed in for the first time, it is not finished. The learner is expected to revise and reflect on it in a meaningful and useful way the second time or sometimes a third time. And the teacher will have more time spent getting valuable feedback from pupils' work and provide more guidance and support to the learners by "writing constructive, corrective, informative, and encouraging comments" (Smith, 2002) instead of simply correcting and grading the learners' regular homework. With the use of portfolios, we pay more attention to the quality rather than the quantity of assignments. Therefore, the tasks chosen for the portfolio should be well thought out, meaningful, motivating and challenging to the learners.

A final note about using portfolio: we need to think about the best time and the most appropriate stage of learning for us to bring in portfolios. Portfolio is mainly a folder or file for keeping something either in written forms or in picture forms. Therefore, for beginning learners, who have not developed many writing skills, it may only include pictures related to language learning. For lower beginners, we can invite children to draw some pictures by themselves to express their feelings and attitudes towards English learning. Also we can draw very simple stick figures with speech bubbles to go with it so that children can fill in the bubbles with some simple English they can write and also they can color some pictures. With learners who have developed some written language skills, it would be a good idea to set up a portfolio for collecting written work. Furthermore, with portfolios, teachers need to think about where to keep them and how. You also need to decide when you would ask your learners to select their samples and how you are going to discuss with them the reasons for selecting the particular samples. It can be time-consuming, but is definitely a worth trying method for assessment.

8.4 How can we give feedback to learners about their learning?

The first question you may have might be what feedback means. Feedback is everything that we do to tell our learners how they are doing. For example, we praise our learners when they do well; we write comments on their written work; we also correct the errors the learners make. These are all different kinds of feedback we provide concerning our pupils' learning. We can also find out how our pupils feel about our teaching and this is the case when we get feedback from our pupils. So, as teachers, we frequently give feedback to our pupils and at the same time we can also get feedback from our pupils concerning our teaching.

8.4.1 What are some of the ways for teachers to give feedback to pupils?

The most common way for teachers to give feedback to pupils is to give them a mark or grade. Besides this, have you tried or can you think of other ways of giving feedback to pupils about their learning or progress?

TASK 8.4.1

Read the following kinds of feedback forms and discuss the advantages and disadvantages of each type in a group.

Forms of giving feedback	Advantages	Disadvantages
• Give grades or marks based on paper-and - pencil tests.	• Easy to see where each child is compared to others.	• Difficult to see the problems with each child and difficult to use such information to improve teaching. • The atmosphere among pupils is tense. • Damages some pupils' motivation and interest in learning.
• Explain the test results, e.g. why certain answers are wrong.		
• Praise		
• Rewards		
• Exchanges		

Discussion Point

Besides paper-and-pencil tests, there are many other ways that we use to give feedback to pupils about their learning. They can be both formal and informal. As far as formal feedback is concerned, we can have individual meetings or group meetings with some pupils to discuss with them their strengths or weaknesses in learning. We can ask the pupils to set targets themselves for learning and then meet them as agreed to. We can talk about their progress or problems they may have in trying to achieve such targets. Obviously, this type of feedback allows teachers to focus on individual pupils and can provide help where needed. Pupils also can get more concrete information about their own learning and will feel more encouraged to work harder. Other ways include giving pupils written comments about their performances in tasks or in project work, etc. through a form of record, so that they know clearly how they have performed and how the teacher has assessed their efforts. Informal ways would include direct praise or punishment to the pupils who do well and who do not do well. Also we may use observation notes to record in class how particular pupils carried out the task during the activities as we have discussed earlier.

Now, we simply need to be aware that we can provide feedback to our pupils in different ways and there are advantages and disadvantages for each of them. We should select the most appropriate ways for our teaching and learning contexts and make our feedback more systematic and more accessible to the pupils. We can also involve parents and the pupils themselves in the assessment and let them give their feedback as well. The advantages of informal ways of giving feedback are obvious as it is less threatening to the pupils and tend to be more closely related to teaching and learning activities. This kind of feedback will motivate learners on a day-to-day basis rather than a test result which comes only at the end of the term when everything is too late to be improved or changed.

8.4.2 What is the role of self-assessment and how can we design self-assessment tasks?

Many teachers may think that children at primary level are not able to do self-assessment. However, research seems to have found that this is not the case. According to Katz (1995), from kindergarten on, most children can be encouraged to assess the general progress of their own learning. He also believes that in principle unless children are consulted about their own views of their own progress, they cannot learn to take some responsibility for learning (ibid). In other words, only when children are engaged in assessing themselves, can they develop the ability to take responsibility for their own learning or become more independent learners. Teachers may ask "How can we ask children to do self-assessment when they are still so young and can hardly express themselves in written language?"

TASK 8.4.2A

The following is an example of a self-assessment sheet for children to reflect on their own learning. In your learning experience, have you ever tried to assess yourself about your own learning? Do you think children are able to do so? Do you see any point in asking your learners to self-assess themselves? Discuss with another student.

Name ____________ Date ________________

I can say hello.	☺	☹
I can say yes and no.	☺	☹
I can introduce myself.	☺	☹
I can ask how someone is.	☺	☹
I can say how I feel.	☺	☹
I can count to 10.	☺	☹
I can count to 20.	☺	☹
I can say the days of the week.	☺	☹

How do I feel about my English?

A. ★★★★ B. ★★★ C. ★★ D. ★

________ Signed

Discussion Point

The point we would like to make is that pupils may not be able to understand the meaning of self-assessment at the beginning. When we have focused a lot on teaching English, there is hardly any teaching done about how to learn. Pupils, as a result, have little idea of how to do self-assessment or how to plan their own learning. Therefore, it takes time and patience to help our pupils achieve such awareness and ability because this requires a change in our pupils' own understanding of learning (Black, 1998).

We have to understand and also we need to help our pupils understand that summative assessments (tests) of the pupils are for the schools' and their parents' benefits, and do not really mean very much for the teachers and the pupils themselves. The purpose of such tests is to make the pupils work harder, but often without telling them how to work harder. Pupils then often feel a source of pressure from such tests, which makes them anxious. On the contrary, formative assessment and self-assessment are ways to help teachers see how they can improve teaching and how they can help pupils better themselves and to help pupils to see what they have achieved and what needs to be worked on more. Through formative assessment, we hope our learners will become more aware of themselves as learners and will know exactly where the problems are and how to tackle these problems through their own efforts and the teacher's help.

TASK 8.4.2B

Work in groups, choose one section of the textbook based on which you would like to assess your pupils' learning. Develop a series of assessment tasks and decide on ways of keeping records. Write a short rationale for your design of the assessment and be prepared to share your project with the whole class.

8.4.3 How do you feel about doing a self-assessment task yourself?

TASK 8.4.3

To assess your own understanding of the main issues we discussed in this section, we invite you to complete the following task in the form of a self-assessment. Please choose an answer which best reflects your learning. After you complete the task, work in groups of four and share your experiences and reflections. What have you learned from this?

(1) How would you assess your own learning in this section?

☐ I learned a lot. ☐ I learned a little. ☐ I am totally confused.

(2) I understand the differences between assessment, testing and evaluation.

☐ Clearly. ☐ Quite clearly.

☐ Not quite clearly. ☐ Not at all.

(3) I can tell the difference between summative and formative assessment.

☐ Yes. ☐ Somewhat. ☐ No.

(4) I understand better the purposes of assessment.

☐ Yes. ☐ Somewhat. ☐ No.

(5) I understand the relationship between teaching and assessment.

☐ Yes. ☐ Somewhat. ☐ No.

(6) I can plan better for assessment in my lesson planning.

☐ Yes. ☐ Somewhat. ☐ No.

(7) Please write a short learning diary based on the following questions:

i. What do you think you have learned from this section?

ii. What are your main difficulties in understanding this section?

8.5 How can we use tests to assess learning?

In recent years we have seen many new methods and ways of evaluating and assessing learning performance and language ability. However, pencil-and-paper tests still remain as the main instrument in most teaching situations across China for various reasons. Well designed, valid tests provide useful information about what learners know about and can do in English. However, not all tests are well designed. Some can produce unreliable information about our learners' ability and language performance. What is more damaging is that they often exert negative backwash on both learning and teaching.

8.5.1 What are some common types of tests?

TASK 8.5.1

Tests are of different kinds and may be used for various reasons. The following are four commonly used tests. Please match them with their right definitions. What other tests can you think of? What is the purpose for them? When can you use them in teaching?

Placement test	Proficiency test	Achievement test	Weekly/monthly tests
This test is used to determine learners' general level of proficiency in relation to the requirements of certain standards. For example, the 2022 Curriculum. The result is also useful for evaluating teaching and learning in different schools.	Such tests are used to find out how well learners are doing after a lesson or unit is finished. The purpose is for the teacher to check learning and to decide if extra work is needed so that help can be given to those who need it. The test focuses only on what learners have recently learned.	This test is often used at the beginning of a school year or the start of a program. The purpose is to learn about learners' current level of language ability in order to decide where to put them into appropriate levels of classes so that their later progress can be more appropriately assessed.	This test is used to find out how well learners have learned what was taught after a certain period of time to evaluate the effectiveness of teaching and learning. Teachers as well as learners can use such information to improve their teaching and learning.

Discussion Point

A test is usually carefully designed for a specific purpose and consists of one or more exercises or tasks each with a clear objective. We use tests to assess children's present progress in learning or how well they can do against certain standards. One thing in common among the four tests under discussion is that they all try to evaluate learners' language ability. However, what makes them different is how the results are used: to compare one learner with other learners, to have a record of the beginning level so that they can be put into appropriate levels of classes or their later progress can be assessed, or to find out how well they have learned what was taught, or obtain a general picture of their achievement against certain pre-set standards.

As we all had the experience of being language learners or teachers ourselves, we had taken or used all these kinds of tests but perhaps we were unaware of these terms or unclear about their different purposes. With an understanding of their purposes and uses, we will be able to use them more carefully and sensitively.

A test can focus on different aspects of learning or learner performance. For example, we can test our children's listening, speaking, reading and writing skills or vocabulary development as well as cultural knowledge.

As regarding the forms of tests, pencil-and-paper tests are easy to design and deliver, so they are still being widely used in everyday teaching. They are a quick and easy way to get information about how well a learner does with the language, especially when there are a large number of students. Tests also have a powerful backwash on everyday teaching. In other words, what is being tested will largely determine what is being taught or emphasized in teaching and learning, and how. Sometimes it is good but more often it will lead teaching astray since in most cases students' knowledge about a language instead of their communication ability is being tested. Therefore, only understanding the different functions of tests is not enough. We also need to be able to develop appropriate tests to achieve our purposes.

According to Cameron (2003) , tests used for children need to be different from tests for adults. They should reflect characteristics of children and how they learn. Our tests should meet children's physical, linguistic, social, and conceptual levels of development. What is more, tests should at their best reflect the teaching methodology we adopt in teaching—interactive use of games, songs, rhymes, stories, and writing, because it is important for tests to serve teaching rather than for teaching to serve tests although in most cases, it is the test which drives teaching. Teachers, for various reasons, are forced to teach what is going to be tested. Therefore, it is important that we design or select the right kind of tests for the purpose of promoting teaching and learning.

8.5.2 How can we test listening?

TASK 8.5.2

There are many ways of constructing a listening test depending on both the purpose and the level of the language tested. The following are three examples. Work in groups and discuss what each of them is testing and how they are different from each other.

Example 1

Example 2

Example 3

Discussion Point

The first example focuses on children's ability to relate sounds with meanings and the focus is on vocabulary. Such an activity is commonly used at the lower or beginning level to test children's recognition of sound and meaning of a word by recognizing the right pictures. This can also take the form of written words or sentences, in which the learners are required to single out the one they hear on the tape.

The focus of Example 2 shifts to the meaning and function of the language where learners need to listen and comprehend the sentence. They observe the pictures at the same time in order to choose the right picture which matches what they hear.

The last example is similar to the second, but it is more demanding since the task is more complicated and with a short dialog or discourse.

8.5.3 How can we test speaking?

In most classrooms the test of speaking is usually left out for the reason of time and management. It is not an easy task to test a large class with sixty learners in one single lesson. However it is still practical to include speaking in a test if it can be carefully designed and properly managed.

TASK 8.5.3 A

Work in groups and list some practical ways for teachers to test speaking in primary schools. Pull all your ideas together and see how many you have. Discuss in groups which ones are more practical and which are not? Why?

Discussion Point

The following are some common ways we can use to test children's speaking:

- Sing a song/say a chant: at the beginning level, you could ask learners to choose to sing a song or a rhyme learned from the textbook. Although just singing a song would not provide information about learners' real communicative ability in speaking, it could encourage learners to speak and help them feel and acquire the rhythmic patterns of the English language. It also helps to develop their confidence in speaking. That is very important to very young learners because at the primary level the purpose of English teaching is to cultivate learners' interests and build up their confidence in English learning.
- Oral interview: In this exercise learners answer teacher's questions or express their ideas on certain topic or topics. The questions could be pretty simple about personal information or on topics that are familiar to them. Or they could be more comprehensive and longer so that the students need to provide more detailed information about the same topic.
- Talk about pictures: It is similar to the example of oral interview but the teacher needs to prepare pictures as prompts. The children look at the pictures and answer teacher's questions on the facts about the pictures. For higher graders, they can look at a series of pictures and tell the story with simple sentences.
- Role-play: Children work in groups and do a role-play about a story learned before. Although there might not be much creative use of language in the role-play, it is a

good opportunity to observe whether children can use the language correctly and appropriately. Besides, role-plays can provide children with a relaxing atmosphere which can reduce significantly their test taking anxieties.

TASK 8.5.3B

Now based on the primary English textbook available to you, design a listening or a speaking test to be used at the end of a semester for the right level. What kind of test will you design? Share them together in class and decide for what age and level of learners they are more appropriate for?

8.5.4 How can we test reading?

TASK 8.5.4

Look at the following exercises for testing the skill of reading (Figure 8.5.1–Figure 8.5.3). What ability are they trying to test? How are they different from each other? Which level of learners are they appropriate for?

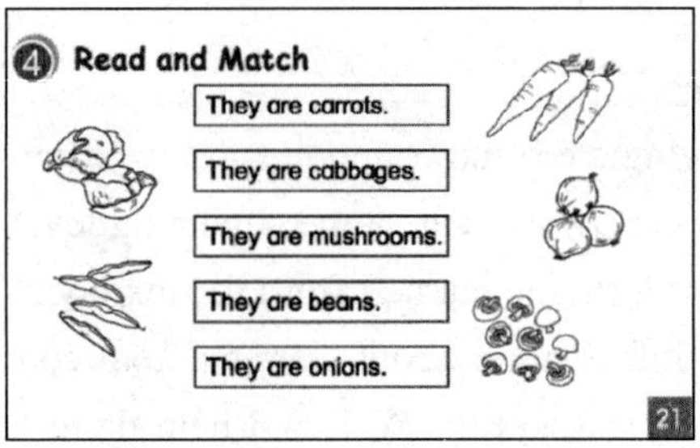

Figure 8.5.1 Read and Match①

Figure 8.5.2 Read and Check②

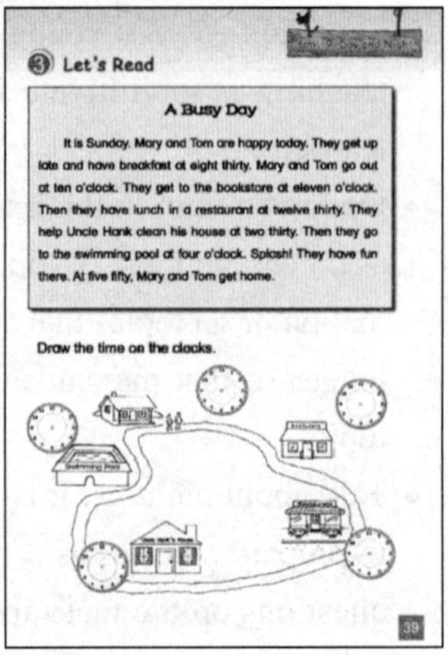

Figure 8.5.3 Let's Read③

---

① 选自北京师范大学出版社的义务教育教科书《英语》（三年级起点）三年级下册Unit 8、Unit 4。

② 选自北京师范大学出版社的义务教育教科书《英语》（三年级起点）。

③ 选自北京师范大学出版社的义务教育教科书《英语》（三年级起点）五年级下册Unit 9。

Discussion Point

Generally described as a receptive skill, reading is often included in a pen-paper test. Although it is easier to design reading tasks for a test, the difference between lower level and higher level reading ability at the primary level sometimes are overlooked and should be reconsidered and balanced.

As you can see from the above examples, tasks in a reading test vary a lot in the form and focus regarding lower and higher levels. The first example is designed to assess the ability of word recognition which is the foundation for reading ability since automatic and accurate word recognition ensures fluent and fast reading at a higher level. The next example focuses on the sentence level for checking comprehension of sentence meaning. The test takers will also need to use their observation ability in order to finish the task. The third example is a passage designed for higher graders. It provides meaningful context and discourse with the purpose of testing reading comprehension and the skill of searching for specific information. At the beginning stage of primary English, the purpose of a reading test is to ensure that learners are able to understand the printed message to make them believe that they "can read" in another language. When they move to higher grades, using simple and appropriate reading strategies should be given more attention. However, we all need to remember that the overall purpose of primary English emphasizes nurturing learners' confidence and interests in learning to read and their confidence and interests only come from their progress and success in learning the language. Therefore, tests should provide them with the opportunity to experience success.

8.5.5 How can we test writing?

Task 8.5.5A

Now, based on your understanding of a reading test for both lower and higher graders, work in groups and try to design two tasks for testing writing to be used for both lower and higher graders in a primary school.

Discussion Point

Among the four skills, writing might be the most difficult skill to be developed. The testing of writing ability is not an easy task either.

When designing a writing test you need to consider what your students can write. Have they just learned how to write alphabets or have they been writing sentences that are logically connected to each other? What is more important for a teacher is that she/he should understand what pupils are supposed to be able to write according to the curriculum Standards. With all these questions answered, you can then set out to design a writing test.

The writing tasks provided here are not perfect ones. They are only examples to illustrate different levels of writing tasks. The first example is obviously for beginners, possibly for those who started their first-year English at grade one or two. Students need to trace the dotted words first and then copy the sentence correctly. It helps children develop the basic concept of writing such as capitalization, spacing, punctuation and spelling. Such an exercise is not usually seen in a test since most teachers would consider it too easy. To make writing more "difficult" for higher graders, you may replace the dotted words with pictures and have the students write out the words or sentences themselves. It does not mean that beginners cannot or should not write sentences. To make writing more meaningful, we can design a task to ask them to complete their personal information in a form or card with some key words provided.

- Example 1

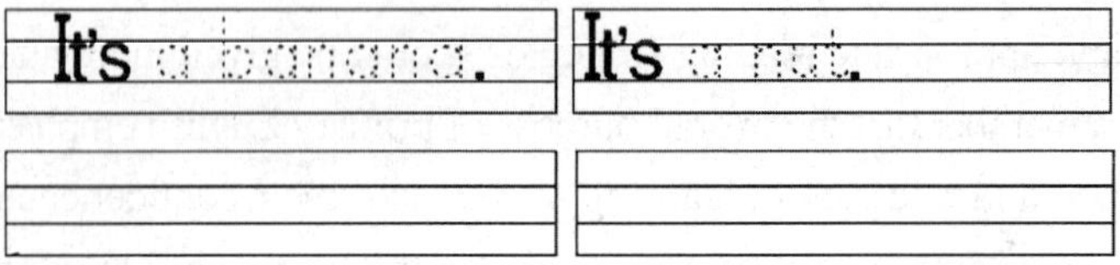

In the second example, students are expected to complete sentences with information provided in the pictures. The exercise focuses on a specific grammar area. Though they are presented together, they are actually unrelated to each other. Such a task assesses whether learners are about to write meaningful sentences that are grammatically correct. However, it could not assess their logical thinking and the ability to use these sentences appropriately in approximate situations.

- Example 2

1. Last year we______________
______________.

2. Yesterday he ______________
______________.

3. Last week she______________
______________.

4. On Sunday they ______________
______________.

The last example provides both a context and discourse for the grammar point to be tested. However, it focuses more on grammar rather than writing. As a modification for more advanced learners, such a passage could be designed into a form of an E-mail, and students can then write a simple response letter. Another idea is to provide several pictures in a random order and pupils can be asked to write a story consisting of 4-6 sentences which should be logically connected. Such kind of writing tasks can be more motivating and can provide a context to support students' writing than simply giving a title having children write a passage which goes far beyond the requirements for primary learners.

- Example 3

Write the verbs in the past tense.

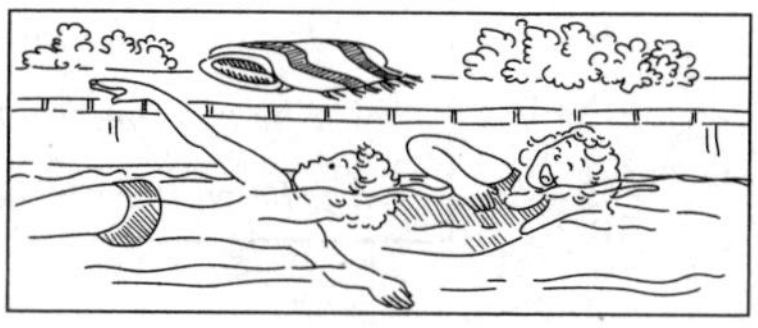

Last summer Ann and Ken were on vacation. They (visit) 1.________ their Aunt Tina. They (go) 2.________ by train. It (is) 3.________ the first week in August. It (is) 4.________ very hot. Aunt Tina (have) 5.________ a swimming pool in her garden. Ann and Ken (like) 6.________ the swimming pool a lot. They always (go) 7.________ swimming in the morning. They often (have) 8.________ a race. Ann usually (win) 9.________ the race! After swimming they (eat) 10. ________ ice cream in the garden. It was fun at Aunt Tina's house.

An important purpose for using a test, among all others, is to have an idea of what they have already learned in the near past period of time. Therefores , they should be tested only on what they learned. It makes them become aware of the progress they made and what they can do well in English.

TASK 8.5.5B

Compare the following two test examples and find out how they are different from each other. What ability does each test assess? If you are going to use one of them, which one will you choose? Why?

Test 1

1. Listen and check the sentence that you hear.

   1) [ ] a. He ate the banana too quickly.
      [ ] b. He hit the ball hard.

   2) [ ] a. What did you do at school yesterday?
      [ ] b. Where did you go yesterday?

3) [ ] a. This storybook is more interesting.
[ ] b. This science book is more difficult.

2. Listen and write out the missing words.
1) He ________ at the table next to the window.
2) She coughed and coughed. She ________ breathe.
3) The waiter ________ the man on the back.

Tape scripts:

1. Listen and check the sentence that you hear.

1) He ate the banana too quickly.

2) Where did you go yesterday?

3) This science book is more difficult.

2. Listen and write out the missing words.

1) He sat at the table next to the window.

2) She coughed and coughed. She couldn't breathe.

3) The waiter hit the man on the back.

3. Translate the words.
1）拜访，访问：________________.
2）清洁，打扫：________________.
3）击，打：________________.
4）breathe: ________________.
5）planet: ________________.
6）prize: ________________.

4. Which one is different? Read and circle the word.

1) [s]	a. seven	b. sock	c. six	d. bees
2) [is]	a. boxes	b. miss	c. catches	d. cheese
3) [k]	a. nice	b. book	c. kite	d. cat

5. Complete the sentences with the words given in the blanks.
1) Yesterday morning, there ________ (is) a big football game here.
2) He ________ (do) watch TV last night. He read a storybook.
3) Mary's family ________ (move) to another city last month.

6. Read the passage and answer the questions.

Jack and his friends entered the swimming race. Jack won third prize. It was a notebook. David won fourth prize. It was a pen. Ken won second prize and it was a storybook. Who was first? It was Matte. He won a gold medal!

1) Who was first? ________________.
2) What was the second prize? ________________.

3) Did Jack win the third prize? ____________________ .

Test 2

1. Speaking. (You need to choose ONLY one of them.)
   1) Choose a story from your book and read it out aloud.
   2) Answer teacher's questions about you.
   3) Talk about your family in five sentences.
2. Listen and check the correct picture.

Tape script:

Look. This is Mary's family. Mary is a student. Her mother is a nurse and her father is a policeman.

3. Listen and choose the right answer.

1) ______ a. I went there with some of my friends.
2) ______ b. We went there by bus.
3) ______ c. I went to the seaside.
4) ______ d. We played football on the beach.

Tape script:

1) Where did you go last weekend?

2) Who did you go with?

3) How did you go there?

4) What did you do there?

4. Read and choose the word that doesn't belong to the group. Circle the word.

1)	hard disk	speaker	keyboard	screen
2)	beautiful	careful	decide	interesting
3)	policeman	teacher	dancer	post office
4)	Saturday	July	March	November

5. Complete the sentences with the words in the box.

poor	old	sell	buy

Long long ago, there was a man in a small town. He was very ______. He was often hungry but he had no money to _____ food. He had an _____ cow. The man wanted to _______ the cow but no one wanted his cow.

6. Read and tick the correct answer.

Last night Lucy had a funny dream. She was at a birthday party and it was for her. Her parents were at the party and her friends came, too. Her friends were nine years old but she was only one! She couldn't talk. She couldn't eat the cake. She couldn't play with her friends. Lucy didn't like the dream.

1) In the dream, she was at ☐ *a birthday party* ☐ *a hospital.*

2) It was Lucy's ☐ *first* ☐ *ninth* birthday party.

3) Lucy was the ☐ *youngest* ☐ *oldest* girl at the party.

4) Lucy ☐ *liked* ☐ *didn't like* her dream.

7. Read the following questions and write your real answers in the space given.

1) Who is the youngest in your family? ____________________.

2) Who is the oldest in your family? ____________________.

3) Who is the tallest in your family? ____________________.

Discussion Point

There are obvious differences between the two tests:

- Test 2 has listening comprehension and sentence writing sections;
- Test 2 tries to set a topic or choose a specific situation for each exercise, but sentences in Test 1 of the same type of exercise are unrelated to each other.
- In Test 1 each area of grammar is tested separately, while in Test 2 the grammar points are mixed naturally into a discourse with other language skills.
- Obvious efforts have been made in Test 2 to make the content more interesting and meaningful.
- Test 2 focuses more on children's ability in communication, while Test 1 seems to focus more on what students know about the language, or whether they can produce the correct form of the language.

With the second test you are more likely to get the information about what the test takers can do in all the four skills, since it has tasks on all of them. With the first test, the result will not put you in a position to judge how well students can do in communication in the specific grammar areas. The reason is that knowing about a structure does not ensure the ability of using it appropriately—when and where it supposed to be used. Therefore, these exercises may be useful for early practice in learning a new structure but they are not really valid in the final test with a communicative objective.

Different from Test 2, Test 1 included sections that test learners' vocabulary and phonological knowledge. However, you will probably agree that they are not successfully deigned. As what has been discussed in previous chapters, few textbooks choose to present IPA at the primary level, since it requires both special training and analytical ability. A test item on phonological knowledge would have a negative backwash to teaching, as both teachers and learners would spend extra hours learning IPA, which is inappropriate, difficult and boring to them, just to ensure a better performance in such kind of tests. As we all know, children, in general, are strong in listening and speaking but weak in analytical skills.

Unit 9

Adapting and Evaluating Textbooks

Aims of the unit

In this unit, we are going to focus on the following:

9.1 How to evaluate textbooks

9.1.1 What factors need to be considered when choosing or adapting a textbook?

9.1.2 What are the features of good textbooks?

9.2 How to select textbooks

9.2.1 What are the components of a textbook?

9.2.2 What are the criteria for choosing a textbook?

9.3 How to use textbooks effectively

9.3.1 How can teachers make adaptations to a textbook?

9.3.2 How can we evaluate the presentation of vocabulary, grammar, and pronunciation in a textbook?

9.3.3 How can we evaluate the development of skills in a textbook?

9.3.4 How can we evaluate the organization of a unit?

9.3.5 How can we evaluate the topics, difficulty level and other issues in a textbook?

In most primary English classrooms, teaching is often carried out based on a pre-determined textbook, although in some cases exceptions do exist. These textbooks are normally complied by educational experts and experienced teachers of English with contents and topics appropriately sequenced and structured to include a wide range of materials aiming to meet the requirements set by the national English curriculum. The booming textbook market has provided a wide selection of primary English teaching materials for teachers. Although it is mostly true that teachers would not be involved in decision-making as to which book to use at a school, it is necessary for teachers to be able to make proper judgment about the strengths and weaknesses of a pre-determined textbook so that adaptation can be made to meet the needs of a particular group of learners that one teaches. In this case, teachers need to learn how to evaluate and adapt textbooks.

9.1 How to evaluate textbooks

9.1.1 What factors need to be considered when choosing or adapting a textbook?

TASK 9.1.1

Suppose you are an English teacher in a local public school. In groups, make a list of possible requirements or expectations from the local educational authorities, school principals, teachers, learners as well as parents regarding English language learning. What implications can you draw?

Requirements from educational authorities:
Requirements from the school principal:
Learners' needs:
Parents' expectations:
Teachers' expectations:

Discussion Point

The 2022 Curriculum Standards issued by the Ministry of Education is the official document that guides the practice of English language teaching in China. The 2022 Curriculum specifies the goals and purposes of having English as a school subject and sets up specific standards to be achieved for different grade levels. Therefore, the selection of textbooks for students in public schools should be carried out to adhere to the spirit and concept of the 2022 Curriculum Standards.

Besides Curriculum, school requirement also needs to be considered when evaluating or adapting a textbook. As schools are located in different economic and geographic regions, their starting age for English differs and time allocation may also differ. For example, some urban schools may offer English at the age of six while other school at eight. While most schools allocate 2 forty-minute lessons a week for English, some schools may allocate 4–5 forty-minute lessons. Therefore, different schools may expect different levels of achievement by the time children graduate. Textbooks need to be selected with different requirements in mind.

Moreover, children's needs should be taken into consideration. Young learners are more inclined to indirect learning than direct learning. They learn best when they are "playing" . They are quite active and care much about whether they can "have fun" during the process of learning. They cannot sit still for long and they always expect activities that allow them to think, to imagine and to involve them physically to "do" things with English.

Parents' expectations can also be an influencing factor for selecting or adapting a textbook, which unfortunately has often been overlooked, as parents' attitudes can either be a helpful support for teaching and learning or as an obstacle. English teachers are not unfamiliar with complaints like, "Why doesn't my child have homework?" "Why couldn't my child write or say any English at home?" Perhaps, we should not blame these parents for not understanding the nature of teaching and learning. All parents would expect their children to be able to demonstrate the skills and knowledge gained immediately after learning.

Teachers also have preferences for which book to use. They are concerned about questions such as: Does the book have clear instructions? Does it provide enough supporting materials so that no or less extra time is needed to make preparations? Does the methodology suggested in the book reflect the recent development in ELT research both at home and abroad? Among others, these questions should be considered before setting out to evaluate textbooks for use.

9.1.2 What are the features of good textbooks?

TASK 9.1.2

Choose an English textbook that you think is good. Why do you think it is a good textbook? What characters does it have? Discuss in groups and list out at least 5 characters of good English textbooks.

Common characteristics of good textbooks

1.
2.
3.
4.
5.
6.
7.

Discussion Point

There are some commonly shared characteristics of good textbooks. Tomlinson (1998) proposes that good textbooks should:

- attract the students' curiosity, interest and attention. Therefore, the textbook should have attractive layout, interesting content, etc. They should make sure that learning really takes place when the students use the textbook. It is not necessarily enough that students enjoy the textbooks.
- help students feel at ease. The layout of presentation, tasks and activities, texts and illustrations should all look friendly to students.
- help students develop confidence. Good textbooks help students build up confidence with activities that are within students' language ability.
- meet students' needs. What is covered in the textbooks should be relevant and useful to what students need to learn and what they want to learn.
- expose students to language in authentic use.
- provide students with opportunities to use the target language to achieve communicative purposes.
- take into account that the positive effects of language teaching are usually delayed.
- take into account that students differ in learning styles.
- take into account that students differ in affective factors.
- maximize learning potential by encouraging intellective, aesthetic and emotionally involving tasks which stimulate both right-brain and left-brain activities.

9.2 How to select textbooks

9.2.1 What are the components of a textbook?

Task 9.2.1

Find a primary English textbook together with its teacher's book. Look through them and examine the structure, layout, material, methods, etc. in pairs. Then fill in the following table. Disscuss in groups: What level is it designed for? What are the objectives? How is each unit or lesson structured? What methods are suggested and what teaching resources are provided?

Structure (objectives, content, sequence, lesson or unit divisions)	
Layout (typical organization of each lesson or unit, format and presentation of the main content)	
Types of material (including activities and exercises)	
Methodology and procedures (suggested use of the book indicated by the types of activity, instructions, and the teacher's book)	

Discussion Point

Before looking into the details of a textbook, we usually go through a textbook quickly to get a general impression of what the book is like. This is important because this will give us an overview of the structure and organization of the book. Usually this is called an **impressionistic overview**. In an impressionistic overview, we will know for what level of students the book is intended and what level of proficiency the book is designed to reach. Such information may also be placed in the teachers' book.

From the content page of a textbook, we should be able to get an overview of the book regarding the topics, language knowledge and skills, functions, and the sequence of the topics, units and lessons. You may also need to look for other special features of the book and additional support materials that are available for teachers. Most textbooks may also have workbooks alongside them. Finding out all the information about a set of textbook is the basis for evaluation and selection.

9.2.2 What are the criteria for choosing a textbook?

When choosing a textbook, every teacher wants to choose the best one available. But a good textbook may not be the most appropriate one for your students.

Task 9.2.2

Suppose you are a teacher of a local school.Your students are 3rd-year pupils and have no experience of learning English. Find a set of textbook that is used in your area and examine it carefully.Then decide if you will choose it for your pupils. Why and why not? Use the checklists provided below to help you.

A checklist for selecting a textbook for your learners:

1. Is it right for your pupils?
- their age, education, interests, and needs,
- their motivation and attitudes towards the English language and its culture,
- the price.

2. Does it suit you as a teacher in the school?
- your level of experience and training,
- your ability in English,
- your interests and your culture.

3. Does it meet the requirements of the 2022 Curriculum?
- suitability for the number of teaching hours available,
- the teaching objectives of your school,
- the requirements from the local educational authorities.

4. Do you think you will choose this textbook for your pupils? Why and why not?

Discussion Point

Before selecting a textbook we need to evaluate it first. We will need to consider the needs of our students and their language levels. We also need to take into consideration many other aspects before we make our decisions. Grant (1987) provided a three-part questionnaire for textbook selection. It examines how a textbook is appropriate for the intended students, the teachers, the syllabus and the examinations.

Choosing a textbook: questionnaire (Part 1–Part 3)

Part 1: Does the text book suit your students?

Questions	Yes	Partly	No
1. Is it attractive? Given the average age of your students, would they enjoy using it?			
2. Is it culturally acceptable?			
3. Does it reflect what you know about your students' needs and interests?			
4. Is it about the right level of difficulty?			
5. Is it about the right length?			
6. Are the course's physical characteristics appropriate?(e.g. is it durable?)			

continued

Questions	Yes	Partly	No
7. Are there enough authentic materials, so that the students can see that the book is relevant to real life?			
8. Does it achieve an acceptable balance between knowledge about the language, and practice in using the language?			
9. Does it achieve an acceptable balance between the relevant language skills, and integrate them so that work in one skill area helps the others?			
10. Does the book contain enough communicative activities to enable the students to use the language independently?			
Score: 2 points for every Yes answer. *1 point for every Partly answer.* *0 for every No answer.*			

Part 2: Does the text book suit the teacher?

Questions	Yes	Partly	No
1. Is your overall impression of the contents and layout of the course favourable?			
2. Is there a good, clear teacher's guide with answers and help on methods and additional activities?			
3. Can one use the book in the classroom without constantly having to turn to the teacher's guide?			
4. Are the recommended methods and approaches suitable for you, your students and your classroom?			
5. Are the approaches easily adaptable if necessary?			
6. Does using the course require little or no time-consuming preparation?			
7. Are useful ancillary materials such as tapes, workbooks, and visuals provided?			
8. Is there sufficient provision made for tests and revision?			
9. Does the book use a "spiral" approach, so that items are regularly revised and used again in different contexts?			

continued

Questions	Yes	Partly	No
10. Is the course appropriate for, and liked by, colleagues?			
Score: 2 points for every Yes answer. *1 point for every Partly answer* *0 for every No answer.*			

Part 3: Does the text book suit the syllabus and examinations?

Questions	Yes	Partly	No
1. Has the book been recommended or approved by the authorities?			
2. Does the book follow the official syllabus in a creative manner?			
3. Is the course well-graded, so that it gives well-structured and systematic coverage of the language?			
4. If it does more than the syllabus requires, is the result an improvement?			
5. Are the activities, contents and methods used in the course well-planned and executed?			
6. Has it been prepared specifically for the target examination?			
7. Do the course's methods help the students prepare for the exam?			
8. Is there a good balance between what the examination requires, and what the students need?			
9. Is there enough examination practice?			
10. Does the course contain useful hints on examination technique?			
Score: 2 points for every Yes answer. *1 point for every Partly answer.* *0 for every No answer.*			

9.3 How to use textbooks effectively

9.3.1 How can teachers make adaptations to a textbook?

Although published textbooks are generally written by experienced and better-qualified people, it is impossible for any one textbook to meet the needs of every student. Since each individual student varies in terms of his/her learning abilities, styles, interests, etc., it requires that the teacher adapt the textbook for the benefits of the students. It is important that a teacher should not just TEACH a textbook but USE it creatively by making necessary adaptations according to the context.

TASK 9.3.1

The following are some suggestions about ways of textbook adaptation. Match the definitions with the terms on the left.

- Omission
- Addition
- Replacement
- Reordering
- Rewriting/modification
- Reduction
- Extension
- Branching

- Teachers may decide the order in which the textbooks are presented. They can then decide to plot a different course through the textbooks from the one the writer had laid down.
- Where the teacher shortens an activity to give it less emphasis.
- Teachers may decide to rewrite materials, especially exercises, to make them more appropriate, more or less challenging, for the learners.
- Where an activity is lengthened in order to give it an additional dimension.
- Text or exercise material, which is considered inadequate, for whatever reason, may be replaced by more suitable material from other resources.
- Teachers may decide to add more content to the textbooks, either in the form of texts or activities, if there seems to be inadequate coverage.
- The teacher leaves out things that are inappropriate, offensive, unproductive, etc., for the particular group of learners.
- Teachers may decide to add options to the existing activity or to suggest alternative pathways through the activities.

Discussion Point

Adaptations may take two forms: macro and micro. Macro adaptation is needed when some parts of the selected material should be supplemented, replaced or omitted. Micro adaptation takes place at the unit level which is often made during the teaching process. Micro adaptation may involve reordering activities, shortening or omitting activities, adding supplementary material, etc. There are also adaptations at the activity level when the design of an activity is not appropriate for the learners or it is poorly designed. For effective adaptations of a textbook, proper and systematic evaluation is needed before adaptations.

9.3.2 How can we evaluate the presentation of vocabulary, grammar, and pronunciation in a textbook?

In the following, we will take a more detailed look into the specific evaluation of language knowledge in a textbook. It includes the presentation of vocabulary, grammar, and pronunciation. This is an important step for micro adaptation. It should be done based on specification of objectives, principles and procedures.

TASK 9.3.2A

Choose one or two units from a textbook that is available to you and think about the following questions: Does it have a vocabulary learning section? If so, where is it located in the unit and why? How are new words presented and what methodology does it suggest? Share your findings in pairs.

Discussion Point

For beginning level learners, vocabulary seems more important than grammar. Most primary English textbooks have a vocabulary learning section, although they may differ in their ways of presentation.

A typical way to present new vocabulary is to use a combination of words and their illustrations. In this way students can get the **meaning** directly from the illustrations. The word printed below tells them what the word looks like **(word form)**. And **pronunciation** is often presented separately in the audiotape that goes with the textbook. For higher level learners, the presentation of vocabulary may take a different form.

Vocabulary learning does not stand alone in a unit. It relates to other activities in many ways. It usually comes with a listening or reading text which provides a context and discourse for understanding vocabulary. After the words are presented and learned, they should be recycled in later learning activities and in later units under similar or related topics. Therefore, evaluation should take recycling into consideration.

TASK 9.3.2B

Is there a special section for teaching grammar in the book available to you? If so, how is it presented? What beliefs underline such a presentation?

Discussion Point

Every textbook has to teach grammar. However, the ways of presenting grammar vary. Some textbooks present grammar explicitly while others present it implicitly with grammar mixed up with other learning tasks or activities. It is justifiable either to have or not to have a formal presentation of grammar at the primary level.

Since the primary objective of learning is to develop and maintain learners' interest in learning, grammar is not the focus. They are often presented in a context and learners need to discover the meaning and form in that context. Designed in this way, textbooks can provide an opportunity for learners to learn grammar with their main focus on meaning. However, following an initial understanding of meaning, the activities and exercises that follow should help to highlight the structure of the target grammar. Learners then are encouraged to think and observe to see if they can sense the intended rules. There is no need to use special grammar terms or terminologies in such a presentation, since an analytical way of grammar learning is neither necessary nor appropriate for learners at this stage.

TASK 9.3.2C

Look at a textbook that is available to you. Examine if it has a section on pronunciation. If yes, what is the purpose? Does it help children develop their spoken language?

Discussion Point

We should make it clear that the teaching of pronunciation at the primary level should focus more on aspects such as stress, rhythm, weak form, intonation, etc. instead of the correct pronunciation of an individual word. In real situations, successful communication does not depend on the correct sound of a word but the proper handling of sentence stress and intonation. English is a stress-timed language and variations in stress may effectively change the intended meaning. This does not mean that the correctness of individual sound is not important, on the contrary, it is, but it should not be overemphasized. Raising children's awareness of sound and spelling relationships can be helpful for children to develop their ability to read and write, but we should avoid teaching phonics which complicates the process of learning.

9.3.3 How can we evaluate the development of skills in a text-book?

TASK 9.3.3A

Look at the textbook at your hand and discuss the following questions in pairs: Does it have listening, reading, writing and speaking activities in each unit? Are they balanced? Which skill/skills are left out? Why?

Discussion Point

The language used in real life involves all the four skills and they are often used in an integrated way. For example, when we have a conversation with a friend, we need to both listen and talk. And if our friend tells us something important, we may need to take notes. If we do not understand, we need to ask questions. In evaluating a textbook, we need to consider how the four skills are integrated. However, different skills may be given different emphasis at different stages of learning. For example, for beginning learners, learning may focus more on listening and speaking. Then, reading and writing can be added with increased integration.

TASK 9.3.3B

Now, take a look at the textbook you have and examine how it develops the four skills. Take notes where appropriate.

Skills	Listening	Speaking	Reading	Writing
Is the skill included or left out in the book? If so, for what reason?				
Is the skill presented in an integrated way? If yes, how? If not, why not?				
How is the skill developed and practiced throughout the book?				

continued

Skills	Listening	Speaking	Reading	Writing
What support does the book provide to develop the skill?				
Does the language practiced sound natural and real?				

9.3.4 How can we evaluate the organization of a unit?

TASK 9.3.4

Now look at the textbook at your hand and think about the questions: How are materials organized into a unit? What's the sequence and order of the materials? How are language knowledge and skills interweaved? What methodology does such an organization suggest? What do learners need to do and what are their roles in learning?

Discussion Point

Learner needs are an important factor to be considered in textbook evaluation. Some related questions may include: what is the role of the learner in the process of learning? Do they have to remember, imitate and repeat all the time? Or is there any material provided that requires them to observe, to think, to express their own idea and relate to their own experience? All these questions can tell a lot about the textbook to be examined.

The way how materials are put together implies the method to be used in teaching. It demonstrates whether learners need to observe, to explore the language during which they focus on meaning and function before language form or the other way round. The former is an active learning process that involves learners' active thinking and it will contribute to the development of learners' overall language ability in the long run.

9.3.5 How can we evaluate the topics, difficulty level and other issues in a textbook?

TASK 9.3.5

Examine the primary English textbooks that are available to you and discuss in pairs: What topics does the book cover? How much do the topics relate to learners' life and their experience? Does the difficulty level of the book increase gradually? Does the order or sequence of grammatical items reflect a gradual move from being easy to difficult? In what order or sequence are grammar items arranged in the whole series?

Discussion Point

The scope and sequence of a textbook can be used as a shortcut to answer these questions. Usually scope and sequence are presented in teachers' book, but some are included in students' book on the content page which tells you what topics are covered and how they are arranged. We need to take into consideration our students' experiences, interests and cognitive levels of development when evaluating the appropriateness of the topics. These issues should also be considered when we evaluate the grading of the difficulties in grammar presentation. Generally speaking, those items that are closely related to children's life should be introduced earlier. For example, present continuous and past tense are included in almost all primary English textbooks, because children are more likely to talk about the things they are doing and what they did in the past.

The difficulty level needs to move up gradually. The input should be one step ahead of the learners' current level of ability according to "i+1" theory (Krashen, 1985). In this way children can make progress in a supportive environment. Sudden changes in the difficulty level are likely to put learners at the risk of turning away from learning.

Recycling is another element that need to be considered. Language learning is a war again forgetting and what was learned needs to be recycled constantly. Early learned topics in a good textbook will surely reappear in later stages so that learners can build up their knowledge and skills step by step.

References

ATKINSON D. Teaching monolingual classes[M]. London: Longman, 1993.

BLACK P J. Testing: friend or foe? The theory and practice of assessment and testing[M]. London: RoutledgeFalmer, 1998.

BREWSTER J, ELLIS G, GIRARD D. The primary English teacher's guide[M]. London: Penguin Books, 1992.

BROWN H D. Principles of language learning and teaching[M]. 4th ed. London: Longman, 2000.

CAMERON L. Teaching languages to young learners[M]. Cambridge: Cambridge University Press, 2001.

CAMERON L. Challenge for ELT from the expansion in teaching children[J]. ELT journal, 2003, 57(2): 105-112.

CANT A, SUPERFINE W. Developing resources for primary[M]. London: Richmond, 1997.

CEL-CEMURCIA M. Discourse analysis and the teaching of listening[M]// COOK G, SEIDLHOFER B. Principles & practice in applied linguistics. Oxford: Oxford University Press, 1995.

CHEATER C, FARREN A. The literacy link[M]. London: Center for Information on Language Teaching and Research, 2001.

CHRISTISON M A. Applying multiple intelligences theory in preservice and inservice TEFL Education Programs[J]. English teaching forum,1998,36(2): 2-13.

COOK V J. The comparison of language development in native children and foreign adults[J]. International review of applied linguistics in language teaching, 1973, 11(1): 13-28.

CROSS D. A practical handbook of language teaching[M]. New York: Prentice Hall, 1992.

DAVIES P, Pearse E. Success in English teaching[M]. Oxford: Oxford University Press, 2000.

DEAN J. Organising learning in the primary school classroom[M]. London: RoutledgeFalmer, 2001.

DESHATTY D D, MOKASHI V. Mind maps as a learning tool in anatomy[J]. International journal of anatomy research, 2013, 1(2): 100-103.

EHRMAN M E, LEAVER B L, OXFORD R L. A brief overview of individual differences in second language learning[J]. System, 2003, 31(3): 313-330.

GARDNER H. Frames of mind: the theory of multiple intelligences[M]. New York: Basic Books, 1983.

GARDNER H. Multiple Intelligences: the theory in practice[M]. New York: Basic Books, 1993.

GARDNER R C. Social psychology and second language learning[M]. London: Edward Arnold, 1985.

GRANT N. Making the most of your textbook[M]. London: Longman, 1987.

HALLIWELL S. Yes—But will they behave? Managing the interactive classroom[M]. London: Center for Information on Language Teaching and Research, 1991.

HALLIWELL S, JONES B. On target: teaching in the target language[M]. London: Centre for Information on Language Teaching and Research, 1991.

HALLIWELL S. Teaching English in the primary classroom[M]. London: Longman, 1992.

HARMER J. The practice of English language teaching[M]. 4th ed. London: Longman, 2007.

HEDGE T. Teaching and learning in the language classroom[M]. Oxford: Oxford University Press, 2000.

KRASHEN S D. The input hypothesis: issues and implications[M]. London: Longman,1985.

LARSEN–FREEMAN D, LONG M H. An introduction to second language acquisition research[M].London: Longman, 1991.

MALEY A. Squaring the circle-reconciling material as constraint with material as empowerment[M] // TOMLINSON B. Materials development in language teaching. Cambridge: Cambridge University Press, 1998.

MOON J. Children learning English[M]. Oxford: Macmillan Heinemann English Language Teaching, 2000.

NATION I S P. Teaching and learning vocabulary[M]. New York: Newbury House Publishers, 1990.

O'SULLIVAN M C. Teaching large classes: the international evidence and a discussion of some good practice in Ugandan primary schools[J]. International journal of educational evelopment, 2006, 26(1): 24-37.

PECCEI J S. Child language[M]. New York: Routledge, 2000.

PHILLIPS S. Young learners[M]. Oxford: Oxford University Press,1993.

SARASIN L C. Learning style perspectives: impact in the classroom[J]. Journal of chemical education, 1999, 76 (12): 1629.

SCRIVENER J. Learning teaching: a guidebook for English language teachers[M]. Oxford: Heinemann, 1994.

SENIOR R M. A class-centred approach to language teaching[J]. English language teaching journal, 2002, 56(4): 397-403.

SHARPE K. Modern foreign languages in the primary school[M].London: Kogan Page Limited, 2001.

SLATTERY M, WILLI J. English for primary teachers: a handbook of activities and classroom language [M]. Oxford: Oxford University Press, 2001.

SMITH K. Learner portfolio[J]. English teaching professional, 2002, 22(10): 39-41.

TANN S. Developing language in primary classroom[M]. London: Cassel, 1991.

TOMLINSON B. Materials development in language teaching[M]. Cambridge: Cambridge University Press, 1998.

VALE D, FEUNTEUN A. Teaching children English[M]. Cambridge: Cambridge University Press, 1995.

UR P. A course in language teaching: practice and theory[M]. Cambridge: Cambridge University Press, 1996.

MCTIGHE J, WIGGINS G. Understanding by design[M]. Expanded 2nd ed. Alexandria: Association for Supervision and Curriculum Development, 2005.

WILLIAMS M, BURDEN L R. Psychology for language teachers[M]. Cambridge: Cambridge University Press, 1997.

BROOKES A，GRUNDY P. 英语写作教学 [M]. 刘道义，导读 . 北京：人民教育出版社，2000.

HARMER J. 怎样教英语 [M]. 田贵森，导读 . 北京：外语教学与研究出版社，2000.

KATZ L G. 与幼儿教师对话：迈向专业成长之路 [M]. 廖凤瑞，译 . 南京：南京师范大学出版社，2003.

陈则航，王蔷．在小学英语阅读教学中培养学生的批判性思维培养 [J]. 中小学外语教学（小学篇），2016（5）：1–5.

梅德明，王蔷．义务教育英语课程标准（2022 年版）解读 [M]. 北京：北京师范大学出版社，2022.

王蔷 . 国际小学外语教学研究及其启示 [J]. 课程 · 教材 · 教法，2005（1）：84–90.

王蔷 . 我国小学英语课程政策与实施分析 [J]. 中国外语，2011（4）：47–54.

王蔷 . 深化改革理念，提升课程质量：解读《义务教育英语课程标准（2011 年版）》的主要变化 [J]. 课程 · 教材 · 教法，2013（1）：34–40.

王蔷．在英语教学中开展读写结合教学的意义及实施途径 [J]. 英语学习，2020（5）：26–32.

王蔷 . 英语教学法教程 [M]. 2 版 . 北京：高等教育出版社，2006.

王蔷，敖娜仁图雅，陈则航，等．小学英语分级阅读教学：意义、内涵与途径 [M]. 北京：外语教学与研究出版社，2017.

王蔷，胡亚琳 . 英语学科能力及其表现研究 [J]. 教育学报，2017（2）：61–70.

王蔷，李亮 . 推动核心素养背景下英语课堂教 — 学 — 评一体化：意义、理论与方法 [J] 课程 · 教材 · 教法，2019（5）：114–120.

王蔷，钱小芳，周敏．英语教学中语篇研读的意义与方法 [J]. 外语教育研究前沿,2019(2)：42–48.

中华人民共和国教育部 . 义务教育英语课程标准：2022 年版 [M]. 北京：北京师范大学出版社，2022.

中华人民共和国教育部 . 义务教育英语课程标准：2011 年版 [M]. 北京：北京师范大学出版社，2012.

中华人民共和国教育部 . 全日制义务教育英语课程标准：实验稿 [M]. 北京：北京师范大学出版社，2001.

读者意见反馈

为收集对教材的意见建议，进一步完善教材编写并做好服务工作，读者可将对本教材的意见建议通过如下渠道反馈至我社。

咨询电话　400-810-0598

反馈邮箱　gjdzfwb@pub.hep.cn

通信地址　北京市朝阳区惠新东街 4 号富盛大厦 1 座

　　　　　高等教育出版社总编辑办公室

邮政编码　100029